THE BHAKTI MOVEMENT
Renaissance or Revivalism?

This is a Comprehensive Survey of the Bhakti Movement as it sprang in South India to spread across the subcontinent in independent and multifarious manifestations yet marked with amazing commonalities. Spanning a period of 11 centuries starting from the 6th CE, the movement encompassed in its sweep a vast range of dimensions; Social, political, economic, religious, cultural, linguistic, ethical and philosophical. Among the multifarious movements which contributed to the formation of India and its Culture, the Bhakti was undoubtedly the most pervasive and persistent, says the author. Besides its sweep and depth, what proved most remarkable about the movement was that it arose almost everywhere from the masses who belonged to the lowest class and castes. Though spirituality was its leitmotif, Bhakti proved to be a stirring song of the subaltern in their varied expressions of resistance and revolt. A seemingly conservative phenomenon became a potent weapon against entrenched hierarchies of orthodoxy and oppression, in a wonderful dialectical expression. This qualifies Bhakti movement to be reckoned on a par with European renaissance as it marked a massive upsurge in the societal value system to directly impact a range of fields like arts, politics, culture or religion. Even as he takes note of the elements of reactionary revivalism that also marked the Bhakti movement, the author convincingly argues that those of renaissance and progress far outweighed the former.

P. Govinda Pillai (b.1926) graduated from St. Xavier's College, Mumbai. He became a full time political, social and cultural activist after his student life and was elected four times to the Kerala State Legislature, first as a representative of the Communist Party of India and later, the Communist Party of India (M). He was the Chief Editor of *Desabhimani,* the CPI(M)'s mouthpiece in Malayalam, for more than two decades. He has headed many institutions including the Kerala State Film Corporation, Centre for Imaging Technology, Kerala State Press Akademi etc. He is the author of about 35 books based on a range of subjects including Marxist asesthetics, literarture and culture, social movements and science.

THE BHAKTI MOVEMENT
Renaissance or Revivalism?

P. GOVINDA PILLAI

Routledge
Taylor & Francis Group
LONDON AND NEW YORK

AAKAR

First published 2023
by Routledge
4 Park Square, Milton Park, Abingdon, Oxon OX14 4RN

and by Routledge
605 Third Avenue, New York, NY 10158

Routledge is an imprint of the Taylor & Francis Group, an informa business

British Library Cataloguing-in-Publication Data
A catalogue record for this book is available from the British Library

Library of Congress Cataloging-in-Publication Data
A catalog record for this book has been requested

ISBN: 978-1-032-36471-1 (hbk)
ISBN: 978-1-032-36473-5 (pbk)
ISBN: 978-1-003-33215-2 (ebk)

DOI: 10.4324/9781003332152

Typeset in Palatino

by Sakshi Computers, Delhi

AAKAR

Contents

Preface

This book on the *Bhakti* movement in India does not claim to be exhaustive. Many individual protagonists of the Bhakti movement as well as some sects and sub-sects deserving mention have been left out for reasons of space. The aim was to keep the book within limits notwithstanding the massive dimension of the subject. If the responses of the readers are for a more exhaustive treatment of the subject, we may do so in the next edition. One difficulty that the author faced was the diversity of languages in which the bhakti literatures appear. Friends who knew these languages have helped me to understand and translate them into English.

Following Dr A.K. Majumdar who wrote about Bhakti Renaissance and Dr Savithri Chandra Sobha who dwelt upon bhakti in Hindi poetry, I was originally inclined, without any doubt, to characterise the movement as pure Renaissance. However, after studying the subject more, I came to realize the complexity of the phenomenon. Finally, I came to the conclusion that the movement cannot be portrayed as Renaissance alone but that it contains a strong element of conservative Revivalism as well. In the concluding chapter, I have dealt with this problem in detail. This is an aspect which deserves more research and study.

Had it not been for the help of my friend, L. Parameswaran, both in research and production, this book would not have been realized. I thank him for his assistance. The excellent DTP work done by D.K. Premalatha also needs to be acknowledged.

In spotting out and collecting the necessary books and other materials, Dr Ravi Sankar S. Nair's service is invaluable.

My son M.G. Radhakrishnan, a senior journalist, read through the entire manuscript and edited it. The bibliography prepared by him provides additional value to this work. Though he does not expect me to thank him formally I cannot resist the temptation to acknowledge his services.

It will not be out of place if I express my profound feelings of gratitude to my friend Shri N.E. Sudheer for providing me with necessary references and for all his efforts in bringing out this book.

Gandhi Jayanthi 2011 **P. GOVINDA PILLAI**

Part I

THE HISTORICAL BACKGROUND

1

The Cult and Movement

After the rise and growth of Buddhism in the country between the 6th century BC *and 2nd century* AD, *the medieval Bhakti movement was undoubtedly the most widespread, far-reaching and many a faceted movement that appeared in India. The Bhakti movement influenced almost the whole country, at different times, and had a definite impact not only on religious doctrines, rituals, values and popular beliefs, but on art and cultures as well. In turn, these had an impact on the value structures of medieval state and the ruling classes. At a certain stage of its development, the Bhakti movement was sought to be used as a platform by the forces opposing centralizing Mughal state. In the cultural field, the growth of regional languages, devotional music, dance, painting, sculptures et cetera, became closely related to the Bhakti movement.*[1]

Satish Chandra

Among the multifarious religious, philosophical, social and political movements which contributed to the formation of India and her culture, the Bhakti of the medieval period (fourteenth to seventeenth centuries) was undoubtedly the most pervasive and persistent. To mention only one of its various impacts, all the modern Indian languages—except perhaps Tamil—were given their modern form and style by the immortal bards of this *movement* by trans-creating the ancient Sanskrit epics and *Puranas* especially the *Ramayana, Mahabharatha* and *Bhagavatha* into regional languages. Thus we have Kamban's *Ramayana* in

Tamil, Ezhuthachchan's *Adhyatma Ramayana* in Malayalam, Krithivasa's *Ramayana* in Bengali, Madhavakandali's Assamese *Ramayana,* and Tulsidas's *Ramacharithmanas* in the Avadhi dialect of Hindi.

Among the *Mahabharatha* writers were Nannayya-Tikkana in Telugu, Pampa in Kannada and Sarala Dasa in Oriya. Though the authentic prestige and hoary tradition of these two epic poems were never in doubt, the *Bhagavatha Purana,* a comparatively later work, formed the basic text of Vaishnavite bhakti—which was more pervasive and influential than those of their rivals, the Saivites. The former sect worshipped God Vishnu and his incarnation Krishna, while the latter revered Siva. The undercurrents of these two trends are evident in the works of Bhakti poets mentioned above in tune with the subjective predilections. Besides their *Ramayanas* and *Mahabharathas* some of them had also ventured to retell or translate the *Bhagavatha.* However, Pothana in Telugu, Eknath in Marathi and Premananda in Gujarati are known mainly for their *Bhagavatha*s.

This new prestige and competence acquired by the languages of the common people constituted a long step toward their empowerment, as against the elite classes and castes who jealously guarded their monopoly over the knowledge and hegemony in social and political discourse, and of course, the rituals and forms of worship. Language is not simply a means of communication; it is also a powerful instrument to keep intact the structures of power relations. Hence all revolutionaries and innovators shun the language of the powers-that-be and choose instead the regional and popular languages. Gautama Buddha, the first rebel to challenge effectively the hierarchical caste structure of Hindu society, had adopted the popular Prakrit or Pali language for his teachings in preference to the prevailing Sanskrit of the ruling castes. By the same token, the first thing a victorious conqueror or nation did was to impose his language on the vanquished. It is well known how T.B. Macaulay (1800–59), the Law member in Governor General's Council had sought to build up a new intelligentsia in India—brown in skin but toady white men at hearts—through the imposition of a medium of English education.

As said earlier, Tamil was a possible exception to the general pattern of the emergence of Indian languages in the wake of the Bhakti movement. For the first sprouting of the Bhakti movement in India had taken place in the South, especially in Tamil Nadu by about the sixth century of the Common Era (CE), and by that time, Tamil was already a flourishing language with a remarkable corpus of developed literature of the so-called *Sangam* Age spanning from the third century before CE (BCE) to the third century CE. So, Tamil is arguably the oldest living language not only of India, but most probably the world as a whole. However, it would be counter-productive to stretch the argument to the extreme and make the divergence of paths absolute. *Sangam* literally meant a group or collective. In this instance, it means either a royal court or an academy under royal auspices. The literary works were first presented before this collective and subjected to debate and evaluation. Usually the works were passed on to a larger public (that, too, would have been very limited due to highly restricted literacy rates) after overcoming these hurdles. The *Sangam* classics like *Chilappatahikraam, Manimekhalai* and others were composed in highly ornate court language, which by modern standards would be seen as elitist and archaic. The vocabulary, syntax and idioms of modern Tamil were contributions of Bhakti poets and saints called Saivite Nayanars and Vaishnavite Alvars, many of whom were wandering minstrels, who sought orally to communicate to the lowliest strata of society. So the vigour and vibrancy, simplicity and beauty of the present-day Tamil were a contribution of the Bhakti movement. Hence it is only legitimate to issue a note of caution against bestowing Tamil too much of an exceptional status.

Language and Power

On the question of language and the power structure of society, we may well begin with the views succinctly expressed by Pierre Bourdieu (1930–2002), the French philosopher. His collection of articles translated into English is called *Language and Symbolic Power*. Its editor, John P. Thompson, gives a competent summary of Bourdieu's view. The introduction begins as follows:

> All competent speakers are aware of the many ways in which linguistic exchanges can express the relations of power. We are sensitive to variations in power. We are sensitive to the variations in occults, intonation, and vocabulary, which reflect the different positions in social hierarchy. We are aware that individuals speak with different degrees of authority, that words are loaded with unequal weights depending on who utters them and how they are said, such that some words uttered in certain circumstances have a force and conviction that they would not have elsewhere. We are experts in the innumerable and subtle strategies by which words can be used as instruments of coercion and content, as tools of intimidation and abuse, as signs of politeness, congessence and content. In short we are aware that language is an integral part of social life with all its abuses and injustices and that a good part of social life consists of linguistic expression in the day to day flow of social interaction.[2]

This line of investigation has recently become widespread in academic circles. The same conclusions were arrived at with different lines of arguments by Norman Fairclough, too, in *Language and Power* (Longman 1989). The fast expanding area of socio-linguistics also provides ample proof for this line of thought as seen in *Language and Society* by Suzanne Romaine (Oxford 1994). From all these, the conclusion is inevitable that the Bhakti movement succeeded in bestowing a new respectability and competence to regional languages spoken by the common people as against the aristocratic but dying Sanskrit which had served as an instrument for Brahmanic caste domination. However, it was hardly as simple as that. The transactions and recreations of ancient Sanskrit texts by the new Bhakti poets had also helped to propagate the upper caste ideologies among the common people. It was a dialectical process.

The Sweep and the Depth

From the partial listing of the Bhakti poets itself it is clear that the movement embraced not only the present-day India, but also the entire subcontinent including the areas ceded to Pakistan. In the medieval period, Islam added to the spectrum of the diversity and variety of Indian religions, apart from its ascendance to state power.

Buddhism and Jainism were in decay and decline during the period. Their space was appropriated by the progressively rising tide of reforms as well as the resurgence of traditional Hinduism. Though the trend began with the sage Badarayana and his work *Brahmasutra,* generally credited to the early centuries of the CE, we will move on to the resurgence of Hinduism after a few more lines and also an account of its transformation which overtook Jainism and Buddhism.

A unique feature of the Bhakti movement, as also with Buddhism, was the rejection of caste and gender hierarchy and its associated forms of discrimination. The movement was led not just by a small section of Brahmins but also many devotees from the lower castes—shepherds, tailors, dalits and also former robbers and bandits. Thiruppan Alvar and Nandanar among the Alvars and the Nayanars of Tamil Nadu, Namdev and Chockamela of Maharashtra were just a few among the lower caste saints of the movement. Andal and Karaikkal Ammayar in Tamil Nadu, Akka Mahadevi in Karnataka, Meerabai in Rajasthan and Lal Ded in Kashmir were among the most famous bhakti poets and mystics. Their personal careers and contributions are discussed later in this book.

Another remarkable feature of the movement which gave it an unusual depth was the participation of Muslims mainly through the Sufi sect. Though there were also Muslim poets and mystics not connected with the Sufis, who also contributed to the non-sectarian continental awakening, the Sufi input was significantly deep and enduring in the bhakti tradition. It may be said that the Sufis were Muslim counterparts of the Hindu bhakts. This does not mean the two were parallel streams with no point of contact whatsoever. It only points towards the common origins of their inspiration. Both these streams joined and mingled with each other as Yamuna and Ganga at Prayag and majestically flowed home to the sea—the sea of India's composite culture and ethos. The Sufi movement among the Muslims had begun in twelfth century CE with Muhammed Chisti, who was credited with the fatherhood of Urdu. Nizamuddin Aulia was another luminary. Abdur Rahim Khan of the Pathan clan, Dadu Mulla and Malik Muhammed Jayasi were among the mystic Hindi poets who preached religious tolerance and a devotional cult. The Muslim weaver of Banaras, Kabir, was the foremost outstanding figure in the movement.

It is interesting that even some Buddhists had joined the Bhakti movement especially in Orissa. Of course, Buddhism was a declining force with only some scattered followings here and there. By this time in Orissa, the masses claimed Lord Jagannath as an incarnation of Gauthama Buddha and worshipped him as did the followers of Chaitanya Mahaprabhu. Chaitanya himself was described by the Buddhists as belonging to a Buddhist *sangha* as a disciple or *bikshu*.

2

Declining Buddhism, Resurging Hinduism

The ancient Gupta Empire which marked "a golden age" in Indian history covered the northern Indian hemisphere approximately during the period from 320 to 550 BCE. This period witnessed the resurgence of Hinduism. Buddhism was delivered a great ideological blow during the early years of the CE by Adi Sankaracharya (788–820 CE), triggering a Hindu resurgence with his articulation of the formidable philosophical thought of *advaita vedanta*. However, the great victory of Sankara as having rendered a 'death blow' to Buddhism may be an exaggeration, for Sankara also had absorbed in his scheme many aspects of Buddhism like its opposition to elaborate and wasteful sacrifices, rituals et cetera. A close study of any movement of renaissance or revolution will show that the inspiration it affords and its essentials survive in new forms much longer after its nominal decline and fall. We know that the French Revolution of 1789 had collapsed within four years with the coup d'état of Napoleon Bonaparte. However, who can deny that the French Revolution had heralded the beginning of the eclipse of feudalism and gave way to the rise of capitalism? Its slogan—Liberty, Equality and Fraternity—had an enduring influence in the nineteenth century not only in Europe but also in faraway Latin America and Asia. So, too, is Buddhism which in spite of its banishment from India, its birth place, many centuries ago, remains an undying inspiration even today to many in India as well as other countries. Many of the symbols of the Indian republic such as the Ashok Chakra and the three-lion pillar, are borrowed from Buddhist tradition. And Buddhism or its many sects remain among the four major religions of the world with the majority of its adherents in China, Japan and Sri Lanka.

In spite of his strong advocacy of the *varnasrama* hierarchy which was stridently condemned by the Buddha, Sankara was foresighted enough to absorb into his system many tenets of Buddhism. It was Mahavira and Buddha who successfully revolted against the barbarian custom of animal sacrifice (often human too) and advocated non-violence as the ultimate *dharma (ahimsa)*. Sankara, too, had vehemently opposed such sacrifices attaching primacy for seeking knowledge or holding aloft *jnanayoga* above *karmayoga*. He began his mission and attracted admiration with his victorious verbal duel against Kumarilla Bhatta and Prabhakara Bhatta, both strong defenders of the sacrificial style of Hinduism adumbrated in the Brahmanas of Vedic literature. Once having defeated Kumarilla and Prabhakara in the debate, Sankara's triumphant tour of India and as the legends say, his ascendancy to the *sarvajnapeetha* (the pedestal of omniscience) were foregone conclusions.

Along with these eminently sensible and radical elements in Buddha's teachings, Sankara also took over some abstruse and subtle concepts of some taller sects of Buddhism like Sunyavada of Madhyamikas and their chief protagonist, Nagarjuna. Sankara's absolute idealism and his denial of material reality under the mask of *Mayavada* owe much both to Nagarjuna's Madhyamikas and Sunyavada.

For this far reaching reconstruction of Hindu theology, Sankara sought to establish the primacy of the *Upanishad*s, Badarayana's *Brahmasutra* and the *Bhagavad Gita*. The three are referred to as *Prasthanathraya*. By holding aloft the *Upanishads*, he was throwing the *Veda*s into the dustbin of history. *Upanishad*s being the fourth part of the *Veda*s, he called the system he enunciated as the end product of the *Veda*s, the Vedanta. It may also mean the essence of the *Veda*s. The former three parts of the *Veda*s, which in effect were rejected by Sankara, were the *Mantras*, *Aranyaka*s and *Brahmana*s. The *Upanishad*s which do not advocate sacrifices and concentrate on philosophical issues with an implicit monotheism came in handy for Sankara for his monistic theology (Advaita Vedanta). *Upanishads* formed a growing corpus of philosophical writings and their number runs to more than 200. Sankara, by selecting only ten of them for his commentary, established their authority. These ten are:

1. *Brahadaranyaka Upanishad*
2. *Chandogya Upanishad*
3. *Aitreya Upanishad*
4. *Taitriya Upanishad*
5. *Isa Upanishad*
6. *Kena Upanishad*
7. *Katha Upanishad*
8. *Prasna Upanishad*
9. *Mundaka Upanishad*
10. *Mandukya Upanishad*

Though Sankara adopted many of the precepts and practices of Buddhism, he did not accept the opposition of Buddha and Jaina to the *varnasramadharma,* the Hindu caste system. Sankara's critics like Madhvacharya condemned him for being a '*Prachanna* Buddha' or crypto Buddhist. In his commentary on Badarayana's *Brahmasutra* which also advocated the caste system, he endorsed the denial of the right of Sudras to learn sacred texts like the *Vedas*. Sankara, with his monistic theory which extolled the unity not only of humankind but also the entire universe, found it very difficult to come to terms with Badarayana's theory of caste hierarchy and discrimination. Sankara resorted to a weak subterfuge by quoting *Manusmrithi* to justify the caste system. This was akin to quoting criminal procedure code to defend a philosophical position.

All these go to prove that Sankara's system in many ways fulfilled the vacuum created by the decline and near-demise of Buddhism and Jainism and to that extent it contained some elements of renaissance. Yet the movement as a whole certainly contained more elements of revivalism than of renaissance.

Some saints and poets of the Bhakti movement and even many modern writers seek the roots of Bhakti in Sankara's system. However, it would be grossly incorrect to describe it as a continuation of the resurgent Hinduism. As we will argue later, the Bhakti movement was directed much against the abstract philosophical speculations of Sankara and their social consequences.

As seen the Bhakti movement had spread to all parts of the subcontinent. However, this process of expansion had not taken place simultaneously, for even as the movement was sprouting forth in some parts, it was on decline in other regions. Still as a continuous chain of related events, it had encompassed the subcontinent with occasional time lags for about ten centuries.

3

The Problems of Origin and Nature

Many modern scholars who have gone deeply into the origins of the Bhakti cult and movement find their roots in the most ancient scriptures like the *Veda*s, epics and *Purana*s. Some even venture to discover their traces in the Harappan pre-historic relics. Some try to construct the unbroken thread of *bhakti* running—though with ups and downs—through the five thousand odd years of Indian culture and civilization. A.K. Majumdar's *Bhakti Renaissance* (1965) and K.C. Varadachari's *Aspects of Bhakti* (1956) may be cited as examples of this proclivity. The beginning of Bhakti may be traced to hymns of the *Rig Veda* (I 62.11). Says Majumdar:

> 'Longing Prayers are said. Indra who is longing just as a wife with desires gets her husband'. This idea is amplified in another hymn (X-43.1) which says: 'All my hymns in unison praise Indra as wives embrace their husbands. So do my thoughts embrace Indra the divine bestower of gifts: For the sake of a favour they cling to the liberal God (Indra) as wives do their Lords (or as a woman) does her handsome lover'. In another hymn (VI 45.26) Indra is addressed as a friend and it is said that there is a limit to his friendship and he gives cows to those who want cows and horses to those who want horses. In many other passages of Rig Veda, Indra is referred to as a Suhrud or a friend. Scholars have argued whether this attitude is that of a bhakta or devotee basing their definition of the terms as conceptions which developed much later. Without entering into this controversy, it may be stated that even if the attitude of Bhakti in all its implications was not present in Rig Veda hymns, the germ was already there.[3]

Though Majumdar sticks to his view of the Vedic origins of Bhakti, he hints at the possibility of the growth of the concept and practice in post-vedic periods. Further ahead he locates the middle ages as the juncture of its resurgence. But others like Varadachari do not even make Majumdar's concession. They would have us believe that the bhakti sentiment which is innate in the very being of homo sapiens and 'eternal consciousness' are likely to animate humans till their evolutionary span ceases and enters its next stage. Opines Varadachari, an authority on ancient Indian lore and philosophy in his lectures delivered at the University of Mysore under the auspices of Department of Indology, headed by the historian K.A. Neelakanta Sastri:

> Bhakti pre-eminently is the religious approach to God or the Supreme Reality. It is the religious consciousness or rather the religious mode of consciousness. Though it is related to the affective mode of consciousness, it is something more than that which is merely a subjective experience. There is the relationship to the Object which demands a relationship with it, though it is apparently not a simple affective relationship. It entails a complex sentiment of awe, fear, holiness and dependence. It is capable of being felt in certain moments of spiritual disclosure to the individual. It may be sensed as a superior power, luminous and compelling, as a law supernatural and even impersonal, as a universal sense and meaning of all existence or something surpassing all the categories of experience.[4]

Thus proceed the luxuriant narratives that smack more of sophistry than facts and logic. However, this much of Varadachari's prose is enough to acquaint us with his style of presentation and argument. Often Varadachari seems to be more mystically inclined than even the mystis of bhakti. Varadachari has reduced the Bhakti movement which gathered momentum and popularity as a society's collective celebration of arts under the leadership of the wandering minstrels to the subjective and individuated experience and ecstasies of a few inspired souls. Varadachari does not enlighten us about why and how such subjective experience of individuals could sway the entire society for about a thousand years from the seventh century to the sixteenth century CE. He concludes:

> Bhakti thus is a phenomenon of exceeding complexity but expressing one of the fundamental needs of the human soul not only as an expression of the soul itself in its integral nature but as being a means to its highest destiny of full freedom. It is the transfigured or sublimated emotion or sentiment of love directed to the highest Object, God in all its richness and fullness.[5]

Another writer on the Alvars of Tamil Nadu, S.M.S. Chari, goes even further than Majumdar and Varadachari. The name of his book itself, *Philosophy & Theistic Mysticism of the Alvars*, proclaims his views on the Bhakti movement. He treats the movement as a highly academic exercise of an intellectual elite. Thus he begins his preface.

> This book is devoted to the study of the Tamil hymns of the Vaisnava saints of South India known as Alvars who lived between the 6th and 8th centuries of the Christian Era. It's main objective is to present the philosophical and theological teachings as contained in the hymns and to evaluate the extent to which they have contributed to the Vishishta Advaita Vedanta and Vaisnava theology as expounded at a later period by Ramanuja and his successors. Right from the time of Nath Muni (9th century) the Vaisnava Acharyas have given great importance to the four thousand hymns of twelve Alvars collectively known as Nalayira Divya Prabhandam. They have accorded it a stature equal to that of Sanskrit Vedas as it contains the quintessence of the Vedic teachings.[6]

Chari's headlines of the chapters too betray his propensity to impose abstract philosophical concepts to the simple and melodious songs of the Alvars who were wandering minstrels chanting folksy songs of wisdom for their own enjoyment as well as to entertain their listeners. Some of the Alvars were Brahmins but others were illiterate peasants and Dalits. There was even an Alvar considered mad, that is, *Pay* Alvar, literally "mad Alvar". It could be that the minstrel's wild expressions of ecstasy were taken as a sign of madness! However, Chari would have us believe that they were all 'great philosophers' on the lines of Nagarjuna, Sankara, Ramanuja and others. Look at some of his chapters' titles: *The Doctrine of Ultimate Reality, The Doctrine of God, The Doctrine of Individual Self, The Doctrine of Sadhana* et cetera.

As seen earlier, Varadachari extricates bhakti from its historic and social contexts and ascribes it as eternal and the innate aspect of the human soul. The presumptions of Majumdar, Varadachari and Chari were responded to by another outstanding scholar Dr David N. Lorenzen. In an essay on Kabir Panth, Dr Lorenzen writes:

> No ideology can be properly understood without analytically locating it in its specific historical, economic and political context. However common sensical this statement may appear, academic discussion of Indian religion often seem to delight perversely ignoring its structure and consequence. Nowhere is this more evident than in the chronic tendency to exaggerate the undoubtedly real and remarkable continuity of Hindu tradition and to correspondingly minimize its discontinuities. For instance, while few modern scholars wholly accept the traditional view that the essence of Hinduism is to be found in the four Vedas, many do not hesitate to accept the incredible theory that the worship of mother-goddess in medieval Tantric cults represents a resurgence of the popular civilization, not withstanding the lapse of some two to three thousand years in which no serious evidence for the continuity of such a cult exists.[7]

Lorenzen, a member of the Center of Oriental Studies at El Colegio de Mexico in Mexico City was associated with many universities in the US and Europe. Unlike many Western scholars, he is very sympathetic to Indian traditions and customs. His book on '*Kapalikas and Kalamughas*' sects which were painted very negatively as barbarians and savages by others unveils their positive aspects. He considers the Bhakti movement in India as among the victims of unhistorical assessment. He says:

> The concept of bhakti or devotion is a frequent victim of such anachronistic or de-contextualised analysts. Some form of devotion is obviously central to or at least present in all religions. The superficial similarity of the devotional sentiments expressed in different stages of Hindu traditions, in say the Vedas and Puranas, tends to disguise serious contextual and functional differences.[8]

Therefore in order to avoid the pitfalls pointed out by Lorenzen, let us briefly examine the historical and social contexts which gave birth to the Bhakti movement in India.

4

The Chronology and Geography

The cult of bhakti continues to be a force in the 21st century India, too. Its proof lies in the living practice of the ritualistic reading of *Mahabharatha, Ramayana* and the *Bhagavatha,* translated or created by the bhakti poets in Hindu homes regularly or in specified months. The practice of modern poets and novelists to compose their works on the basis of these epics and the *Purana*s too illustrates the enduring presence of the cult. The onslaught of modern technology and media has only helped to sustain its influence.

A few years ago, the serial presentation of the *Ramayana* on the state-owned (Dooradarshan) TV won high popularity. Many devout Hindus used to pay obeisance with folded hands when the gods and goddesses appeared on the TV screen. A recent book by Christian Lee Novetzke, Professor in the South Asia Program at the University of Washington on Sant Namdev, the thirteenth century bhakti saint from Maharashtra explains its theme as follows:

> This book is about how a religious figure of fourteenth century India has been remembered over seven centuries, through multiple media including performance, writing and film. The figure is Namdev, a saint important to Hindus and Sikhs in central, western and northern India. The book focuses primarily on the cultural history of Namdev's legacy in the area co-terminus with modern Maharashtra. The theoretical fabrics used to understand this long tradition of recollection through multiple media are encompassed by the term 'public memory' and are derived from

> both the study of 'publics' of various kinds and the study of memory particularly in ways similar to what Jan Assmann has called 'memory history' or the 'history of cultural memory.'[9]

Although the survival of medieval phenomenon is certainly remarkable and deserves deep study and detailed analysis, it would be the height of folly to assume that the cult continues without any let up or hindrance. It may be true that large sections of people in India of different denominations are still addicted to the rituals and other practices associated with Bhakti. However, it is also a fact that the twentieth and twenty first centuries have not produced counterparts of Alvars, Nayanars, the Veerasaiva Vachana poets, Namdev, Meera, Surdas et al. So what we have today is not so much a vibrant and continuous presence of the bhakti cult as they are reverberations of a bygone age.

When did the Age of Bhakti begin and when did it come to a close? There are certain types of events in history for which it is possible to fix the dates or on some occasions even the hour of their occurrence. However, it would be a foolhardy or hazardous venture to try to fix a date for the beginning and ending of deep-rooted social and cultural transformations like the European Renaissance which marked the eclipse of the middle age and the Indian Bhakti movement which, in turn, signaled a breach with many a tradition made sacrosanct by scriptures and conventions. Yet for the purposes of analysis and comparison some chronology is required however approximate and slippery it may be. Here is the Sanskrit passage often quoted by scholars somewhat indicating the geographical contours of the movement:

Utpanna dravide bhakti
vriddhim karnatake gata
kvachit kvachin maharastre
gujjare pralayam gata

This may be roughly translated as follows:

The Bhakti movement began in Dravida country.
It grew in strength and entered Karnataka.

From there it passed on to Maharashtra.
And declined and vanished from Gujarat.

This passage certainly refers to the birth of the Saivite Nayanar and the Vaishnavite Alvar movements of about the sixth or seventh centuries CE. The movement's phase in Karnataka refers to the Veerasaiva movement of Basava and his followers and the parallel movement led by Pampa, Kumara and Purandhara. The third stage was in Maharashtra which began with Gnaneswara and blossomed forth with the devotees of Vittal at Pandharpur like Tukaram, Chokhamela and Namdev. The fourth stage is indicated as the final step of the movement into Gujarat where it is supposed to have declined and vanished.

The statement that the Bhakti movement had declined and vanished after entry into Gujarat is not entirely correct. Poets like Narasimha Mehta did carry the torch of Bhakti in Gujarat during the subsequent period. However, there is reason for the pronouncement of the movement's doom in Gujarat for the sharp break in the continuity of the movement by the time it reached Gujarat was quite evident. By the twelfth and thirteenth centuries, the movement in the south and south-west India had become a spent force. The movement in the north-west, North and north-east took two or three centuries more to spring up with Meera in Rajasthan, Ramananda in the Gangetic belt, Kabir in the north, Chaitanya in the east and Guru Nanak in the Indus belt. The Sanskrit verses appearing in some of the Puranas might have been composed during the interval between the decline of the movement in the south and west on the one hand and its rise in the North on the other. The last outstanding figure of the Bhakti movement was perhaps Guru Nanak (1469–1539) the founder of the Sikh religion. Hence it is only fair to conclude that the history of the rise and decline of the Bhakti movement spanned around a thousand years between the seventh century and the sixteenth century.

Though the tempo of social changes in ancient and medieval periods was very much slower than in the later modern periods, the two thousand years which witnessed the rise and fall of the Bhakti movement was not at all stagnant. The campaigns and conquests on Indian soil by the Afghans, Turks and finally the Mughals had begun by the time of the decline of the Alvars and Nayanars of Tamil Nadu. These conquests had deep impacts on Indian society and politics. Tirumular Nayanar, who may be considered as the pioneer of the Tamil Bhakti movement and Guru Nanak, the last major figure of the movement faced extremely different situations and problems during their lifetime. As already seen, the Sufi sect, too, had a major role in the Bhakti movement. The first Sufi saint-poet belonged to the twelfth century. The Guru Granth Sahib which is supposed to contain the original words and ideas of Guru Nanak borrows heavily from Koran.

However the Bhakti cult in the south has not revealed any links with Muslim traditions. Chekkizhar, a scholar and Minister of Chola king in his *Periya Puranam* composed in the twelfth century narrates the story of the sixty-three Nayanars and their teachings. Almost simultaneously the *'Nalayira Prabhandam* of the songs of 12 Alvars were also collected and published. This encyclopaedic work does not indicate that he was in any way aware of Islam or the Koran. Nath Muni who did a similar work *Thevaaram* giving details about the twelve Alvars and their teaching also was not very much worried or fascinated by the Islamic teachings or intrusions. Their concerns were Buddhism and Jainism which drew their ire. They desperately castigated their adherents as *Sramanas*. To sum up, though the Bhakti and Sufi movements had certain inalienable common characteristics from the beginning to the end, there were also a variety of divergences and differences as well.

5

Social and Political Background

We have been saying repeatedly that the Bhakti movement was a social, religious and literary phenomenon of the medieval period. This period was almost taken for granted as a stage in Indian history between the sixth and sixteenth centuries CE. However, this is only a relatively recent assumption. Colonial historians from James Mill onwards had taken another view. They made the periodisation of Indian history on the basis of the religion of the ruling dynasties. Thus they had designated ancient India to the Hindu period and medieval India to Muslims. Perhaps due to ideological and political reasons they did not call the British period as Christian age. This distorted periodisation though suited the imperial strategy of Divide and Rule had ignored the basic concepts of historical evoluation and social change.

Modern historians assign the interim period of transition from ancient India to medieval India as between the fourth and seventh centuries CE. R.S. Sharma after effectively refuting the colonial historians' prejudicial periodisation presents the modern view as follows:

> It would thus appear that between the 4th and 7th centuries, ancient Indian life was in a stage of fermentation and transformation. Momentous changes appeared in polity, society, economy, language, script, art and architecture and in religion and intellectual life. It is very difficult to take their total view and locate and explain their convergence. But it is necessary to make an attempt in this direction. The concept, content and origins of

> medievalism need to be analysed and clarified. This can be done not through a survey of political and dynastic developments but through an integrated study of all the strands in Indian life in different parts of the country.[10]

From this it is clear that the transitional period covers the closing years of the Gupta dynasty (c. 320–547 CE) to the reign of Harsha-vardhana (r. 606–47) of Kanauj. A number of factors contributed to the transformation of Indian polity and social structure. Most important features of this transition period include the decline of the imperial power, decentralization of administrative structure and the rise of feudal chiefs as intermediaries located between the central power on the one side and the peasants and other producing classes at large on the other. In social and historical terminology, this new system is called 'feudalism'. It may seem strange that this decline of central authority had begun during the reigns of the powerful Guptas and Harsha. R.S. Sharma, Romila Thapar and others have located the beginning of this disintegration of central power in the system of 'land grants' or the 'land gifts'.

The Gupta dynasty's rise to imperial power was coeval with two contradictory developments—the decline of Buddhism and Jainism and the consequent rise of Brahmanical Hinduism with its *varnasramadharma.* The official and academic language was Sanskrit which during the ascendancy of Buddhism was relegated to an unfair position by Prakrit and Pali. Many historians would have us believed that the Gupta era was the Golden Age of Indian history. Though this claim is not accepted by modern historians, it shows certain aspects of Gupta suzerainty. It was a flowering age of art and literature and the restoration of the lost glory of traditional Brahminic Hinduism. It was in this new situation and new configuration of social classes and caste that the royal power gave land as gift to the Brahmins for their priestly and scholastic services. Land was also allotted to soldiers and government officers in lieu of cash remuneration. As Kautilya describes in his *Arthasastra,* the salary of officials should be paid in cash and the taxes should be collected by the agents of the royal authority. With the later Guptas and Harshavardhana this practice began to be very rare.

The taxes were to be collected by the land grantees who were also entrusted with the duty of maintaining the law and order and punishing criminals. Land was also gifted to temples especially in South India and they became centers of feudal power and Brahmin dominance. Armies were also maintained by the feudal chief when the king or the emperor wanted to wage a war or defend his domain against any attackers. They called upon the feudal chieftains to contribute army personnel who would return home after the battles ended.

All these new developments were not the results of subjective decisions or the volitions of the powers that be. This period had witnessed a deep social and economic crisis and the new set up was a response and an attempt to solve it. It is this crisis that gave rise to the concept of repetitive cycles of social development – *Kritayuga, Threthayuga, Dwaparayuga* and finally *Kaliyuga.* And after Kaliyuga, the society or the world would re-enter Krithayuga and the process would be repeated *ad infinitum.* The *Purana*s and the *Dharmasastra*s of the early centuries of the first millennium CE give detailed characteristics of these *yuga*s. Kritayuga was supposed to be the perfect haven of peace, piety, prosperity and dharma. Then onwards in the following three ages, the glories of *Kritayuga* and *Dharma* progressively degenerated and the worst was *Kaliyuga* which coincides with the historical category of the medieval era.

Basing himself on the various Puranic texts and epics including the *Aranya* chapter of the *Mahabharatha*, Sharma summarises the main features of *Kaliyuga* as follows:

> The main elements of Kali in the texts assigned to the third century AD and probably the beginning of the 4th century can be enumerated as the mixing varnas (varnasankaras) hostility beween shudras and brahmanas, refusal of vaishyas to pay taxes and offer sacrifice, oppression of people with taxes, wide-spread theft and robbery, insecurity of family and property, destruction of livelihood, growing importance of wealth over ritual status and dominance of mlecha princes. In short widespread social disorder adversely affected society and security of privileged orders.[11]

Some of these may be considered symptoms, others as causes and yet others, as consequences. Whatever that be, it was the crisis of the existing social order which affected mainly the ruling upper castes and classes. The ruling classes never tolerate such challenges to their privileges with equanimity. The law books composed by the Brahmanas and other privileged classes strictly forbade such deviations from the prescribed paths of behaviour and assigned duties, and even threatened with dire punishment in this world and eternal damnation in the other. Krishna, in the *Gita* advises Arjuna to stick to *swadharma* even if it is inferior to *paradharma,* that is no one should transgress the duties assigned to his caste and adopt the duties of other classes.

The new administrative reforms initiated by kings and emperors like land gifts, delegation of powers to a rising class of feudal chiefs were also responses to the emerging scenario. Though we have stated that these administrative changes led to evolution of the feudal system, a modification of the concept and establishment of the system is called for. D.D. Kosambi divides feudalism into two categories— 'feudalism from above' and 'feudalism from below'. This is how he differentiates the two types:

> Feudalism from above means a state wherein an emperor or a powerful King levied tribute from sub-ordinates who still ruled in their own right; and did what they liked within their own territories—as long as they paid the paramount rulers. These sub-ordinate rulers might even be the tribal chiefs, and seem in general to have ruled the land by direct administration without the intermediary of a class which was in effect a land owning stratum. But feudalism from below is meant the next stage where a class of land owners developed within the village between the State and the peasantry, gradually to wield armed power over the local population.[12]

So the feudalism of the period we are discussing was in the second stage of development, that is, feudalism from below which was actually a logical development of the stage of feudalism from above. This final stage was certainly more oppressive as far as the peasantry was concerned and set in motion sporadic resistance on their part. This feudalisation and resistance were not confined to some areas—it was a subcontinental phenomenon with local and time variations.

Some historians of South India like K.A. Neelakanta Sastri,

and Burton Stein tend to speak of this period of rural life as tranquil and orderly and tacitly assume a peasant society without landlords. Kesavan Veluthat successfully demolishes this idyllic picture of rural life on the basis of original inscriptions and other evidence. He writes:

> The copper plate records of Pallavas and the Pandyas in the 7th and 8th centuries AD provide information on the various shades of rights on land concomitantly the position of different sections of society depending on the nature of the right that enjoyed on a particular piece of land. Most of the Pallava copper plates record the grant of land to Brahmanas. Inevitably they are related to the creation and transfer of certain superior rights over land. This is expressed in the case of a few Pallava as the expression Kutineekki, which means literally removing the previous occupants. The same idea is expressed in another expression Mun perrarai marri found in a couple of Pallava records. Both these signify that the recipient of the land were at liberty to evict the earlier occupants of their own choice.[13]

This new agrarian social structure which had robbed the traditional rights of the peasantry did not go unchallenged. The producing classes resisted the exploitation of the rentier idle classes in various ways ranging from humble submission of complaints to violent outbreaks and even self-immolations. Sharma gives numerous instances of such peasant resistance. Litigation, too, was another form of resistance. However, the law givers of the period amended the *Dharmasastras* to include defiance of the *Raja Sasanas* (Royal Orders) too among the anti-Dharma activities. Thus the attempts to redress the peasant grievance through litigation against royal land gifted to Brahmanas were doomed to fail. Many of the heroic stories found in Karnataka and other neighbouring areas bear inscriptions which prove that the heroes were often martyrs who laid down their lives in the struggle against landlords' oppression. Many later Jataka tales of Buddhists give numerous instances of such resistance. Though ultimately the power of the landlords prevailed over the peasants, the wide spread resistance added to the instability of the feudal order besides some paltry benefits gained by the peasants here and there.

6

'*Kali*': A Curse or Blessing?

Sharma's description of the Kali Age is based mainly on the *Santhi Parva* of the *Mahabharatha* which explains that it was an age of decay and crisis. From his description it is also clear that the crisis had affected mainly the ruling caste hierarchy and its values. In history the decay of the existing order paves way for the foundation of renewal and reconstruction. So the *Kali Age* actually prepared the ground for Bhakti Renaissance. It is interesting to note that the *Kali Age* was not condemned as a curse by some Puranic texts and commentators.

> *At the advent of the present age, Kaliyuga, which traditionally dates from the death of Krishna on the 18th of February in the year 3102* BC, *only a quarter of the original* **Dharma** *is still present. Conversely,* **Adharma** *has grown to replace the lost three quarters. After this point the decline of virtue is a foregone conclusion....*[14]

Kaliyuga within this concept is a fertile ground for the rise of new religion or the timely transformation of the old. Bhakti movement can be considered either way. This interpretation is not in consonance with the general idea among the Hindu or the Indian public at large as it has been a common practice to ascribe all that is unsavoury to the Kaliyuga. As said earlier, some Puranas give a different perspective of Kaliyuga. In the important spiritual text *Vishnu Purana,* the sage Parasara, in the course of clearing the doubts expressed by Maithreya, says on Kaliyuga:

> ...Being thus addressed by the Munis, Vyasa smiled and said to them, 'Hear excellent sages, why I uttered the words "Well done, well done". The fruit of Penance, of continence, of silent prayer, and the like, practiced in the Krta age for ten years, in the Treta for one year, in the Dvapara for a month is obtained in the Kali age in a day and night; therefore did I exclaim, "Excellent, excellent, is the Kali age!". That reward which a man obtains in the Krata by abstract meditation, in the Treta by sacrifice, in the Dvapara by adoration, he receives in the Kali by merely reciting the name of Kesava. In the Kali age a man displays the most exalted virtue by every little exertion; therefore, pious sages, who know that virtue is, I was pleased with the Kali age. Formerly the Vedas were to be acquired by the twice- born through the diligent observances of self-denial; and it was their duty to celebrate sacrifices comfortably to the ritual, Then idle prayers, idle feasts, and fruitless ceremonies, were practiced but to mislead the twice-born; for although observed by them devoutly, yet, in consequence of some irregularity in their celebration, sin was incurred in all their works, and what they ate, or what they drank, did not effect the fulfillment of their desires. In all their objects the twice-born enjoyed no independence, and they attained their respective spheres only with exceeding pain. The Sudra, on the contrary, more fortunate than they, reaches his assigned station by rendering them service, and performing merely the sacrifice of preparing food, in which no rules determine what may or may not be eaten, what may or may not be drunk. Therefore, most excellent sages, is the Sudra fortunate.
>
> Riches are accumulated by men in modes not incompatible with their peculiar duties, and they are then to be bestowed upon the worthy, and expended in constant sacrifice. There is a great trouble in their acquisition; and great grief for their loss. Thus, eminent Brahmanas, through these and other sources of anxiety, men attain their allotted spheres of Prajapathi and the rest only by exceeding labour and suffering. This is not the case with women; a woman has only to honour her husband, in act, thought and speech to reach the same region to which he is elevated; and she thus accomplishes her object without any great exertion....[15]

Parasara's description of the opportunities Kaliyuga offers to the subaltern section of society is almost similar to the contributions of the radical poets and saints of the early Bhakti movement. All these prove that the Kaliyuga was a curse only for the ruling classes in society but a blessing for the oppressed and downtrodden.

Though Kaliyuga is supposed to continue to this day, it is assessed here as referring to the early centuries of the first millennium of the CE.

7

The Warring Princes and Foreign Conquerors

It was briefly discussed earlier that the decline of trade and towns and the consequent paucity of metal coins were the chief factors which led to land gifts and feudalisation of society. It was also noted that this had led to a form of decentralisation of powers and the rise of a number of independent and semi-independent states. D.N. Jha says that as many as hundreds of such entries may be counted and listed. This fragmentation of polity was a by-product of the decline of trade and towns.

As we have seen this process of feudalisation was not confined to North India especially the Gangetic valley. With variations in form and time, the feudal relations were spreading throughout the length and breadth of the subcontinent. Sharma and other historians point to the paucity of coins as an evidence of this decline. The all-India trade routes, caravans and transactions in coins instead of commodities and barter are parts of a frame on which large states and empires are built. The urban centres functioned not only as trade centres but also as hubs of military and state power. With the decline of urban centres and trade, power had receded to rural areas resulting in a type of decentralization of power structure which led to the rise of smaller states and principalities. After Harshavardhana's time, his empire broke into a number of smaller states always involved in mutual spats for supremacy. This predicament continued till about 1526 CE when Babar occupied the Delhi throne and the Great Mughals resurrected the old imperial glory till the death of Emperor Aurangzeb in 1707 CE.

The period (about a thousand years) between Harsha's death and conquest of Delhi by Babar may be divided into two phases. The first phase came to a close with the establishment of the Delhi Sultanate by the Turkish conquerors in c.1200 CE. This first phase saw the rise of a number of new States, mini empires, their vassals and autonomous feudal chieftains who handled not only tax collections but administration of their domain.

The main contenders for dominance of north India between the seventh and tenth centuries were the Palas of Bengal, Pratiharas of Gujarat and the Rastrakutas in the Vindhya region. When these three mini-empires were engaged in the struggle to step into the shoes of Harsha, many powers were rising in the central and southern regions. The Chalukyas in the Deccan, Cholas, Pandyas, Pallavas and Cheras in the deep south– some making intrusions into the north and crossing the eastern seas to South East Asia and beyond. In north-west India too new kingdoms were rising with resurgent Hinduism under a new mysterious race called the 'Rajputs'. Their origins are still a matter of controversy but a larger consensus favours the migrant tribes of the Huns from the far west of West Asia as the predecessors of Rajputs.

The Huns—a violent tribe from central Asia—had invaded India in the fifth century, settled in the arid regions of Rajasthan (previously called Rajaputana, the home of Rajput), made India their home and adopted the traditional Indian religion. Later their descendents, the Rajputs came to be even considered as the stalwarts of Indian tradition, religion and heroism.

After the collapse of the Maurya Empire—c.322–180 BCE—there was no north Indian empire which extended southwards beyond the Vindhya ranges. The Deccan was almost isolated from the north. As already mentioned, north India had become a constant warfield of three important dynasties, the Palas of Bengal, Prathiharas of Gujarat and the Rashtrakutas of Central India during the eight to eleventh centuries. Though Samudra Gupta (335–75 CE) of the Gupta dynasty did make some forays to the south, it was ephemeral. The succeeding Harsha Gupta's (606–47 CE) empire too did not extend to the south with its heartland in the Indo-Gangetic Plain. The western and eastern Chalukyas had their territories close to Vindhyas. The Kakatiya kingdom was in present day Andhra with Warangal as the capital. Karnataka was ruled by the Hoysala dynasty while the western Chalukyas occupied most of the rest of Karnataka. By the fourteenth century the Vijayanagara kingdom rose to prominence and became a centre of Hindu renaissance. The deep south was dominated by three kingdoms or empires as many historians designate them—the Pandyas, Cholas, and Pallavas. Of these the Pallavas were the most durable though the Cholas had their glory under Rajaraja Chola (985–1014 CE). That was the age of Moovarasar or the three kings. There was also a Chera Kingdom extending from Kodungalloor to Palakkad and Coimbatore. Veluthat gives this brief summary of the political and social structure of this period:

> The earliest known phase in the history of South India, which is generally taken to have come to a close by the third century AD, is thought in the conventional literature to have been separated by the next known phase of the monarchies under our study, i.e. the early seventh century, by a 'long historical night'. This disjunctive character of the age of Pallavas has been rightly questioned in recent years. Continuity there certainly was, but what is equally important was a series of change that had been effected in the social and economic spheres which had reflected itself in the form and content of the political organisation. A totally new ideology, which suited the new social formation, had been developing, and this helped reinforce it in a big way. Thus, even when one does not agree with the conventional view of the disjunctive character of the age of the Pallavas and after in the history of South India, these sea changes should not go unnoticed.
>
> As stated earlier, our information regarding the social and economic processes in the age of the Pallavas from the seventh century AD is to be gleaned from the very few epigraphic records, which present only a narrow, one-sided picture. A number of large scale agrarian settlements opened up on the river valleys of the Pennar and Palar. A distinctive feature of these settlements was the existence of a managerial class of non-cultivating intermediaries, superimposed over the cultivating peasantry and enjoying superior rights over the land and having direct links with the state.[16]

According to Veluthat and some other scholars like M.G.S. Narayanan it was the Bhakti movement which galvanised and legitimised the social and political structure of the day. Though it would be hazarduous to try and set specific dates for the birth and demise of a movement like bhakti, there can be no dispute that these centuries, as mentioned by Veluthat, represented the high watermark of the Bhakti movement in south India, especially Tamizhakom. Veluthat assesses the impact of Bhakti as follows:

> It has been brought out that the Bhakti movement legitimised the entire gamut of relationships in the social, economic and political spheres. The graded hierarchy of economic relations with various shades of right in land, the equally graded hierarchy of social relations with different shades of ritual status and the corresponding graded hierarchy of political relations with different shades of power and authority—this was reflected and legitimised in the religious world. While the Bhakti movement has been presented by earlier historians as representing a veritable social reform movement spearheaded against caste and other forms of inequality, our analysis shows that this helped in consolidating the new social and political order in South India in the early medieval period. It strengthened and gave support to the new monarchy; and by favouring the ideology of the Brahmanised sections in society, it helped the entire upper class to send its roots deeper in society. As for the ruling class, the identification of the necessary apparatus of legitimation was indeed possible through this ideology. The socio-political milieu in which this ideology took shape in northern India had evolved a ready-made framework for itself and, once the ideological standards of that milieu were adopted, it was also easier to adopt the apparatuses of political legitimation as they had developed there.[17]

Veluthat's views on this question cannot be totally brushed aside. However, this altogether negative view of bhakti does not accord either with the history or the character of the bhakti leaders.

The Foreign Impact

Some scholars are of the view that the Bhakti movement was in part a response to the invasion by the various races and people and the intermixture of their faiths with Indian traditions. Though this argument cannot be fully accepted, it can hardly be denied altogether either. Many Muslim saints like Kabir and the Sufi sects were part of the Bhakti movement, especially in north India.

After short forays into the north-western India by Mahmud Ghazni and Mohammad of Ghori, a series of invasions took place through the Khyber pass and Hindukush ranges by the Turks, Afghans and Mongols (whose descendents came to be known as Mughals) by the twelfth century CE. The Turks conquered India and the Delhi sultanate was established. Next was the turn of the Afghans. These conquerors quarreled for the dominance of India, and in the process, came into and went out of power periodically untill 1526 when Babar conquered India and captured Delhi to establish the Mughal dynasty. The Mughal Empire began to disintegrate by 1707 with the death of the last great Mughal Emperor, Aurangazeb.

In 1498, the Portuguese navigator, Vasco da Gama, sailed round the African continent, crossed the Arabian Sea and anchored at Kappad, a few kilometers north of Kozhikode (Calicut), and laid the foundations of the Western dominance of Asia. The influence of Muslims and Christian rulers paved the way for two more religions to the mosaic of Indian faiths.

Though the traditional Indian religions were Hinduism, Buddhism and Jainism, they were all fragmented into sects and warring groups. Many bhakti leaders tried to galvanise these groups and sects and cast them into a united community living in harmony with a common faith. However, as we will see the ultimate result was that the movement itself was split into different castes or faiths to add to the existing plethora. Adding further to this confusing scenario were the newly imported religions like Islam and Christianity which brought in their own sub-divisions and sects. Of course, their fragmentation was far less in number than that of the Hindus but it can hardly be ignored.

The Bhakti movement addressed all these problems with varying measures of success, as we shall see. Here also Veluthat's blanket negation of any progressive content in the movement seems to be exaggerated.

8

The Triumvirate and Duumvirate

It is a hazardous task to select a few among the innumerable gods and goddesses of the Hindu pantheon for any special study. Some texts go even to enumerate them to 330 million. The number of gods and goddesses goes on multiplying as many local deities and tribal gods, once derided by the orthodoxy, are canonised and admitted to the pantheon. This process of canonisation takes varied forms. Some of these local deities are absorbed into one or two of the existing godheads, some are merged into the existing ones and new myths are woven around them. They are either co-opted into the existing *Purana*s or new texts are composed to give them new authenticity.

All these varied methods of identification, absorption, co-option and synthesis are exemplified in the evolution of the three most important deities of Hindus; Brahma, Vishnu and Siva. Like an organism of nature, the gods and goddesses also undergo a process of evolution with life cycles like birth, growth and death. The death may be a complete transformation of the original concept into its opposite or at least to a different form with hardly any resemblance to original. The histories of religious practices are replete with such instances. In India, an outstanding anthropologist and Indologist Professor G.S. Ghurye gives many such examples in his study *On Gods and Men* (Bombay 1992). It is well known that Gautama Buddha, who grew in stature and spread his doctrines in opposition to Vedic religious dogmas and practices, was later absorbed and co-opted into the Hindu pantheon and was designated as either an *avatar* or synonym of Vishnu. So also R.S. Sharma argues *Tantricism* which became a part of Hindu rituals and later Buddhism was borrowed from tribal practices as some tribes were absorbed into the fold of the all consuming Hindu social system. As we said all these varieties of transformation, synthesis and symbiosis are discernible in the evolution of the Hindu Triumvirate collectively and individually.

The Triumvirate

The concept of the supreme position assigned to the Triumvirate evolved around the idea of Brahma the Creator, Vishnu the Preserver, and Siva the Destroyer. Unlike in monotheistic religions like Judaism, Christianity, and Islam, which assign the power of creation, preservation and destruction to their single Godhead (Jehova and Allah), the Hindu tradition assigns the power for the task of *srishti, stithi* and *samhara* to the triumvirate or the *trimurthis,* which in certain ways, is akin to the theory of the Trinity in Christianity. The theology of the Trinity was never preached by Jesus Christ or his twelve disciples, but was concocted by later theologians and divines who were eager to bestow the great teacher's simple and humanistic teachings with an aura of philosophic intricacies. The Muhammadan teaching was no different.

The Rise and Decline of Brahma

The name of Brahma as a God (not as meaning the Universe, *Brahmandom*) does not appear in the earliest texts of the four *Veda*s, called *samhithas.* It appears only in later additions called *Brahmanas, Aranyaka*s *and Upanishad*s and that too in a subdued manner. For example, the first mention of Brahma appears in *Satapatha Brahmana* as just a name in the long list of other gods. *Aranyaka*s and some *Upanishad*s also make references to Brahma. Brahma's elevation to the central stage in the Hindu pantheon began with the *Ithihasa*s and *Purana*s certainly composed later than Vedic texts. However, the *Ithihasa*s and *Purana*s with constant extrapolation and editing, the confusing medley of stories and legends in them had changed the role previously assigned to gods, a few more were added to the list and the protocol of status was re-written. In this process, Brahma also was downgraded in many ways. The story of Brahma's birth in a lotus grown from the navel of Vishnu itself places Brahma on the second rung. The story that Brahma had originally five faces (*panchamukha*) and that Siva, in order to teach him a lesson, plucked one of them and left him with four was yet another strategic step to push him down in the divine heirarchy.

As a consequence, a situation arose when the era of the triumvirate gave way to the duumvirate. The configuration as described by Greg. M. Bailey is as follows:

> Although it would be supremely difficult to define an epic and puranic pantheon (or pantheons) very strictly, it is obvious from a cursory reading of these texts that some gods were accorded a higher position in relation to others. Vishnu and Siva are clearly regarded as very important gods in this literature; whereas others like Indra, though still important are often depicted in myths in a position subordinate to the first two gods. Several Although it would be supremely difficult to scholars using text-critical methods that developed by W. Kirfel have obtained results which have considerable implications for establishing Brahma's relative position in the pantheon.
>
> In a series of articles, P. Hacker has drawn attention to the results which can be obtained for the reconstruction of Indian religious history by constructing a history of the texts. By adhering to a rigorous philological method, which aims to determine the relative ages of texts and portions which correspond almost literally, later interpolations and reworked passages can be isolated, leaving what may be an 'Ur-text'. Utilizing Text Groups 2A and 2B of Kirfel's four fold division of the Puranic Cosmogonic passages, he has sworn the existence in these passages of three different textual layers each expressing its own religious idiosyncrasy. Hacker concludes: 'The oldest layer is a Brahmaism (or Swayambhuism) associated with the ideas of the original Waters and the World Egg. In the second layer an attempt is made to harmonize these beliefs with Samkhya Philoszophy which at that time was intellectually attractive; .... In it the theism remains Brahmaism. Finally, in the third layer, Siva or Vishnu is the highest god.[18]

Bailey gives a detailed account of the worship of Siva in many parts and especially in the northern and the Gangetic plain and

Rajasthan. A famous temple devoted to Brahma is located in Pushkar of northern Rajasthan (near Ajmer) which is still a popular centre of worship and pilgrimage. When we consider hundreds of thousands of temples scattered all over India, the number of Brahma temples is very few and far between. In Thiruvananthapuram on the western side of the Sri Padmanabha Swamy temple, there is a minor temple, which seems to be an ancient one where the trimurthis are installed for worship. Usually the trimurthis including Brahma are not installed together in Hindu temples. All these are rare exceptions which prove the rule that a sharp decline in Brahma worship began around the sixth century CE. This century witnessed the beginning of the rise of the Bhakti movement in the deep south which subsequently travelled in the west coast of India and encompassed the subcontinent as we have already seen. It is also significant that the Bhakti movement was composed of two important streams of Vishnu and Siva worshippers. In the south, the Siva worshippers were headed by 63 Nayanars and Vaishnavas were led by 10 to 12 Alvars. We have already noted that Brahma was the Creator, Vishnu, the Preserver and Siva, the Destroyer according to the Hindu tradition. But the story of Brahma's birth in the Lotus which grew from the navel of Vishnu had resulted in assigning a subordinate position to Brahma. The literal meaning of Vishnu is *one which continuously spreads out*, that is, Vishnu is the expanser to all aspects of the universe. So his field of activity and influence is co-terminus with the universe, if such boundaries can be attributed to the endless universe. The Hindu thought, rituals and most of the gods are related to Vishnu. Many of the gods of the Hindus are *Avatars* or incarnations of Vishnu. Generally Vishnu is supposed to have descended from heaven in ten different incarnations—the *Dasavatara*—at different periods of time. Some texts relegate Dasavatara to a final phase and claim there was a first phase when Vishnu adopted the human form in another eleven Avatars. His consort is Lakshmi, 'the Goddess of Prosperity'. Some texts state that he had two other consorts, too, Ganga and Saraswathy. Saraswathy is the 'Goddess of Learning' and Ganga, a celestial goddess, who descended to the earth to flow as the epomynous and eternal river into the sea. Ganga was brought down as a big torrent into the wild *jada* (matted head) of Siva. However, Ganga did not overflow from Siva's jadas and remained there forever, in order to fulfill the wishes of his devotee the King Bhageeratha. When Siva shook his head, droplets of water fell on the earth and they flowed on as the holy river Ganga. But there is also another story which says Ganga made the wild stretches of Siva's jada her permanent abode. Hence Siva's another name 'Gangadhara', the wearer or carrier of Ganga. Another story woven into this fabric is that Ganga is the daughter of Brahma. These apparent contradictions —glorious and imaginative of course—and paradoxes abound the ancient scripts which once again prove their literal interpretation a futile exercise.

Among Vishnu's dasavatara are *Narasimha* (the man-lion), *Vamana* (the dwarf), *Parasurama* (the Conqueror with an axe), *Sri Rama*(the righteous ruler of Ayodhya) and *Sri Krishna* of the Yadava Vrishni community who is a warrior, lover, philosopher and the charioteer of Arjuna, the heroic Pandava in the Kurukshetra War. All of them have their own *Purana*s, other mythologies and are worshipped by Hindus as individual gods in their own right. To sum up, Vishnu is an all embracing divinity who is worshipped by Hindus in many divine and human forms in which he made himself appear to the humanity.

It is these versatile and multifarious attributes which make Vishnu the central deity of Hindus and naturally the pivotal figure in the Bhakti Movement. The major trend in the Bhakti movement was Vaishnavism born in the south with the Alvars as its prophets. It has already been noted that the hymns of Vaishnavism composed by the 10 or 12 Alvars formed the basic texts of the Vaishnava cult called the *Nalayira Divya Prabhandams*, They consisted of 4000 verses in Tamil and were compiled by Nathamuni in the twelfth century CE.

Siva, the Destroyer

Among the Hindu pantheon of gods and especially among the Triumvirate, Siva is the most mysterious and fascinating figure. He does not find a place in Vedic literature as Siva. The Vedic figure who can be considered closest to the later Siva is Rudra.

This does not mean that he is a later addition to the ever-lengthening pantheon. Actually there is ample evidence among the idols, terracottas and the coin-like relics of the pre-Vedic Harappa sites that a god closely resembling Siva was a popular deity of prehistoric people.

The Vedic deity, Rudra, who in due course evolved into or merged with Siva, is not considered a prominent god in the *Veda*s. Mahadev Chakravarti who has made a thorough study of Rudra Siva evolution says:

> Brahma is comparatively a minor though a physically attractive atmospheric god in the Rigvaeda with only three entire hymns to him and seventy three casual references in all. But in the course of ages, this minor deity has developed, as a result of fusion with a number of non-Aryan divinities into the great and powerful god Rudra-Siva, the third deity of the Hindu triad. The concept of Siva was built up by the Vedic faith and type of tradition alone, but we have already a proto type of Triambika.[19]

Besides the pre-Vedic origins, Siva's fondness for wild forms of dance (he is called Nataraja, king of dance) his wearing live serpents or skulls as garlands or his robe made of cheetah's skin, keep him distinct from the ken of Hindu or Aryan deities. His field of action is the high Kailas mountain of the Himalayan ranges. He also lives in cemeteries and pastes himself with the ash from funeral pyres. Siva's wife, Parvathy, has a synonym, *Aparna,* which also means *one who is without clothing*. How did such a sharply distinct and 'alien' figure come to be a deity of the Brahminic Aryan race? Its answer lies in the rich, diverse and even contradictions-filled composite tradition of Indian culture. Rudra of the *Veda*s and later *Purana*s is depicted as a 'fierce figure, destructive like a terrible wild beast, the swift, the red boar of the sky, the cow-slayer, the man-slayer, the lord of animal sacrifices, the sworn enemy of Kama, the god of love'.

Perhaps these fierce and destructive attributes of Rudra were transposed onto Siva to make him the god of destruction—*Samhara* Rudra. Yet, it seems curious that Siva does not live up to his fierce reputation of the destroyer always in the epics and *Purana*s. Besides the features we have detailed, there is another very important attribute that adds to the wild persona of Siva—the third eye on his forehead. The third eye is supposed to be always closed and the moment that eye opens, the powerful rays that emanate from it will destroy the whole universe. Yet, he has not done it in the long series of contradictory episodes in the *Puranas*. With all these contradictory and confusing alien attributes, he was finally synthesised with Rudra and adopted by the Aryan orthodoxy. How and why this was done is explained by Chakravorty.

> ...The story of the admission of Siva to the Brahmanical pantheon is part of the biggest story of the absorption of non-Aryans, after conflict and compromise, into the Aryan society. The Indian people is a 'Mixed people, in Blood, in Speech, and in Culture of the four races' namely Austro-Asiatics, Mongoloids, Dravidians and Aryans. Similarly the cult of Siva accommodated multifarious Aryan and pre-Aryan faiths and beliefs ranging from the Austric notions of Phallus Zoomorphic deities (particularly the Bull and Serpent cults), the Dravidian conceptions of a great Father God and a Mother Goddess, the institutions of Yoga, Pooja and Bhakti and both Austric and Dravidian myths and legends relating to petty godlings and hero-worship. Thus the concept of Rudra-Siva is an amalgam of the proto -Siva of the Harappan civilization, Rudra of the Vedic literature and several other gods conceived during the post-Vedic period.
>
> That Rudra did not comply with the ideal of a Brahminic god even in the Vedic literature can be proved by a number of concurrent testimonies.[20]

The Brahmins not only set to rest their prejudices and adopted Siva with full heart to their pantheon, but accorded him a higher pedestal than the other gods. They called him *Parameswara* (the supreme god), *Maheswara* (the great god) et cetera. The word 'great' (*maha*) is also used as an epithet for Vishnu though not for Brahma.

Though Vaishnava faith was born in the south, the Saiva cult seems to have had its origin in the northernmost part of India like Kashmir. It was the royal ascetic, Vasugupta, who is credited with the introduction of Siva worship in Kashmir which could be only partly true. The Saiva worship and rituals grew sporadically among the tribals of the Himalayan ranges and Vasugupta may have codified its practices and given it a sophisticated form.

9

Heartland Moves South

What is considered today as Indian civilization including its culture, religion and literature had its origin in the Indo Gangetic Plain in north India. Generally speaking, the Aryans who began their migration to India from the north west regions were the main architects of this civilization although the pre-Aryan, Harappan, Negroid and Dravidian civilizations had mingled with the Aryan contribution in which Astraloid, Mongols and other secondary streams also flowed in. The concept of Aryan race is now disputed by historians and ethnologists. The correct description of the Aryan race is 'Sanskrit speaking' people, according to Romila Thapar, Upinder Singh, R.S. Sharma and others.

Another important factor to be taken into consideration here is the concept of Aryans as a race. The very concept of race is an invention of the nineteenth century colonial scholarship. Modern scholars including Thapar and others oppose this and assert that Aryans were a people who spoke Sanskrit, i.e., it is a linguistic differentiation. Misled by the 'race' theory archaeologists like Mortimer Wheeler who played a great role in digging and describing the Harappan sites put forward the hypothesis that it was the Aryans who concequered and vanquished the Indus civilization. The *Veda*s and *Purana*s have extolled Indra as a leader who is supposed to be the king of the gods in heaven. One of the synonyms of Indra is Purandara. The Sanskrit composite term Purandara means the 'Destroyer of Cities'. From this, Wheeler comes to the conclusion that Aryans were destroyers of the Indian cities and also the civilization. Modern anthropologists like Ashley Montagu condemn this idea of race as dangerous.

> The idea of 'race' represents one of the most dangerous myths of our time and one of the most tragic. Myths are most effective and dangerous when they remain unrecognised for what they are. Many of us are happy in the complacent belief that myths are what primitive people believe in but of which we ourselves are completely free. We may realize that a myth is a faulty explanation leading to social delusion and error but we do not usually realize that we ourselves share in the mythmaking faculty with all men of all times and places, that each of us has his own store of myths which has been derived from the traditional stock always in ready supply of the society in which we live. In earlier days we believed in witchcraft. Today many of us believe in 'race'. 'Race' is the witchcraft of our times. The means by which we exorcise demons. It is the contemporary myth. Man's most dangerous myth.[21]

Refuting Wheeler's views, modern archaeologists and prehistorians put forward other reasonable hypothesis regarding the demise of the Indus civilization. They say that there are sufficient grounds to believe that Indus civilization had declined and disappeared due to climate changes, natural calamities and flood in the river valley.

Next to the Aryan contribution, the most important element in the present composite culture of India is the Dravidian element. Though there are grounds for doubts, it is generally believed that the 'Aryan conquerors' or more correctly the migrants, pushed the Dravidians southwards and south India became their homeland.

The *Vedas*, *Upanishads*, *Ithihasas*, *Puranas*, *Creative Literatures* and various other texts were all, with very few exceptions, born and propagated in India. Till about the fourth or fifth century CE, Buddhists' and Jains' sacred texts and tales were also products of north India. We see a reversal of these roles of north and south by the late centuries of the first millennium CE. Neelakanta Sastri describes this reversal as follows:

> ... In the sphere of religion as generally in all matters of spiritual culture, South India began by being heavily indebted to the North; but in the course of centuries, it more than amply repaid the debt and made signal contribution to the theory and practice of religion and to philosophic thought in its various aspects. Its saints and seers evolved a new type of bhakti fervid emotional surrender to God which found its supreme literary expression in the Bhagavata Puranas, a bhakti very different from the calm, dignified devotion of the Bhagavatas, of the early centuries before and after Christ in northern India. Again from South India arose the two schools of Vedic exegesis – Mimamsa – that go by the names of Kumarilabhatta and Prabhakara. The founders of the three main systems of Vedanta – Sankara, Ramanuja and Madhwa – also hailed from southern country. Yet another prominent philosophical system–the Saiva siddhanta also found its exponents in the Tamil country. Lastly, the Vedas were commented on more than once in this part of the country and the constant study of the ritual manuals of the different Vedic Schools was kept up...[22]

An examination of this intellectual advance in the south overtaking in the North is in many ways very significant in the study of the Bhakti movement, which as we saw, had begun in the Tamil-speaking regions. After Buddhism and Jainism which were born in the north and spread to the South including present Sri Lanka three centuries before CE, this new wave of Indian culture and language was making new forays into the south. Along with the second wave new forms of worship, rituals and concepts also made their entry. Then a question arises as to who or what made way for this. There are some scholars who consider that the Bhakti movement which dominated south India, including the Tamilakom, Karnataka and Andhra, drew their first inspiration from the Schools of Vedanta, namely, Sankara's *Advaita Vedanta,* Ramanuja's *Vishishta Advaita,* Madhwa's *Dwantavada* and the related theories of Yamunacharya, Nimberka and others. We have already found how weak was the idea that the Bhakti movement had owed its origins to Sankara. The same is true of Ramanuja and Madhwa.

It was not so much these Sanskrit texts and philosophy which influenced the Bhakti movement as it was the other way around. We would also argue that it was during the process of absorbing and articulating the implicit and nascent philosophical ideas in the regional languages into Sanskrit language and academic idiom, that the Bhakti movement began its decline.

Part II

A THOUSAND-YEAR STORY

10

Bhagavata Purana

The *Bhagavata* is considered most important among the *Purana*s and a basic text for Vaishnavite Bhaktas. In the Bhagavata (chapter XI 5.38.40) it is said that the great devotees of Vishnu will appear in the south on the banks of Tamraparni, Kratamala (Vaigai), Payaswini (Palar), Kaveri and Mahanadi (Periyar). It is interesting to note that the Alvars, Namma Alvar and Madhura Kavya Alvar were born in the Tamraparni country, Periya Alvar and his adopted daughter Andal in the Kratamala, Poygayalwar, Bhullathalwar, Pey Alvar and Thirumarisaipiran in the Payaswini, Tondaradipodi Alvar, Tiruppan Alvar and Tirumangai Alvar in the Kaveri and Periy Alvar and Kulasekhara Perumal in the Mahanada countries.

From all this, Prof. Surendra Nath Dasgupta conclusively establishes that Bhagavata was not only a post-Alvar composition but also was written in the Dravida south. Friedhelm Hardy, in his exhaustive and thorough study of *Viraha Bhakti,* agrees with Dasgupta with more details and some differing views. He summarises his findings on *Bhagavata* tradition as follows:

> ...The picture which the previous sections have attempted to delineate covers almost the whole of the first millennium AD. In the light of Parts 3 to 5, it emerges clearly that this picture is too large and that only certain facets of it would have been sufficient for an understanding of the origins of emotional bhakti in South India. Yet for various reasons this detailed analysis undertaken

> in Part 2 need not be considered superfluous. Certain assumptions which were made concerning the few early sources would hardly have been convincing without the corroborative evidence of later works; only a well structured account of the Northern situation will allow us to determine possible stimuli from the North and possible lines of influence from the South concerning the Alvars and the Bagavatha Purana and finally if we were to pursue the post Bhagavata Purana developments,we would notice that also in the North the independent traditions merge together in typical expressions of emotional Krishna bhakti. But above all Part 2 has shown that in the North emotional bhakti is unknown until AD 1000.
>
> Our analysis has shown that the development of the Gopi myths was not monolinear, but took place in a number of independent traditions. The word 'tradition' itself has been used in two slightly different meanings, denoting either a series of individual poems et cetera which follow traditional conventions and themes, or a sequence of additions and interpolations in a 'text' or text nucleus. Synchronically, these traditions can be regarded as different milieux; our material showed that there was relatively little interaction between these different milieux, and this situation makes it unlikely that the South should have come to know all different versions of the gopi myths.[23]

These changes in the philosophical landscape of India also point to the question related to the 'creators of philosophy'. Till the period we are discussing, the creators especially in Sanskrit were known as *rishis* or sages. Later tradition calls them the *acharya*s or teachers. Though we may identify certain rishis from the *Puranas*, *Ithihasa*s and *Upanishad*s like Vasishta, Narada, Viswamitra, Vidhurar and a few others, their works do not carry their individual names and more often than not, all of them were assigned to Vyasa. Whether the name of Vyasa is a proper noun has also been disputed by scholars. 'Vyasa' also means an editor, a compiler or publisher. However, from this period onwards, we have acharyas or teachers like Sankara, Ramanuja, Madhva, Nimbarka and many others. Their works were invariably in Sanskrit.

The rise of these southern acharyas in the history of Indian philosophy and Hindu religion had two effects on the Bhakti movement. As we have seen, the Bhakti movement was absorbed into the main stream Sanskrit philosophy. That seems to be its victorious climax. But it also has diluted the movement's character as a popular movement that thrived in the ethos of the regional culture. As we shall see later, the elements of resistance and dissent which marked the Bhakti movement appear to vanish with its absorption into the mainstream Sanskrit philosophical corpus to gradually transform into the ideology of upper classes. In certain areas including Tamil Nadu, the Bhakti movement also suffered the encroachment of caste hierarchy, the social expression of feudal inequality.

11

The First Blossoms from the Deep South

To seek the origins of Bhakti movement in the *Veda*s and the *Upanishad*s and such ancient lore is a highly misleading exercise though a limited and critical use of such sources may be useful to trace some continuities. Scholarly opinions and concrete historical evidence prove that the Bhakti movement was born, had blossomed and ultimately declined in response to specific historical, social, economic and political situations which prevailed in medieval India between the seventh and the seventeenth centuries of CE.

This does not mean that the movement was manifest simultaneously across India. Even as it was being born in certain cultural or linguistic areas, the movement was already in full bloom in certain other locales and on its decline in some others.

Thirdly, the movement had blossomed first down south or the Tamil country—Tamizhakom as it is generally referred to. The Tamil Bhakti movement's time span could be placed between the seventh and ninth centuries CE. Some scholars extend it back to the sixth and some extend it forward to the tenth centuries. There were two streams in this movement—Saivaite and Vaishnavaite—sometimes running parallel and at times at cross-purposes as well. Traditionally, 63 Nayanars were said to have been the founders and leaders of the Saiva movement, the worshippers of Siva. The other stream was Alvars—mainly 12 of them—who were devotees of Vishnu. Before examining the details of their faith, teachings and songs, let us have a general view of the political, social and religious situation which gave rise to this movement.

The Background

The dates of ancient Tamil classics are still a matter of controversy more on account of political interests than scholarly evidence. The Dravidian movement and its political offshoots like the different Dravidian Kazhakoms under the mistaken conception of *old is always good* try to push back the dates of classics and their authors to many centuries BCE. However, there are a few like Prof. S. Vaiyapuri Pillai, editor of the *Tamil Lexicon* who refused to accept the false claims of chauvinists and stuck to strict scholarly norms.

It is a general consensus that the Tamil Bhakti movement's origins belong to the seventh century CE. The period just preceding it is generally referred to as the age of 'Didactic Poems' which include Sangam epics and other *Thokais* (anthologies) like *Chilappathikarami, Manimekhalai* and *Jeevaka Chinthamoni.* These, though contain entertaining and gripping plots, do not try to hide their religious—Jain or Buddhist—motives. Besides, there are important Buddhist works in Sanskrit on philosophy, logic, et cetera, too. However, unlike earlier Buddhists who wrote in Pali (Prakrit) these scholars changed their discourses in Sanskrit under the influence of Mahayana and its esoteric tendencies. Nevertheless, the Jains in the South chose the local language—Tamil—for their propaganda and disputations. Therefore Buddhism in Tamizhakom at this period was comparatively elitist, while Jainism was more popular and had more adherents.

The best example of this Jain parlance in simple and chaste Tamil is the justly famous *Kural* written by Thiru Valluvar, a Jain saint of the seventh century CE, who was a contemporary of Appar, an outstanding Saivaite bhakta who was also a Jain to begin with. *Kural* is written in an aphoristic style which is fundamentally on life and without mentioning any deity or such concepts. *Kural,* consisting of 1330 poems under 133 chapters is broadly divided into three parts—*Aratupal, Porutupal* and *Kamathupal* respectively dwelling on duty, wealth and love.

From the titles of the parts, it is clear that the *Kural* does not deal with heaven or soul or god, but is entirely on worldly affairs. Still, the validity of most of the aphorisms attest to the greatness of *Kural*—even after 14 centuries of is composition. Vaiyapuri Pillai gives a graphic account of the religious and philosophical background of this period:

> The smooth and gently flow of harmony that existed till the end of the 5th century was ruffled by the logicians. Their erudition, their pride in their own learning and their thirst for victory over their rivals and alien religionists created an atmosphere tense with acrimonious controversies. Dignaga was the founder of Buddhist logic and one of the foremost figures in the history of Indian Philosophy; but among his successors we may mention Dharmapala's pupil Chandrakirti (6th century) born in Southern India. Among Jain logicians, Unasvati and Siddhasena Divakara (533 AD) are well known. Pakshilasvamin Vatasyana and Uddyotkara (AD 620) are Hindu logicians. Though these are all Sanskrit writers, they seem to have exercised great influence over their co-religionists in the Tamil area also. Challenges and controversies were frequent. There was one element which fanned the flame of controversy to red-heat and that was bhakti. This movement began in the 6th century, caught the imagination of the people and spread rapidly. The controversy which had hitherto had been conducted on a generally intellectual level became now coloured with emotion and the sectarian spirit consequently deepened. It gathered momentum as time passed and changed to purely emotional level. The common people took it up at this level and the bhakti cult became a popular movement.[24]

The Bhakti movement, as we have seen, had many positive and negative impacts on philosophical and religious life as well as good structures. Among them was the revival of Hinduism. Hindus were the leaders who had led the struggle against the dominance of Jains and Buddhists. Buddhism, as we have seen, was an intellectual and hence largely an elitist movement. So it is not difficult to understand why it had to give way to the popular and emotional bhakti. However, Jainism, with its popular style and writers like Valluvar, also got submerged in the rising tide of emotional bhakti.

To find an answer to this problem requires examination of

the sociopolitical changes in Tamizhakom and their impact on Jainism. These changes may be linked to the decline of the urban economy that had given rise to the formation of feudal relations. We have already examined the process of feudalism in the south and north, relying on the seminal works of R.S. Sharma and Kesavan Veluthat. Buddhists and Jains were patronised mainly by the trading classes and artisans in urban centres and the kings who depended on these classes for political and financial support also joined them. The decline of urban centres and the consequent weakness of Buddhism and Jainism and the emergence of new religions and worship forced the kings and chieftains to the new religious forms represented by the Bhakti movement. So we see the Pallavas, Pandyas and Cholas and such ruling dynasties throwing their lot with the new movement and often persecuting their old clients. Dr Ramendra Nath Nandi describes these changes and their social roots as follows:

> The Jain literature of the medieval period shows that fundamental changes were taking place in doctrines, rituals and monastic organization of the different Jain sects, particularly in the southern region. Probably the deviations bear a relationship to the changing social and economic milieu of the early middle ages characterized by the decline of a market economy of towns and the rise of a small scale subsistence economy of agriculture.
>
> The decay and desertion of towns forced a large section of the urban monastic community to settle down in the neighbouring countryside and mobilize direct access to peasant surpluses. The urban decline also restricted the mobility of individual monks and groups which earlier travelled long distances in quest of urban promoters. Inevitably, the monks also grew unwilling to subject themselves to the rigours and uncertainties of a wandering ascetic life.[25]

These changes in the mode of life and rituals of Jain monks and nuns invited fierce controversies among them. Nevertheless, propelled by social environments and human weaknesses for a life of ease and pleasure, the changes came to stay. However, the pristine purity and spiritual values which gave the monks an authority over the followers began to drain in the process. The well-endowed settlements and monasteries in the countryside replaced old forest dwellings, living on alms for food and continuous travels to preach and propagate their doctrines by monks gave way to luxury and comfort in the company of equally comfort-loving nuns. Nandi sums up in the following words, the result of this transformation of the monks which led to the disenchantment with their spiritual leaders:

> Hemachandra, a Svetambara author of the 12th century, remarks that the provision for loding (upasraya) is most beneficial to the ascetics, for an upasraya furnishes them with food, drink, clothing and beds, and protects them from heat, cold and insects. Devendra, another Svetambara author of the 13th century states that the best form of charity (dana) is the gift of a dwelling place (vasati) for, in addition to food and shelter, this gives opportunity for study, meditation and development of religious life. In response to the wishes of the Jain fraternity, therefore, the wealthy clients including kings and nobles undertook to build residential houses for the monks and furnish them as best as they could.
>
> The changing character of monk's life necessitated a reformulation of the monastic laws. However, most seriously affected was the monastic ideal of non-possession or non-attachment (aparigraha). The wandering monk who broke journey only temporarily was looked after by his host, and therefore did not need to possess any personal belongings. But now, since the monk had permanently settled down at a place, he needed certain necessities on a permanent basis. Possession of attachment to worldly things was, therefore, almost inevitable.[26]

Though the gift or *daana* and hospitality are provided by the householder of his volition, gradually householders became resentful. The *aparigraha* or non-possession commitment of the monks began to thin down and their needs went on increasing. People came to consider this as another form of exploitation or even extortion and their resentment began to rise to the point of resistance.

These developments also contributed to the revival of Hinduism in the garb of the Bhakti movement.

12

Hindu Reformation

Revolution, renaissance and reformation are born in response to specific social, economic and political situations. Movements rise to a climax and after fulfilling their historical functions and when failing to do so, they decline and fade out. Even counter revolutions or counter reformations take place to set the clock back. Yet, what is certain is even as they fade out; many changes they had brought persist and continue as normal features of social and intellectual life. We have explained how Sankaracharya dealing death blows to Buddhism during the ninth century CE was obliged to borrow many aspects of Buddhism and even be thrust the derogatory title of *Prachanna Buddha.*

The revival of Hinduism after the decline of Jainism also had borrowed from Jain precepts and practices even as it opposed the non-Vedic religion tooth and tail. The *yagnas* which disappeared from Hindu rituals were never to return. Though the *varnasrama* hierarchy returned with Brahmanic dominance at a later stage, the early pioneers extolled equality of one and all before the supreme god, Siva or Vishnu. It was certainly a legacy from Buddhism and Jainism whose main plank was opposition to the caste system.

The bhakti pioneers, though, continued to pay lip-service to Vedic literature in its many forms and held the *Ithihasas* and *Puranas* as their basic texts. Throughout the long period of bhakti there were poets who either translated these Sanskrit works or produced adapted versions in the local languages. These regional versions adapted and recreated to suit the new social milieu gave final forms to modern Indian languages. There appears hardly any such attempt to translate or trans-create the *Vedas*, *Brahmanas*, *Aranyakas and Upanishads*. Vaiyapuri Pillai briefly gives as a summing up of the situation which paved the way to Bhakti.

> Let us now hark back to the time when the immortal Kural came into being. There was a bloodless revolution in the Tamil country slowly working its way to a tremendous power. The success of the Jains set them thinking of a rival religious force strong enough to stem the tide of the overspreading Jainism had to be created. The ancient religion of Hinduism served as a power-house generating the requisite force. The Brahmin centres of learning known as 'ghatkas' wee select and exclusive in their constitution. The Yaga performance as still more solemn and it was more rigid in its exclusion of the non-Brahmins. Neither in the 'Ghatkas' nor in the 'yagas' were the people at large allowed to participate. Brahminism had to be transformed into Hinduism in which all and sundry could take part. In this transformation, the Puranic lore was the main plank. People loved to hear the tales of gods and goddesses, often times miraculous and of their still savouring of human weaknesses. An absolute belief in the most extravagant miracles alleged to have been worked by these deities and an implicit acceptance of every monstrous detail of their legendary history were insisted on. The relationship of the human soul to the divine was described in the language of human love, and illustrated with images and allegories, suggestive of conjugal union. The long course of development of aham in Tamil literature and grammar gave peculiar relish to Tamil poets in treating of this relationship. Puranas came to be written for the express purpose of exalting one deity or the other to highest position. Siva and Vishnu and some Puranas did the reverse... [27]

The Northern Hypothesis

M.G.S. Narayanan and Kesavan Veluthat propose as follows in their joint paper about which we have already mentioned.

> Historically, we may suggest that the ideas and institutions which flourished in the more advanced civilizations of the Gangetic Valley, as represented in the Gupta Empire were gradually

> spreading to the South. It is interesting to note that the emergence of a feudalized monarchy with graded systems of samantas or feudators, chartered Brahman settlements and trade corporations, temples of Shiva and Vishnu, the hierarchical order of caste and a spate of devotional literature centered on personified gods, was characterised not only during the Gupta period of the North, but also during the Chalukya period in the Deccan and the Pallava-Pandya-Chera-Chola period in the 'Far South'. Therefore it is surprising that a bhakti movement was not clearly identified in the Hindu-revival of the North under the patronage of the Guptas, variously called 'Hindu Renaissance' or efforescence, 'Classical Period' of Hindu art and literature, et cetera.
>
> Nevertheless, scanning through the Sanskrit literature of that period, with the redacted Puranas dedicated to particular deities like Vishnu, Shiva et cetera and the standardized text of the Mahabharata with the Bhagavat Gita as its epitome, one gets the impression that Bhakti as a distinctive movement had indeed manifested itself there. It must have probably originated in the post-Mauryan period, as exemplified by the famous Heliodorus pillar inscription of Vidisha, recently identified as part of a temple complex. The great cult-centres which developed at such pilgrimage places like Mathura and Varanasi must have given birth to the institution of the temple as an institution that was destined to be the carrier and the rallying point of the cult of devotion. The Bhagavata movement with its agamaic form of worship appears to have reached a climax in the Gupta period, with emperors claiming titles like parameshwara, battaraka, paramabhagavata et cetera is suggestive of their attachment to the cult of devotion.
>
> In the north, Brahman intellectual monopolists had already accepted the path of philosophical awareness or inanamarga almost exculsively for themselves. This they did while chalking out two alternative paths; one of unquestioning dharma–based activity or karmamarga, and the other of blind faith and surrender or bhaktimarga. The path of karma according to one's dharma was generally ordained for all of the castes. The path of bhakti representing a sublimation of the spirit of slavery or dasyabhava was paradoxically enough, especially meant for the exceptional souls in all groups who sought liberation from social restriction.[28]

Friedhalm Hardy also subscribes to the idea. Though the *Bhagavata Purana* was composed in the south in its final version, its legends might have migrated with the Aryans to the south. D.C. Sircar explains in detail how the Guptas, devout

Vaishnavites, propagated Vishnu worship and mythology throughout their empire and beyond. The Chalukyas followed the endeavour and brought it to Deccan and the east. The Chalukyas brought it up to Venkatom and Tirupathi is now a pilgrim centre of great popularity.

The story of Saivism, the other major trend of the Bhakti movement also had a northern origin—especially Kashmir (*History of Shaivism,* Prabhananda Jash, Calcutta, 1974). We have already examined the process of the Vedic minor deity Rudra having been merged with the Himalayan tribal deity to form the god Siva of the Hindu Trinity. The earliest Nayanar, Thirumoolar, was said to have claimed that he had his residence in Kailas (most probably Kashmir) and arrived in the south to meet Agastya to finally settle there in order to write and propagate his *Thiru Mantras* of 3000 poems. The other outstanding Nayanar, Appar and Karaikkal Ammayar also claimed to have visited the Himalayas where Lord Siva appeared before them and asked them to return to the south to carry out their mission.

From these and many other traditions, it is quite correct to trace the ideological origins of Saivism and Vaishnavism to the Indo-Gangetic valley and the Himalayan slopes. However, these were only the ideological origins. Bhakti was a mass movement and not simply an intellectual upsurge. Ideas and their evolution are certainly very important in the study of popular movements. Yet, they do not give birth to the movement on their own; the reverse is the correct perspective. They mutually interact and help in their separate evolutions. We are not attempting here to narrate the isolated history of ideas but the evolution of the movement. Examples cited above do not indicate the birth or spread of a popular movement – but of the production and popularisation of ideas by the elite classes, especially Brahmins and their royal patrons. However, the Bhakti movement in the south headed by the Nayanars and Alvars was quite different from the intellectual Bhakti cult of the north. Emotions played a greater role in the songs, dances and pilgrimages of the Nayanars and Alvars. Therefore it is considered quite proper to begin the story of the Bhakti movement in the south itself.

13

Nayanars

We have already referred to the two streams in the Bhakti movement in Tamizhakom—the one led by 63 Nayanars and the other by 12 Alwars. The former were worshippers of Siva and the latter were of Vishnu. Though these were the dominant streams in the religious life of the Tamils for about three centuries from the seventh century CE onwards, they hardly had any monopoly over people's devotion. Other deities and forms of rituals continued from earlier centuries. Though religion, its rituals and myths had a firm grip over the minds of people and guided their material lives, the passion and vigour associated with bhakti were to appear with the songs, dances, and pilgrimages of Nayanars and Alvars. Neelakanta Sastri gives us this picture which preceded the bhakti poet-saints as follows:

> Till about the fifth century CE, harmony and tolerance characterized the relations between different religious sects. The worship of primitive godlings with offerings of blood and toddy went on side by side with the performing of elaborate Vedic sacrifices; the popular pantheon included Muruga, Shiva, Vishnu, Krishna and others. Buddhists and Jains were found in considerable numbers in different parts of the country following their practices without let up of hindrance. In the story of **Manimekhalai** for instance, we find the heroine is advised to study in Kanchi the philosophical systems of Vedas, Shiva, Vishnu, Ajivakas, Jnana and of Sankhya, Vaisachika and Lokayata.[29]

Sastri goes on further and says that all this harmony began to disappear and acrimony took its place with the emergence of bhakti as the main form of religious life in Tamizhakom from the sixth and the seventh centuries CE onwards. There is no evidence to show that all the Nayanars and Alvars were of this belligerent mood. To what extent this could go, is clear from a Saivite *Purana Halasya Mahatmyam,* which indulges in the most vulgar diatribes to condemn and pillory the Buddhists and Jains.

To describe the life, letters and contributions of all the 63 Nayanars is an impossible task. Even Sekkizhar, a Chola minister and philosopher could not do justice to all of them in his *Periya Puranam,* the basic work on Nayanars. So let us confine ourselves to five or six of the most important Nayanars.

Thirumoolar

The earliest of the Nayanars of whom we have some information, though couched in myths and fantasies, is Thirumoolar. As seen before, he himself claimed that he belonged to Mount Kailas in the Himalayas, the legendary abode of Siva. When he was 'flying' southwards to meet the sage Agasthya, Thirumoolar broke his journey due to the compassion he felt for a herd of cows weeping profusely. He was told that the cows were in grief over the death of their affectionate herdsman, Moolan, whose body was lying nearby. The saint, due to his miraculous powers soon left his body there, his soul entered Moolan's body and Moolan woke up alive to the delight of the cows. The saint in Moolan's body herded the cows to Moolan's house. Moolan's wife could not have understood the metamorphosis and received the saint as her husband. Thus as all things went well, the saint returned to the spot where his original body sans soul was laid. But to his surprise, his original body was found cremated by Moolan's friends. The saint was in a fix! What to do? Then he permanently adopted Moolan's body for himself and also assumed his name—Moolan. When he became accepted as a great saint poet, his admirers and followers respectfully began to call him *Thirumoolar.*

What a student of history could infer from the grains after fanning out the chaff is that Thirumoolar had belonged to a shepherd class considered, a lower caste. There is nothing unusual in this because women and untouchables were common among Nayanars and Alvars as it was among the bhakti poets of other regions. Karaikkal Ammayar was a woman and Nandanar, a *dalit (pariah)* and both were highly respected Nayanaras. The difference between Thirumoolar and them was his erudition and philosophical acumen intertwined with emotional devotion. His massive work *Thiru Manthiram* (sacred hymns) of 3000 verses, besides containing praises of Siva has his versions of bhakti and discussions on *yoga, thantra* and other traditional systems of thought.

Considering their deep devotion to their favourite deity, most bhakti poets in Tamizhakom and other parts of India may be classified as monotheist, though some of them assign minor roles to others in the pantheon. However, Thirumoolar does not make such compromises. One of his verses specifically deplores the act of some devotees to see the *trinity*—Brahma, Vishnu, Maheswara—as a reality, while the only authentic deity is Siva, that is, Maheswara, the supreme godhead. He goes even further and says that 'love is god' (reminding us of the aphorism of Jesus Christ, 'God is Love'). However, Prof. T.P. Meenakshi Sundaram (*A History of Tamil Literature)* invites our attention to the fact that in Thirumoolar's verse 'love' is the 'subject' and 'God' is only an 'object'. That means that all that is noble and true is 'love' and God is only its synonym. Jesu's aphorism is just the reverse.

As we have seen, the mythology says that Thirumoolar left his body and his soul entered Moolan's body. However, his poems give a different view of body and soul. He did not believe that the soul would survive the body. When the body dies, the soul also dies along with it—a view very close to the materialist concept of body and soul. Thirumoolar did not oppose temple worship; but insisted that Siva was not only inside the temple but outside and everywhere. Nature itself was Siva and Siva was nature. Only fools discover a dichotomy between the two. Equally emphatic was his opposition to the caste system. He sang that there was only one god, Siva, and only one caste for all humans.

Thirumoolar was the earliest among the Nayanars and had

flourished about the late sixth and early seventh centuries CE. When he began his mission, the Saivites were divided into different sects—*Pasupathas, Kapalikas, Kalamukhas* et cetera. Thirumoolar's was the first successful attempt to marginalise such sects and put forward a monotheistic Saivism with many radical interpretations and views. Later, Nayanars like Appar and Sundarar would pay him tributes and borrow many of his ideas in their songs.

Karaikkal Ammayar

Karaikkal Ammayar is one of the most famous woman saint-poets in Tamil. She was a contemporary of Thirumoolar, or even prior to him. Some of the ideas of god in Thirumoolar find their echo in Ammayar's poetry—or it could be the other way around as well. It is uncertain who came first. It is said that she began to compose and sing devotional songs from the tender age when she began to speak. Considering the unending flow of her sweet songs in praise of god till her last breath, this story of child prodigy need not be brushed aside. She was a typical mystic such as Akka Mahadevi in Karnataka, Meera in Rajasthan, Lal Ded in Kashmir and St. Theresa in Europe. She had portrayed her relation with her favourite deity almost similar to that of two lovers. Often she lost herself in trances, ecstasy and ethereal weightlessness— all the while composing, singing and dancing. She called herself *'pey'*, that is, a lunatic or a ghostly being or a *'bhootha'*.

Appar

If we consider Moolar and Ammayar as belonging to the first generation of Saivite Nayanars, Appar and Sambhandar belong to the second generation. Sambhandar or Thiru Jnana Sambhandar as he came to be known later was much younger than Appar who was also known as *Thirunavukkarasu* (prince of the sacred tongue). Though Sambhandar was about 35 or 40 years younger than Appar, their lives were very much intertwined, even influencing each other. The story is that Sambhandar, as a child of five or six, met Appar when he was over forty years. Seeing the saint-poet, the child was enamoured and called him '*Appar*', meaning father. In due course, this had stuck and he began to be known to all as '*Appar*'.

According to the *Periya Puranam,* Appar was of the Vellala caste, hailing from Tanjavur. Vellalas are considered to be below Brahmins but a cut above the untouchable caste. In this first wave of bhakti poetry, there were Visoba Khechar, a grocer; Janabai, a maidservant; Savanta, a gardener; Goroba, a potter; Chokha, a sweeper; Kanhopatra, a dancing girl; Narhari, a goldsmith. This wave also attracted Muslims: Shaha Muntoji Brahmani alias Mrintunjaya, who wrote *Siddhasanketa Prabandh, Anubhavasara* and many Abhangas in the fifteenth century. Vellalas generally are working landed farmers. Appar was born to a traditional Saivite family but later converted into the Jain faith. However, his sister, Tilakavati, remained a staunch Saivite and was very much worried about her brother going over to Jainism. The legend is that Appar had suffered a stomach ailment with acute pain. His sister's prayer and intense devotion to Siva was claimed to have cured him. This made Appar turn back to his family tradition of Saivism, enraging the Jains. They tried to ostracize and persecute him in many ways. However, Appar did not waver thereafter and even sought the protection of the Pallava monarchs. Mahendravarman I was then the ruling monarch of Kanchi. Kanchi was then a great centre of learning of all arts and religions, as we have seen already in a reference to the epic, *Manimekhalai.* Appar's teaching and influence converted Mahendravarman to Saivism. Mahendravarman also wrote many books defending Saivism against Buddhism and Jainism. His *Mathavilsa Prahasana* is a burlesque against the Jains and Buddhists. Then onwards, the Pallava kingdom which later expanded into an empire spanning to the west and north of Tamizhakom, became a stronghold of Saivism and the Nayanar creed.

Appar was known as *Thirunavukkarasu.* This name is almost an honorific on him bestowed by his admirers for his famous lyrics and songs. The name his parents gave him was *Marul Nikkiyar* which was almost forgotten.

Appar's works were collected and published in *Devaram* as *Thevaram. Thevaram* contains the songs of two other Nayanars along with Appars. Appar's philosophy of bhakti may be classified as Nirguna and not Saguna. *Nirguna* means that the deity is without any personal attributes and is the all-embracing reality. C. Jesudasan and Hephzibah Jesudasan translated (1961) one of his lyrics although she added a rider that his songs were almost un-translatable. It read as follows:

> He is of Heaven; He is above the Gods; He is Sanskrit
> And Tamil; and the four Scriptures; He baths in milk;
> He is the woodsman who danced with fire in his hand;
> He is the one who blessed the woodsman;
> He is the honey that oozes within the lotus heart of
> Those who think of them;
> He is the darling we may not attain;
> He is Siva; He is the darling who dwells in Sivapuram.[30]

What is Appar's place among the Nayanars? G. Vanmikanathan, a biographer of Appar, says;

> ...Thiru-gnana-Sambhandar, Appar or Thiru-navukku-Arasar, Sundara Moorthi Swamikal and Manikka Vachakar are lovingly called Naalvar, The Four. Manikka Vachakar is the earliest of these four belonging as he does to the 3rd century AD. Thiru –gnana-Sambhandar and Appar were as we saw, contemporaries. Sundara Moorthi Swamikal came a century after them. Manikka Vachakar's major work is the Thiruvachakam, a hand book of mystical theology. It is the account of a soul groping its way to union with the Godhead. Almost every one of the 656 stanzas reduces us to tears. Such is the effect of the pathos, of the yearning, of the self-condemnation, of the faith in God. All these are unparalleled in the volume of devotional literature in Tamil. Great as is the merit of Appar's songs, they do not however have this appeal.[31]

Sambhandar

We have seen that Sambhandar or Thiru-gnana-Sambhandar although a contemperory, was more than 40 years junior to Appar. Though Appar and his songs in praise of Siva had attracted Sambhandar as a child, he was not considered his disciple. Both were very different from each other. While Appar was a humble supplicant before his Lord Siva, Sambhandar was an intellectual supremely confident of his own prowess and powers of debate and persuasion. Appar was instrumental in winning over the Pallava ruling dynasty to Saivism from Jainism which was their traditional faith. However, the Pandyas of Madurai were won over to Saivism by Sambhandar. It was Appar who sent him on a mission to spread stories that the Pandyan king was a Saivite. The king requested Appar to come to Madurai and undertake debates with Buddhists and Jains and convince them of their falsehood and Saivism's validity. Appar requested Sambhandar to undertake the mission and he went to the Pandyan court and conducted fierce discussion and defeated them. The Pandyan king was thus converted and he punished and banished the 'heretical sects' from his country. One story has it that the defeated Buddhists and Jains were hoisted on tridents and exhibited around the city. Another story was that more than 3000 heretics were massacred on the king's orders. Neelakanta Sastri contests the latter episode as unreliable and false. Yet, he does not give us any evidence contrary to the legend of massacre which is even now celebrated in Madurai Meenakshi temple. Certainly Sastri's position could contain a grain of truth. It was quite unlikely that the thousands of heretics were murdered in cold blood after their defeat in the debates by the skilful handling of the issues by Sambhandar. However, to deny that there was any persecution whatsoever against the defeated group also appeared an exaggeration from the other side.

We have already referred to some reasons why people at large had considered the banishing of the heretics with great relief. Ramendra Nath Nandi says:

> ... Much of the sectarian tensions and violence which marked the history of different monastic orders particularly the Saivite and Jains has to be viewed in the context of a low technology and small scale subsistence agriculture which could not provide necessary food surpluses for the multiplying number of monks, priests and mendicants. Apart from the growth of potential literature and the occasional conflicts mentioned in the literature of either sect, there is sculptural evidence of violent Saiva-Jain conflicts on the walls of the Kailasanath temple of Kanchipuram. It is pertinent to mention here that although both the sects

flourished earlier, their conflicts do not surface before the 7th century when the Saivite order began to recognise itself and advance claims on the available social goods...[32]

Sambhandar held his head always high and he did not bow even before his favourite god Siva. He himself claimed as part of his god and that he was born with that consciousness. His poems in praise of his lord are hardly a humble devotee's intense prayer for salvation. In beauty and diction they are not equal to Appar's.

Sambhandar was not a Brahmachari. He was married and had spent many happy years with his wife. That is why he did not even waver in his fate as his senior Appar did occasionally. Professors Jesudasan and Hephzibah explain his personal life as follows:

> ...At the age of sixteen, it is said he married and entered eternal bliss, not only with his bride but also with all those who attended the ceremony. The few years between, he spent in stormy disputes with the Jains, being responsible, if Nambi Andar Nambi's account can be credited, for committing eight thousand Jains to the gallows. He is also said to have miraculously cured Pandiyan Nedumaran of an illness, and won him over Jainism to Saivism, at the request of his queen. While many of these stories are rather tall, Sambhandar was certainly a prodigy who died young. Later references to him almost always bear witness to his extreme youth. In one of his own most beautiful pieces, addressing the Pandya queen who patronised him, he counsels her not to lose heart on account of his tender years, though he was engaging in controversy with the veterans of the Jain religion. We may also accept that Sambhandar, with a band of enthusiastic friends and followers, was partly responsible for the all but complete wiping out of Jainism as a religious force from Tamilnad. He is also said to have argued witgh Buddhist and won them over. Sambhandar was a Brahmin by caste. His native place was Sikali near Chidambaram. He was never guilty, however, of modesty in his esteem of himself. He introduces himself as **Tamilaharan** or 'the ocean of Tamil learning'. Of his scholarship and literary gifts, however, one is of the opinion that posterity would be a better judge than Sambhandar himself.
>
> One is inclined to think that Sambhandar was more of a scholar and musician than a poet. His hymns are indeed very

> powerful when set to tune – so well are they adapted to singing. Of the pans or tunes of the Devaram, nearly all – some 23 – are represented in Sambhandar's pieces. Of their musical value there can be no doubt. Assonance, alliteration, rhyme, rhythm, the free play of liquids and vowels—in handling all these traicks of the trade Sambhandar is a perfect master...[33]

In practical life also he never tried to be a monk and he detested the Jain monks as hypocrites and parasites.Perhaps that is why he was given the epithet *'Thiru-gnanam'*, that is, sacred knowledge.

Sundarar

Among the four stalwarts whom we have mentioned, the next to be considered is Sundarar or Sundaramoorthy Nayanar. He probably lived in the eighth century CE. From his references to Appar and Sambhandar of the seventh century CE, it is certain that he came after them. The *Thevaram* collection of the Saivite poems contains about 1000 verses of Sundarar. Sundarar also mentions Thirumoolar, the pioneer of the Saivite movement and also has a few words in praise of the untouchable Nayanar, Nandanar.

Sundarar's chief lyrics are a mix of his objective thought and subjective experiences and tribulations. Sundarar was a householder who had difficulties in raising and supporting his family. He had two wives—Paravai and Sangili—and his married life was beset with controversies and difficulties which ultimately had to be settled by a court of law. The stories and legends surrounding this episode were less than edifying to modern sensibilities. It is said that as the moment of his wedding approached, a stranger entered the scene and claimed the bride on the strength of a palm-leaf document in his possession. This dubious document turned out to show that Sundarar was his slave. It seems, Sundarar accepted the status of a slave and married Paravai. He agreed with the lowly status and had betrothed her finally. It turned out that the stranger was Siva whose devotee Sundarar became. Later while Sundarar was visiting the Siva temple at Thiruvottiyur, he saw a lovely temple girl employee and fell in love with her and ultimately took her as his second wife who belonged to the Vellala community by birth.

Sundarar lost his eyesight at an early age and his lyrics in praise of Siva are replete with this tragedy. He recites:

> *'I erred, believing that He would forgive'*
> *'You feared not blame, but you have with a film*
> *Obsucred my eye; you, with the dangling ear-jewels!*
> *I asked, 'Are you within the temple? Then*
> *He from within replied, 'Go, we're here'*
> *He with a deer upon His palm.*
> *In another poem, he asks:*
> *'How' can I Bar it, if the womenfolk*
> *Of my house slight me as a blind fellow?*
> *O, three eyed One, if you are determined to take my eye*
> *Can you not give me at least a staff'.*

Besides Sundarar's verses in *Thevaram,* he also wrote another book of poem called *Tiru-thondar-tohai* which means a collection of stories of devotees. We get many details and legends about the Nayanars from Sundarar's collection. Contradictions abound on his life and death. According to one tradition, Sundarar lived only for 18 years. In the light of description above, it is quite clear that this tradition was hardly reliable. There is evidence that Sundarar was a contemporary and most probably a courtier of the Pallava king Narasimha Varman II who flourished towards the end of the seventh century CE. Sundarar's work *Thiru-thondar-thohai* was said to have composed in the second half of the eighth century CE.

Manikkavachakar

Among the 63 Nayanars listed in *Periya Puranam,* four of them are bestowed a place of pre-dominance. They are grouped reverently as the Nalvar or 'The Four' or to be clearer still 'The Big Four'. Chronologically, the last one is Manikkavachakar preceded by Appar or Thirunavukkaraasu, Thirujnana Sambhandar and Sundaramoorthy, the *Thevaram* authors. This chronology is still a matter of dispute. There are those who place him prior to the *Thevaram* group, in the third or fourth century CE. There are some who would even place Manikkavachakar further back in time to the first century CE or even BCE. A modern biographer, G. Vanmikanathan, who had contributed to the Sahitya Academi Series (1976) vehemently tried to establish that Manikkavachakar belonged to the third century CE with sarcastic comments on those who had differed.

However, his arguments were based less on facts and logic than on faith. For example, he dismissed the evidence of Manikkavachakar's contemporary, Varaguna Pandya, who had ruled Madurai and whom the saint praised as a fervent devotee of Siva. This made clear that the saint was a courtier or minister of Pandya kings. Vanmikinathan's argument was that like many Henrys and Edwards, who ruled England, there might have been many Vargunas, who ruled Madurai. Even more flippant was his argument on Sundarar's silence on Manikkavachakar. Sundarar, in his *Thiru-thondar-thohai* gives us a list of Nayanars, omitting Manikkavachakar. The Sahitya Academy author gives us the excuse that Sundarar had many personal handicaps like the responsibility to look after two wives and he didn't travel much and so ignorant of the life and times of Manikkavachakaar. In spite of his personal responsibilities and handicaps, Sundarar was a diligent student of the Saivite tradition and Vanmikanathan's arguments could hardly be seen to carry weight.

Varaguna Pandya had reigned towards the close of the eighth century CE and the beginning of the ninth century. Many scholars place Manikkavachakar's life and mission in this period. Manikkavachakar belonged to the Amatya sub-caste of Brahmanas. 'Amatya' is a Sanskrit word meaning a minister to the king. As many competent others, Manikkavachakar also was a minister to the Pandya king to begin with. His original name has been forgotten forever. The name Manikkavachakar—meaning the 'speaker of gems' or 'gems like valuable thought'—was certainly conferred upon him by his admirers after he had established his name and fame. He was born in a village on the outskirts of Madruai called Thiruvadavur and hence was often referred to as *Thiruvadavurer*. There is ample evidence to prove that he was given the best of education available then to Brahmins. By the age of sixteen, he was an outstanding scholar and had attracted the attention of the king and was appointed a minister. Within a short time Manikkavachakar lived up to expectations and proved his efficiency in administration. The king deputed him on an important mission—to purchase horses for his cavalry. He went south-west and reached the banks of Vaiga River. There he came to hear of a Brahmin sage and took time off to meet him and pay his respects. The sage met him and answered many of his questions on spiritual life. After the long conversation, Manikkavachakar prostrated before him and prayed for his blessings. The young and brilliant minister who had a bright future before him instantly gave up all earthly ambitions and set out on a pilgrimage in search of union with his deity, lord Siva of whom the guru on the Vaiga banks taught him.

The name and other whereabouts of the Brahmin guru are not known. No more of him is heard in bhakti poems or the *Puranas*. Manikkavachakar believed him to be Lord Siva himself, who appeared in human form to search out his potential devotee and shower his graces upon him. This, in short, is Manikkavachakar's life, gleaned out of the accounts of Nambi Andar Nambi and Sekkizhar.

Though he gave up his ministership, he used to go to the court of the Pandyan king occasionally, often at his invitation to conduct debates with Buddhists and Jains. His vast scholarship stood him in good stead in debates to defeat his opponents. His two books in verse on philosophy and hymns in praise of Siva have survived more than a millennium. They are *Thirukaviar* and *Thiruvachakam.*

Thirukaviar is composed in the style of Sangam literature, especially the *Akam* poems on human love. The theme of love was not alien to Manikkavachakar. His poems and hymns touch our hearts with reverberating echoes of human love. However, for Manikkavachakar, this love was the quest of the devotees' heart for union with his deity. Professors Jesudasan and Hephzibah compare Manikkavachakar's lyrics, hymns and their approach to god with certain English devotional poems and poets. It would help a modern reader to comprehend and enjoy Manikkavachakar's perspective and quality of his poems.

Let us quote:

> If the song element is more pronounced than poetry in Sambhandar's verses, the contrary is true of Manikkavasahar. One reason for this may be that the verses of the earlier mystics were intended for congregational singing or for chanting by bands of devotees from temple to temple. Manikka-vasahar's poems were simply offerings of his own soul laid at the altar of his deity, and not intended for congregational singing. The personal element is, therefore, infinitely more marked than in the other mystics. True, Manikka-vasahar has imitated popular songs. Refrains of popular songs have suggested the titles for some of his pieces, like 'Our Lady Fair, Arise', or 'And Breathe His Praise, O Humming Bee!' But a more plausible reason is that Manikka-vasahar's soul was more gifted with genuine poetic sensibility. Between Manikka-vasagar's songs and Sambandar's there is all the difference between the versification of In Memoriam and one of Swinburne's poems. The earnestness, sincerity and pathos of the former stand revealed in every articulate syllable, the very subject-matter of the latter being washed away in dizzy swirl of sounds, through musical sounds. Another difference between Manikka-vasahar and Sam Bandar is the self-abasement in which the former indulges. Throughout an attempt is made to 'decrease' his own self, as the apostle would say. This trait is not so conspicuous in the other three great mystics. 'Me, iron-hearted and deceitful one '1, he calls himself, in the tone of John Bunyan calling himself a sinner. It is not to be accepted that Manikka-vasahar was iron-hearted and deceitful any more than Bunyan was a sinner.[33]

However, by the time he wrote it, Vachakar had completely shaken off the Kavya tradition of Sangam literature. It was not merely an emotional outburst of intense bhakti, though emotion and rhythm give it sweetness and melody of the best Tamil poetry. Philosophy and bhakti, embrace each other to rank it among the great philosophic poems of world literature. Still, as Jesudasans assert, the song element is subdued and philosophy overrides the flow. This is because Manikkavachakar wrote not for a group or for congregational singing. His subjective yearning was so deep that many of his verses acquire the quality of solitary meditation. This meditative mode also points to the decline of bhakti from a popular movement to an elite exercise for individual salvation. That is perhaps the reason that

Manikkavachakar appears at the very end of the movement in the ninth century CE.

Besides the intensive meditational mode of his poems, Manikkavachakar contributed to the decline of popular quality of the Bhakti movement by his theorisation of its ideals. Though as we have seen he had emerged at the fag end of the movement, when the Brahmin Acharyas took over its leadership and began their philosophical speculations and disputes, Manikkavachakar is considered to have laid the foundation of Saiva Siddhanta on a firm basis remaining within the movement. When the simple teachings of Buddha, Jesus and Muhammad were transitioned into abstract theologies by their later followers, the validity of the original simple teachings of good and evil, good conduct and misconduct, et cetera, had disappeared and a priestly hierarchy took over the leadership. The fate of the Bhakti movement was not different.

The mystic experience Manikkavachakkar had or what he had fancied he had, of the union with his deity brims with ecstacy. Read on:

You gave yourself to me and took me
And took me in exchange:
O, Sankara, who, indeed
who indeed is clever of the two?
O, Mightly Lord, who have taken
my mind as your slave,
O, Siva who abide
in Thiruperumthurai.
O, My father,
Lord of the Universe.
My body you have taken
as your abode.
To this I have nothing to offer.

From this mystic experience of union with his deity which includes traces of carnal love, Manikkavachakar rises to the ethereal heights of philosophical speculation with colourful flashes of poetic brilliance.

In the sacred moon
He placed his coolness:

Kindled in mighty
Fire its heat;
In either pure he
Placed his preservative power;
To streams that gleam in shade
Their saviour sweet
And to the extended earth
The strength he gave.

Here, the luxuriant nature with its cool shadows under the greenery and gurgling rivulets on earth below is woven into the texture of a soothing moon and burning sun in the sky to bring to life all-pervasive presence and overlordship of Siva. Seldom does poetry and philosophy mingle with each other to soar so high.

Nandanar, the Untouchable Saint

The last in the short list of Nayanars is the lower-caste and untouchable saint, Nandanar. Though he appears last chronologically, he was not the least. The *Thevaram* poets of the seventh and eighth centuries CE mention him and pay him tributes. In addition, Nambi Andar Nambi, an important chronicler of bhakti saints also gives us some details of Nandanar. However, it is Sekkizhar's *Periya Puranam* which provides us the most detailed account of Nandanar's life and work. As is the case with many other traditional accounts, Sekkizhar's story is also cluttered with legends, miracles and myths. Still, we can sift grain and make out a reliable outline of the life and devotion of Nandanar. Vanmikanathan has published a summary of *Periya Puranam,* with additional notes and references which gives the story of this remarkable saint (*Periya Puranam,* Ramakrishna Matt, Madras, 1985)

Nandanar was born in a *Pariah* family in a colony of untouchables in the outskirts of a beautiful and prosperous village in lower Kaveri basin called Adanur (also written as Athanoor). The chroniclers of Nandanar such as Nambi Andar Nambi and Sekkizhar wrote many verses on the beauty and luxuriant vegetation of this river valley village. For example Nambi Andar Nambi sings on the glory of the village which gave birth to the untouchable saint.

In this great world
people say that Athanoor,
Surrounded by groves
full of mango trees,
Is the native place of him.
who was otherwise called Nalai-ppovan.
A holy devotee of caste
beyond four castes.
Having gained the grace of Lord
in the Hall of Tillai.
Whom every one praise
with their tongues.
And got rid of pollution
of his base beastly profession,
To become a sage,
worshipped by folded palms
By the tree thousand
Brahman as of Tillai

Nambi refers to Nandanar's profession which entailed cleaning up the upper-caste Hindu village, carrying away dead animal bodies, bleaching their leather and even eating the flesh. Even in upper caste temples they had duties like maintenance work, cutting roots, building compound walls and digging tanks. During these duties, a new awakening overcame Nandanar and he wanted to worship the deity, seeing its idol at close quarters. Naturally, the Brahmins and other upper-caste people resisted and Nandanar fell into a deep gloom of despair, and a will to rebel and resist. The fanciful legends and myths prove that Nandanar did not have an easy passage to his deity's presence. The famous story that lord Siva himself asked the granite structure of the big bull, his vehicle, installed in front of the sanctum sanctorum to move aside, so that his devotee could see his idol and worship points to this fact. Then there are legends that Brahmins asked Nandanar to subject himself to a fire ordeal and that he emerged from the test unscathed and purified, as Nambi said, is also a mythologisation of the persecution he had to suffer.

Though the iniquitous and barbarian system of caste

hierarchy was ultimately imposed and maintained by the power of state, it could not have survived for centuries after centuries without the help of an ideology. The ideology in this case was the theory of karma. According to it, humans, after death, are reborn again. The quality and status of humans depends upon what he or she did in the previous life. If the life and activities were meritorious in the previous birth, he or she would be rewarded by being born in higher and privileged castes, with wealth and power. This pernicious ideology was written into law books like *Manusmrithi.* Prof. Sundaram Manickam, a biographer of Nandanar explains:

> The doctrine of Karma and belief in fatalism was so deeply ingrained in the minds of people, that even the untouchable could not feel it as injustice done to them for a long period in so systematic a fashion. On the contrary, they were made to believe all the civil and religious disabilities were only due to their sinful deeds during the previous birth that it was only just and proper to endure them ungrudgingly.[34]

Manickam's assessment of the deeply ingrained faith of the untouchables in karma theory and fatalism is correct. The most important reason for that was the social structure, which needed such ideologies. The most heinous aspect of the class oppression taking the form of castes with untouchability was unique to India. But in other countries also such discriminatory practices in other forms existed. Even in the glorious culture of ancient Greece, slavery existed and was justified by great men like Aristotle and Plato. World history is replete with revolts of slaves and peasants who were most inhumanly suppressed with iron and blood. We had occasion to refer to various forms of peasants' protests and resistance in India which historians like R.S. Sharma have had described. So also is the case with the revolts of untouchable castes. Prophets and reformers like Buddha and Mahavira and Bhakti saints like Thirumoolar, Ramananda and Guru Nanak opposed the caste system. Though we cannot claim that there was any insurrectional upheaval against the caste system, there were certainly sporadic and individual revolts and resistance. Thiruppan Alvar, Ravidas, Chokkala, and Nandanar were among those who had suffered a black-out of their names from history altogether. So Nandanar's revolt against the Brahmanical practices was not a bolt from blue. Sekkizhar's vivid description of the pitiable life of misery and oppression which was the lot of the untouchable was truthful and sympathetic. However, the general trend in *Periya Puranam* is to draw Nandanar into the main stream of orthodox Hinduism, as is also evident in Nambi Andar Nambi's passage we have quoted. How was Nandanar purified by undergoing the ordeal of fire prescribed by Brahamins? After Nandanar stood the ordeal and came out unscathed, three thousand Brahmins were said to sing the praises of the purified Nandanar. Such descriptions hardly do justice to a rebel like Nandanar who wanted to break the caste barriers set up by the upper castes.

Explaining the fate of Marxism in the hands of his pretended followers, V.I. Lenin once wrote:

> What is now happening to Marx's Theory, in the course of history, happened repeatedly to the theories of revolutionary thinkers and leaders of oppressed classes fighting for emancipation. During the life time of the great revolutionaries, the oppressing classes constantly hounded them, received their theories with most savage malice, most furious hatred and the most unscrupulous campaigns of lies and slander. After their death, attempts are made to convert them into harmless ideas, to canonize them, so to say and to hallow their names to a certain extent, for the "consolation" of the oppressed classes and with the object of duping the latter, while at the same time robbing the revolutionary theory of its substance, blunting its revolutionary edge and vulgarising it.[35]

Naturally, the next step can logically be imagined. The rebel is idolised as an icon of the status quo. In the case of Nandanar, the same happened. *Periya Puranam* did the ground work of this transformation of the rebel against casteist barriers to an icon for them to worship. The legend of Nandanar joining the *Sivalinga* in the lime-light of the deity's prowess and disappearance may be a subterfuge after eliminating him by means of worse tactics by the casteist Hindus. He was both a rebel and martyr to his cause.

14

The Alvars

After the brief survey of the Saivite Nayanars, we may turn to the other stream of the Bhakti movement, namely the Alvars who were devotees of Vishnu. Etymologically, Alvar means one who is immersed in devotion, in this case to Vishnu. We have already discussed the ancient Hindu concept of the triumvirate or *trimurthee*, the divine *trio* and how they emerged in the history of Indian religious thought and went on changing their own roles and identities—Brahma the Creator, Vishnu the Preserver and Siva the Destroyer. Brahma, in due course, was relegated to the position of a subsidiary deity, born in a lotus which arose from Vishnu's navel. The creation of the universe was ascribed to Brahma. The Saivites depicted their deity as taking over all the functions of the original three. Vaishnavites obviously did not agree. Though these points and arguments do appear in the hymns sung by Alvars, they are secondary to their intense devotion and quest to unite with their deity. It was left to the author of the *Bhagavatha Purana* and philosophers like Nath Muni and Ramanuja to interpret and explain the role and nature of Vaishnava faith and its role.

The Alvars were mainly twelve in number. Their dates are still matters of dispute. Though some conservative scholars still try to push back the dates of the Alvars to the early centuries before and after the CE, the general concensus now is to place them in the closing centuries of the first millennium of CE, eighth, ninth and tenth centuries. Following are the twelve prominent

Alvars and their probable dates. Their works and the number of verses are also indicated.

	Alvar	Date	Work	Verses
1.	Poygai Alvar	713 CE	*Mudal Tiruvandadi*	100 verses
2.	Putattalvar	713 CE	*Irandam Tiruvandadi*	100 verses
3.	Pey Alvar	713 CE	*MunramTiruvandadi*	100 verses
4.	Tirumalisai Alvar	720 CE	*Nanmukan Tiruvandadi*	96 verses
			Tiruccanda Viruttam	120 verses
5.	Tondaradippodi Alvar	726 CE	*Tiruppalli-elucci*	10 verses
			Tirumalai	45 verses
6.	Kulasekhar Alvar	767 CE	*Perumal tirumoli*	105 verses
7.	Andal	767 CE	*Tiruppavai*	30 verses
			Nacciyar Tirumoli	143 verses
8.	Tirumangai Alvar	776 CE	*Periya Tirumoli*	*1084* verses
			Tirukkuruntandakam	20 verses
			Tiruneduntantakam	30 verses
			Tiruvelukurrirukkai	1 verse
			Siriya Tirumadal	77½ verses
			Periya Tirumadal	148½ verses
9.	Tiruppan Alvar	781 CE		
10.	Periya Alvar	785 CE	*Tiruppallandu*	12 verses
			Periyalvar Tirumoli	461 verses
11.	Namma Alvar	798 CE	*Tiruviruttam*	100 verses
			Tiruvaciriyam	7 verses
			Periya Tiruvandadi	87 verses
			Tiruvaymoli	1102 verses
12.	Madhurakavi	800 CE	*Kanninun-Siruttambu*	11 verses

The source of the verses and hymns written and sung by the Alvars are contained in *Nalayira Prabhandam* which was collected and published by Nath Muni in the ninth or tenth century CE.

The Alvars belonged to different castes—both high and low. Tiruppan Alvar was decidedly an untouchable. Andal was the only woman amongst them. She was an adopted daughter of Periya Alvar. According to S.M.S. Chari,

> ...Coming to the origin of the Alvars, the tradition regards them as divine incarnations. The first four Alvars – Putattar, Poygai, Pey, Tirumalisai - were incarnations of weapons of Vishnu – gada (mace), sankha (conch), nandaka (sword) and cakra (discus) respectivealy. Nammalvar was an incarnation of Visvaksena, the divine angel; Kulasekharalvar of Kaustubha (the ornament worn on the chest of Vishnu) and saranga (the bow of Vishnu)

respectively. Panalvar is considered as the manifestation of Srivatsa, the mole in Vishnu's chest, whereas Madhurakavi is regarded as representing the chief of Vishnugana. In the case of Andal, she is taken as a manifestation of Bhu-devi, one of the consorts of Vishnu.

Apart from the divine origin, the tradition also speaks of a supernatural birth with respect to a few Alvars. Thus, Poygai Alvar is said to have sprung from a lotus flower in the tank near the Yathoktakari Temple at Conjeevaram, Puttalvar out of *madhavi* flower in Tirukkadanmallai (present-day Mahabalipuram) and Peyalvar from a red lotus in a well near Mayurapuri (present-day Mylapore in Madras). Andal was discovered as an infant lying in the flower garden maintained by Periyalvar. There are other miraculous episodes associated with some of the Alvars. Tirumalisai Alvar was born to a sage named Bhrgu who was enticed by a celestial nymph during his penance and the baby born out of this union was deserted by the mother in a jungle, but later picked up by a hunter who reared it. Nammalvar was born to a pious parents belonging to the Vellala family of Tirukkuruhur, now known as Alvar-Tirunagari in the Tirunelveli district of Tamil Nadu (south India). Right from his infancy he entered into yogic meditation under a tamaraind tree in the precinct of the Vishnu temple, where he remained in meditation for sixteen years. Andal was offered in marriage to Lord Ranganatha, the deity at Srirangam temple, and soon after the marriage, she was absorbed into the deity. Similarly, Panalvar belonging to the lowest caste was carried on the shoulders of the temple priest at the command of the Lord Ranganatha but as soon as he entered the sanctum sanctorum, he vanished, becoming one with the deity. Tirumangai Alvar who led a life of a brigand in younger days was transformed into a saint through the marriage with a celestial being who grew up as a handsome young lady in a Vaisnava family.

To a rational mind these stories sound fictitious. Before we brush aside such accounts we have to understand their underlying spiritual significance. According to the theory of avatara, which is distinctive feature of Vaisnavism, Vishnu, the Supreme Being, incarnates Himself in various forms for the purpose of protection of human beings by way of establishing dharma or righteousness and destruction of the evil forces. He condescends out of His will (sankalpa) to come down from His heavenly abode as and when the occasion demands, not only in human form but also in the form of other living beings.[36]

15

Vridhim Karnatake Gata

Utpanna dravide bhakti
Vriddhim Karnatake gata
Kvachit kvachin Maharastre
Gujare pralayam gata

We have seen in the traditional verse quoted above that the Bhakti movement was born in the Dravida country (Tamizhakom) and from there it grew and spread to the Kannada region. As seen before, the Bhakti movement in Tamizhakom had two streams—the Saivite led by the Nayanars and the Vaishanvite led by the Alvars. In Karnataka, the trends were more complicated with more streams. There, too, two streams stand as most prominent. One was the movement working for traditional Hindu reformation. The other was almost a violent revolt against the traditional Brahmanical Hindu social structure and its time-old rituals and caste inequality. This revolt was led by a new sect called the Veerasaivites or Lingayats. The founder and prophet of this movement was Basava, who is also known as Basava Raja or Basava Anna or Basaviswesara et cetera. Before an analysis and description of the history and character of this movement, the following is a brief examination of the situation in Karanataka which necessitated the rise of these two streams of bhakti.

Social and Political Background

During the period between the tenth and the fourteenth

centuries, the area designated now as Karnataka was under different rulers and dynasties. They included the western Chalukyas, Bijapur, Vijayanagar, Hoysalas, Kalachutas et cetera. They also followed diverse religions. There were Jains, Buddhists and Hindus of different strands. Brahmanic Hinduism was the most prominent with its casteist hierarchy, rituals, et cetera. Philosophically Sankaracharya's *advaita*, Madhva's *dvaita* and Ramanuja's *vishitadvaita* had their adherents and sects. Madhwa was a Kannadiga by birth. Though Sankara was a Keralite, he had his followers and a Vidyapeedam in Karnataka. Ramanuja, due to persecution in his home country, Tamizhakom, had fled to Karnataka and had taken permanent refuge there. There were also followers of esoteric faiths like the Kapalikas and Kalamukhas. It is into this land of diversity and contradictions that the Bhakti movement wafted in like a wiff of fresh air which was to change the soul and face of Karnataka.

Arun P. Bali describes the social situation which prevailed when the Veerasaiva movement raised its challenge:

> Social unrest during this period against Brahman domination in Karnataka was characterised by two salient features which made it possible for the emergence of the Virasaiva movement. One was its persistence and continuity, whereby even the passage of time did not weaken but intensified it. For instance, while the underlying causes of social unrest varied in the course of time, they followed each other in such rapid succession that they prevented any relief to the persistent atmosphere of conflict and tension. The second was that the singular cause of social unrest was the Brahman and the social ethos associated with Brahminic Hinduism.
>
> Basically, the Virasaiva movement was against the inequality of men prevalent in society. Inequalities were sanctified by all kinds of ritualisms that served as classic facades to camouflage the realities of exploitation. Society was enmeshed in a labyrinth of rituals tainted by animal sacrifices. By the time of Basavesvara, Brahminic Hinduism was in the iron grip of a rigid and grotesque caste system. The Virasaiva movement was especially against the subordination and exploitation of the lower castes by Brahmans, and it was a forthright quest for equality, liberty and fraternity,

i.e. a quest for equal access of the unprivileged sections to political power, economic share, and for limiting the arbitrary powers so long wielded by Brahmans. The movement posed a serious challenge to time-honoured traditions and systematically rejected the core values and social institutions associated with Brahmans. For instance, in its desire for 'human relationship', it felt it was necessary to break down interpersonal barriers and conventional norms that prevented interpersonal contact on issues like interdining and intercaste marriage, i.e. it discarded the notions of purity and pollution between Brahmans and non-Brahmans. It revealed the realities hidden by rituals, practices, conventions of Brahmans, in order to be liberated from the oppression of Brahman domination. In short, the Virasiva movement was 'a social upheaval by and for the poor, the low-caste and the outcaste against the rich and the privileged, it was a rising of the unlettered against the learned pundit...'[37]

The Beginning of Awakening

The Veerasaiva movement did not mark the beginning of the challenge against Brahmin orthodoxy. The changes had begun with the rise of the Kannada language initiated by a few poets of distinction like Pampa, and other scholars in Sanskrit who had given up Sanskrit in favour of the local spoken languages as their medium. They had translated and often transcribed great Sanskrit epics and the *Purana*s so that the common people could read and understand them. This, in itself, was a blow to the Brahmin monopoly of traditional knowledge and literature.

The first poet who ventured into this was Pampa, followed by Ranna. It is interesting to note that both were Jains. However, their important works were based on Hindu mythology and the *Ithihasas*. Pampa was a court-poet of a minor prince called Arikesari. At the age of 39, Pampa wrote *Vikramarjuna Vijaya,* an important classic in Kannada poetry. It is generally known as *Pampa Bharatha*. As the name *Vikaramarjuna Vijaya* shows, *Pampa Bharatha* is not a verbatim translation or even a summarisation of the original work of Vyasa. Though Vyasa also gave a place of pride to Arjuna's exploits in the Kurukshetra war, he did not go to the extent of idolizing Arjuna as the most outstanding hero of the epic. Pampa does it. Before that, Pampa wrote *Kavirajamarga,* a book on aesthetics. It is in his work *Adipurana* that Pampa fulfills his poetic duty to his own religion, Jainism. *Adipurana* gives the story of a first Thirthankara, the founder of Jainism who was supposed to have had a continuous chain of ancestors in previous births. Together, they are called the Thirthankaras. Some scholars consider that the *Pampa Bharatha* also contains sporadic mention of Jaina teaching though he does not make it a Jainist text. To honour his authoriship of *Adipurana,* Pampa is also called *Adi Pampa.*

The second most important poet of early Kannada is Ranna. Although Ranna, too, based his main work on Vyasa's *Mahabharata* he emphasised the hostility between Bhima the Pandava prince and Duryodhana the Kaurava chief. That is why he called his work the *Gada Yudha,* a duel using clubs.

These descriptions make it clear that the early beginnings of the Bhakti movement in Karnataka were on the traditional lines of Hindu reformation. The next phase is the Veerasaiva revolt.

Basava

In a modern biography of Basava, M. Chidananda Murthy summarises the essence of Basava's contribution thus:

> It is often said that Indian society is basically conservative and hence admits of no grave changes in its sociological set-up. This may be true to a certain extent. But there are instances where rebels have appeared on the scene and acted against the accepted social norms. They could carry society with them in their convictions and mould it according to their dreams. Basavanna was one such rare person in Indian history. To men who believe in his religion, he is a prophet; to students of sociology he is a reformer and a revolutionary; and to some others he is both a reformer and a prophet.[38]

From this it is clear that the Veerasaiva movement was quite different from the evolutionary reform movements of which there are many instances in medieval Indian history.

Objective biographies of saints and prophets are quite rare. Instead, legends and myths abound with exaggerated powers attributed to the hero. However, a fairly good biography of

Basava (also known as Basvanna or Basaveswara) written by Harihara (c.1230 CE) is available. This biography, written almost within a century after Basava's demise, is called *Basava Rajad Evara Ragale*. Of course, according to modern standards, this biography, too, is not entirely satisfactory. However, we may rely on it for a number of authentic facts about the life and times of Basava.

Basava was born in a Brahmin family at Ingaleswar Bagevadi in the district of Bijapur around 1125 CE. His parents were very affectionate and nurtured many hopes on their intelligent and handsome son. However, soon relations between the parents and son began to sour. Even as a boy Basava showed signs of revolt against Brahmanic orthodoxy and rituals. He refused to go through the *Upanayana* ceremony which is supposed to be very essential to a Brahmin. It is considered that a Brahmin boy becomes a true Brahmin only when he is adorned with the sacred thread at this ceremony.

Basava left his house and parents and later even disowned them. Thus began a life of reform and rebellion, the impact of which has not faded among the Kannada people even after eight centuries. Basava and his followers were worshippers of Shiva, symbolised by the *shivalinga*—which they always wore on the body. They did not believe in temple worship and adorned their forehead with sacred ash. Basava's was a new branch or sect of Shaivisam and it came to be known by two designations: Lingayats and Veerashaivas. The followers of the movement prefer the latter designation to the former.

The main centre of Veerasaiva was Kudala Sangama, a lovely retreat where two tributaries merge. Scholars and young Brahmacharies used to meet here at an academic institution called Anubhava Mandala. They would debate and listen to gurus on religious and spiritual matters. Their teacher was Allame Mahaprabhu, a scholar well-versed in various branches of ancient knowledge. Later, he was to be a staunch supporter of Basava and his movement. People used to come not only from the neighbourhood but also from far off places to sit at the feet of Prabhu Deva (as he was also called) and listen to his words of wisdom. Basava was a regular visitor to the Mandala.

To begin with, Basava had an idea to be a permanent inmate and lead a monk's life. Later, however, the call of the wide world and urge for action to ameliorate the plight of the people at large won him over and he gave up the idea of being a recluse. He also found that as far as corruption and social evils were concerned, Kudala Sangama was no better than other places.

Deciding to enter public life, Basava began to look for a job. Adept in mathematics, he got a job as an accountant under King Bijjala of the Kalachutis dynasty. Kalachutis were devoted Shaivaites and their state emblem adorned the figures of Shiva and his vehicle Nandi, the bull. Besides his proficiency in accounting, the Shaivite faith, too, was perhaps a factor for the affection of Bijjala towards Basava who was elevated to the post of Chief Treasury Officer. Bijjala entrusted him with administrative duties also.

Being a very senior officer of the state, Basava's income increased. It could not only sustain his family but could also substantially add to his savings. Basava by this time was a rich man and was at the prime of his life.

All through the thick and thin of his career he had a bosom friend and benefactor called Sidhananda. When he passed away, leaving his two daughters orphaned, Basava married them.They were Gangadevi and Mayadevi also called Nilalochane.

Basava began his mission of spreading the cult of Veerasaivism. He traveled preaching and spending his money lavishly for the cause. His house was both an asylum for the poor as well as a centre of pilgrimage. The medium of Veerasaiva teachings are called *vachanas*. Even before Basava's time, this literary form was prevalent in Kannada. Basava and the Veerasaiva saints like Allama Prabhu, Akka Mahadevi and others by their compositions developed the *vachana* form into a popular and powerful medium. In turn the *vachanas* gave the Kannada language a new vocabulary and melody. His teachings were simple. Read this translation of one of his vachanas:

> Basava's REVOLUTIONARY THOUGHTS had their roots deep in the accumulated popular discontentment regarding the then existing social and religious conditions. It is no wonder then that the majority of people who accepted and acted upon his teachings

came from the poorer sections of society. The established religious as well as the social organizations opposed him and even tried to nip Basava's revolution in the bud. The first thing that Basava did was to declare that anybody could come and join his religion, and no distinction of any kind would be made among them. The religion which he preached and the way he preached it were both simple and appealing.

Though Basava's ideas were revolutionary and his words sharp, his teachings were as simple as could be. They are addressed not to the elite but to the lowly and poor. Here is an example:

Thou shalt not steal not kill;
Nor speak a lie;
Be angry with no one,
Nor scorn another man;
Nor glory in thyself,
Nor others hold to blame.
This is your inward purity;
This is your outward purity;
This is the way to win our Lord
Kudala Sangama.
What sort of religion can it be
Without compassion?
Compassion needs must be
Towards all living things;
Compassion is the root
Of all religious faiths:
Lord Kudala Sanga does not care
For what is not like this.

What you call life
Is a wind-blown lamp;
What you call wealth
Is a market crowd.
Do not, relying on this—
This wealth—destroy you your life!
Do not forget to adore
Our Lord Kudala Sangama.

Behold! between the worlds
Of mortals and of gods

There is no difference!
To speak the truth is world of gods;
To speak the untruth, the moral world.
Good works are Hell—
And you can witness it,
O Lord Kudala Sangama.

Allama Prabhu

The second most important *vachanekara* and Veerasaiva scholar of the twelfth century was Allama Prabhu or Prabhu Deva as his followers called him. We have already mentioned him as the chief guru of Anubhava Mandala. He was born into a rich Brahmin family and was given the best of education available then. Needless to say, the Brahmins were perceived as the repositories of all wisdom and knowledge accumulated through the ages. Though Prabhu considered himself a follower of Basava's Veerasiva movement, Basava considered him as his own guru on account of his vast knowledge and erudition.

Being an extremely eligible young man, he wedded a lovely Brahmin girl, Kamalatha. She was an affectionate wife and their married life was extremely happy. However, Kamalatha's premature death left Allama desolate and gloomy. He almost lost any interest in life and spent his time brooding over the mysteries of life and death. It was a turning point in his life.

Yet, time was the healer of all wounds. After many years of meditation, self-criticism and study, Allama reached a state of enlightenment. He sublimated his love for Kamalatha into love of God. It was a time when Karnataka was beginning to reverberate with the calls of Veerasaivism. Allama did not need to think twice before choosing his god. His god was Siva in the form of the Sivalinga.

This enlightenment had also worked as the balm to sooth him at a time of bereavement. Allama began traveling through the length and breadth of the country composing *vachana*s and singing them to the devotees. However, he had a serious handicap—the burden of knowledge and scholarship. Therefore, his *vachana*s are not simple as those of Basava. While Basava sang to touch the heart of the people, commoners, cobblers, peasants, illiterates and outcastes, Allama was singing to stir the heads of his listeners. Some of his *vahchanas* echo the esoteric Tantric texts. However, he was also singing the praise of Siva, Sivalingam, Kudala Sangmeswara and Mallikarjuna—all of the synonyms of Siva. His *vachanas* expositions meant one thing to one and another to others. It is also said that Allama founded a mystic stream in the Veerashaiva movement which was as clear or transparent as a crystal to begin with.

Akka Mahadevi

Akka Mahadevi is a shining star in the galaxy of women saints of India who include Andal of Tamil Nadu and Mira of Rajasthan. Akka was born in the village of Ballegave in the present-day Shimoga District of Karnataka in the twelfth century. The present Shimoga district was then part of the domain of Kaushik, a powerful feudal chieftain.

From early childhood itself, Akka had a spiritual turn of mind. When she grew up to womanhood, she began to consider herself the bride or spouse of god Siva. So when Kaushik, the feudal ruler wished to marry her and asked for her hand, Akka refused on the plea that she was already a spouse of Siva. Kaushik rejected the plea, calling it a stupid fantasy. He threatened her with his political power. Finally under his threat and most unwillingly she conceded and became his Rani. Akka lived like a loyal wife for some time. However, she soon found that she could not mentally detach herself from her divine spouse. As time passed, she realized that she could no longer lead this dual life. The only way out was parting company with Kaushik. She did it on her own and left the palace and all its splendors. Kaushik accepted his fate and perhaps must have thought 'good riddance'. From then on, she wandered from place to place composing melodious *vachanas* and singing of god and her divine passion. Akka Mahadevi's divorce and wandering, often half-naked or stark naked, were not appreciated by many people. However, Allama Prabhu and Basava and their followers admired her courage and bhakti. She still had not met them or formally joined the movement. She went to Kalyana to meet them and pay her respects.

Though Allama Prabhu had heard about her and had a sympathetic attitude, he again wanted to test her. He asked her many questions on her way of life and faith. Her replies and responses satisfied him and she was duly admitted to the movement. She joined regular get-togethers of faithfuls at Basava's house and debated and sang her vachanas.

We have already in translation seen how simple were Basava's vachanas and how straight-forward his messages. Akka's vachanas in many ways were quite different, though they too were the praise of and absolute surrender to Siva and linga. She refers to Siva as Chenna Mallikarjuna, whom she considers her bridegroom as we saw earlier. Her diction is lyrical as suits love poems. Though her love is divine, the vachanas often transgress the boundaries of divinity and tend to be human, and even carnal.

Dr A.S. Adke who has compiled and edited a volume of Mahadevi's vachanas in English and Kannada assesses her poetry thus:

> And yet, all the while, the person whom she loves (or rather, whom she is in love with) is in the Linga on her palm; and she asks him, archly, with a lover's familiarity, how he could sit there, in her hand, and not speak to her! How can he, who was in her heart before she was fully awake, now hide himself from her? If he is everywhere, she asks, truly everywhere, why not show himself to her alone? When he loves everybody, actually everybody—till his 'mouth is foul with begging of our love'—why does he make himself only scarce to her? Yet she's ready to come back in 'undesired births' because he is her lover. Like a young bride, awake yet unsatisfied, she draws in her fancy little pictures of the marriage rite, complete with 'areca, rice and cocount'! She tosses for him all day and pines for him all night. She pictures a time when, she did not know him, before she was awake; when, however, he was in her—as 'gold's sheen is in the gold'.[39]

Here, what strikes one at the first perusal itself is the humane quality of Akka's love, something common to many women mystics, that is, from the Spanish St Theresa to the Rajasthani Mira and the Tamilian Andal. It is known that Christian nuns call themselves the brides of Jesus Christ. The sublimation of sex and bhakti in mystic women is a favorite subject of speculation among modern psychologists.

Siddharama

Among the followers and colleagues of Basava there were many kinds of people. Among them Siddharama was a remarkable person who was a well known saint of twelfth century Karnataka. He was a social worker devoted to the service of the poor and dispossessed. He was moved even by beasts and birds in distress and tried to help them. By faith he belonged to the Saivite sect of Lakulisha-Pachupathas. He had a monastery and a large following associated with it. The centre of his activities was the present-day Sholapur of Maharashtra state. It was a small village named Shonalige in Siddharama's time. In a few years, his various activities made this village into a flourishing town. He also constructed a beautiful temple with Shiva as the presiding deity. He built a huge reservoir which he claimed was for the benefit of 'men, women, beasts, birds and insects'. The reservoir still exists in Sholapur even after the lapse of eight centuries.

Siddharama could not bear to see a drop of tear. He used to say that his mission in life was to wipe out every drop of tear from any one's eyes, be it man or beast. He tried his best to help the poor not only by giving them alms but also by finding them permanent source of livelihood. He also organised community marriages in temple to reduce the expenditure. He gave respectability to inexpensive marriages. Such were some aspects of Siddharama's social service which he considered part of his worshipping of God Shiva.

Siddharama's name reached Allama Prabhu. He sought him out and had spent many days in conversation with him. Prabhu was able to convince him of the correct path of Veerasaiva and the Linga worship. Siddharama was converted to this new faith. Rest of his life he spent in continuing his social activities and propagating Veerasaivism.

The Twin Sources

There were many more followers of Basava of different types and background. Basava gave perfect freedom to his followers to argue with him if they were so inclined. We have found that Basava's house was always full with guests, followers, opponents and even erstwhile thieves. They argued among themselves about not only Veerasaivism but also about anything under the sun. They could even challenge Basava freely. It is said that the two sources of Basava's inspiration and strength were, God on the one hand and his followers on the other. He did not only teach them but also learned from them and admitted it openly. Chidananda Murthy concludes his book as follows:

> Basava was a man of the masses. He loved people and wanted to be surrounded by them. He drew his energy and inspiration from two sources—from God and from his followers.
>
> *It is a wondrous thing to see*
> *A fish, once out of water, live:*
> *Set me, O Linga, among*
> *The company of the Sharanas:*
> *O good God, here I spread*
> *MY mantle before Thee and pray,*
> *O Kudala Sangama Lord!*
>
> He was like a fish in an ocean of people, and he could not live without them. I turn, the masses too loved him and faithfully followed him.[40]

Like most renaissance movements, the Karnataka movement also had its ups and downs. This is exemplified by the fact that the Veerasaiva movement which began with the aim of doing away all caste and caste discriminations became a caste by itself. Today, the Lingayats constitute a caste with all discriminations associated with the system. When Basava in opposition to the prevailing practice supported and even initiated an inter-caste marriage he was hunted by the conservatives and Basava had to jump into the river at Kudala Sangama to escape from his opponents. However, now, even in the twenty-first century, such inter-caste marriages remain taboo. There are newspaper reports about even riots to prevent inter-caste marriages. So we see that the Lingayat renaissance finally had turned into reaction or revolution turned into counter revolution.

The fate was not different in the case of the traditional Bhakti movement led by Pampa, Purandara and others.

16

Bhakta Mira

Bhakta Mira, the sixteenth century Rajput princess of Chittor is well known not only in Rajasthan and Gujarat, where she wandered in quest of her favorite deity Krishna singing his praises, but all over India from the twentieth century onwards. This recent fame is mainly due to Mahatma Gandhi who resurrected her from the ignominy to which the Rajputs had consigned her. The famous modern singer like M.S. Subbulaxmi, with her melodious recital of Mira's songs, also contributed to her resurrection. However, it is surprising if not unbelievable that there are still conservative sections in Rajasthan who stick to the old prejudices about the saint-singer.

Parita Mukta, who went to Rajasthan in January 1986 to investigate the life and times of Mira, was surprised to hear these condemnations repeated even in these days much after Gandhi tried to Christen her as a saint. Parita Mukta says in the preface of her book on Mira:

> Having grown up in a milieu where Gandhi's evocation of Mira within the nationalist movement had established a pre-eminent place for her within Gujarati middle class culture, I had expected to find, in Rajasthan, visible and identifiable marks of Mira worship. However, the scholars, historians, archivists that one necessarily meets with at this stage of the work (in Udaipur, Chittor, later in Jaipur), were united in their opinion: Mira was not sung in Rajasthan. Did I not know that a figure such as Mira, rejected by the Sisodiya princely power, could not be publicly acknowledged by others in society? That she could not be revered?

> Yes, they insisted, it was not just that, as legend avers, Mira was sent a cup of poison by a Sisodiya Rana in order to bring about her death, but the public humiliation that Mira had inflicted on collective Rajput honour meant that her name could not be evoked without rubbing salt on an old wound. Mira was not seen as a saintly figure in the dominant culture of Rajasthan, to be paid homage to, but as a figure to be excoriated, for the erstwhile rulers of Mewar could not tolerate the veneration of a person who had so directly challenged their authority. Did I not know as well that Mira was a term of abuse leveled at women in Rajasthan, as a charge of promiscuity? (I had not known.)[41]

Rise to Sainthood and Ill-fame

Mira was born in the Rajput ruling family of Mewar. Her date of birth is not certain. Bankey Bihari, who is an authority on the Bhakti movement and Sufis, puts it as 1547 CE. From her childhood itself Mira was spiritually inclined. There are many legends regarding her fascination for her favorite god, Krishna. It is said that once the child Mira was looking through the window as a marriage procession passed along the streets with all the pomp and ceremony. The child in all innocence enquired of her mother who was also watching the procession. 'Mother, who is going to be my bride groom? When is he going to come?' The mother gently smiled at the child's innocence and pointed to the temple nearby where a beautiful idol of Krishna was installed for the devotees to worship. Mira immediately took it to heart and began to consider Krishna as her bridegroom.

As she grew up into a lovely lady, this fascination did not fade but grew with her. She always kept an idol close to her bosom and went about chanting songs in praise of her deity. Mira had been given excellent education at home by hired tutors in language, literature music and the history of the valiant Rajputs, their chivalrous actions and dharma. So Mira was able to write and recite poetry, compose music and sing them melodiously. She spent most of her time in the Krishna temple and sang his praises.

Mira's parents and her community were worried. They feared that if Mira continued this way she would lose her mind. They thought they should find a wayout to save her from this 'affliction'—get her married to a suitable prince. Bhojraj, a valiant prince of Chittor a mighty Rajput state was chosen as her bridegroom.

Mira was very dutiful and meticulous in performing her household chores and serving her husband as was becoming of a Hindu lady. However, once she completed her domestic duties, she would go to the deserted temple in the midnight and sing in praise of Krishna. Her husband would be alone in his apartment waiting in vain for Mira. Early morning after worshipping her deity, she would again be on duty to perform her household chores.

As days, weeks and months passed, the mother-in-law and other members of the royal household began to become jittery. Besides Mira's devotion to Krishna and her indifference to husband, there was also another reason for the Chittor royal family to resent the ways of the bride: the Chittor royal family were Saivaites and worshipped Siva, Kali and Durga. Being a staunch devotee of Krishna, Mira found it impossible to be a Saivaite and refused the entreaties of her mother-in law to worship Durga.

The mother-in-law and sister-in-law went on persuading Mira to be a loyal wife and do her duties as a wife. They lectured on the accepted code of conduct for a dutiful wife and the tradition of Rajput norms and dharma. Mira's response to these pleadings was as follows:

How could I live without Hari, O mother !
For the Dear One I have gone mad; it is like the worm eating out the wood.
Medicines and herbs do not work on me, it appears all madness to me.
As dwells the lotus in the waters, of water born.
As loses the fish its life, when from waters withdrawn.
In search of the Beloved from forest to forest, to catch the music of the flute, I roamed.
Mira, the Blessed one, her Lord Giridhara, the comforter obtained.

Mira sings of her idea of happiness and self realisation as:

In the presence of Giridhara will I dance.
Him I shall please by dancing, and His lovers I shall solicit;

Love and affection shall be the trinkets of my feet and
Remembrance shall be my dancing robe.
The world's regard and the family dignity I shall all discard,
And I shall go and sleep on the bed of the Beloved.
Mira shall dye herself in the colour of her Hari.

Like many other women who have given themselves to their favourite deity, Mira's devotion also takes the form of a bride's love for her groom. She sings:

Now You have to protect me.
For You have accepted me as Thy bride.
The Powerful One, in You I seek my refuge.
Pray let all my works be accomplished.
Vast is the ocean of the world, beyond me to negotiate,
You alone are my ship, for me to cross o'er.
Of the supportless, You are the support,
O Teacher of the World,
And without Your aid every work of the world is ill-performed.
Through ages the pain of Your devotees, O Hari, You have allayed;
And on the world You have conferred salvation;
Mira seeks shelter in Your lotus feet,
Protect her honour now, O Lord.

When all the pleadings and admonitions failed to have any effect on Mira, they resorted to slander. They accused her of loose morals. Mira's opposition to these attempts were really part of a resistance to the Rajputs' ideals of life, their chivalry and what they consider as their dharma. The Rajputs tried to kill her by giving her poison. The legend is that she drank the poison but it did not have any effect on her. Ultimately, she had to leave her parents, husband and seek a life of freedom. Mukta explains the situation in which Mira found herself:

> Mira broke with her **kul**. She broke with the ruling family of Merta and Mewar. She left the fortress of Chittor, swearing never to set foot in the land of Rana. She did not tarry in Merta either, riven as it was with conflict with the house of Jodhpur.
>
> She embarked on a life of an itinerant bhakta, a wandering singer. Thus, she reached Dwaraka. The bhajniks in Saurashtra show a strong empathy with the predicament of Mira the exile. They enter the emotions of Mira the woman in a deep way, paying

heed to her disjunctured ideals and vulnerabilities, so that Mira emerges not just as a rebel of strength, but as a person who having fought a battle against entrenched powers, began the life of an itinerant singer, and was scarred by her experiences. Mira's historical mooring in Saurashtra is as a person who had sundered herself from the community which had oppressed, as well as given birth to her. There is a compassion expressed for her in the bhajans sung in Saurasthra, a sympathy for her situation in exile—and there is an anguish voiced by her at the life of penury she is leading. Hermann Goetz, in his reconstruction of the life of Mira, states that Mira arrived in Dwaraka circa AD 1537 at a time when the Ranchhodji temple there was in ruins, and deserted, after having been sacked by Mahmud Shah I, the Sultan who became known, popularly, as Mahmud Begadha after his conquest of the two forts in Pavagadh and Junagadh. Goetz attributes to Mira the ambition of setting herself up as the 'Gosaiyni' of the temple at Dwaraka, by preaching her own interpretation of the Krishna bhakti (Goetz, 1966:29). Goetz portrays Mira to be a powerful, single-minded person, who might have—if she had not been a woman- become the founder of a sect of her own.

The grandiose ambitions that Goetz attributes to Mira including that of being the architect of Akbar's plan to bridge the gulf between Hindus and Muslims and organizing an empire in which people were expected to find peace and justice (Goetz, 1966:38) are lofty indeed and must be left in that realm. For our purpose, we must, in time, descend to the common recognisable experience of alms-seekers and beggars to make sense of the peoples' Mira as she emerges in Saurashtra.

That Mira should have chosen to go to Dwaraka is not surprising. It was a popular place of pilgrimage—Madhavacharya, Nanak, Kabir, Chaitanya, Jnaneswar had all visited Dwaraka in their lifetime (Thakar, in D.S., n.p.d:67). Mira had already visited Vrandavan and come in conflict with the Gaudiya Vaishnava there. The Vallabh sampraday she had rejected. Whether the Shardapith at Dwaraka set up by the Sankracharya in the eighth century. A.D. welcomed Mira or not is not known.[42]

Giving Mira poison was one attempt that the Rana of the Sisodiya dynasty resorted to. He continued to wreak vengeance on the woman whom he thought had brought humiliation to the family. Though many attempts on her life failed, death claimed her in Dwaraka in 1547. Legend says that she merged bodily into the idol of Krishna, leaving her outer garments wrapping the idol. Many of her followers and modern scholars discount this legend. They say this was a spurious concoction to hush up the crime of the Rajputs and the Sisodiya dynasty. Authors like Parita Mukta go deep into the life and ideals of Mira and find the Dwaraka temple story of her death very unlikely. Mukta explains thus:

> This particular legend could have been started by the Rana's men, given their close links to the Sisodiyas, for whom the hallowing of Mira's name was not tolerable. Certainly the Sisodiyas never utilized Mira's miraculous end to bolster their own power. They did not even in the end claim that she was one of them. As we have seen, the superficial incorporation of Mira by the Rajput establishment was not begun till the nineteenth century, and even that remained disjunctured. The Sisodiyas did not reap the reward of a miraculous death attributed to Mira. They continued to disown her. In a manner true to a feudal principality, they continued to retain a silence about a person who had left their system of values behind. The official history of the Mewar rulers. 'Vir Vinod', (Shyamaldas, 1986:1-2), makes no attribution of sainthood to Mira.
>
> History obscures for us the truth of what happened within the temple at Dwaraka. The only fact that emerges clearly is that Mira did not wish to return to the land she reviled. Did Mira perhaps take her own life rather than return to a life she had abjured? Was Mira eliminated by the Rana's men? Or did she slip away from the temple at Dwaraka, away from the powers who had come to know where she was—and live anonymously in the South as Hermann Goetz avers (Goetz, 1966: 33-40)?
>
> Rational explanations are useful in that they demolish demagoguery. They do not, however, aid us in entering the turbulence of emotions which precedes a sudden death, nor do they enable us to understand the nature of power at particular junctures. The subjectivity of death is not pan-human either, acquiring, in a class society, varying political meanings. Let us take each of the possible ends to Mira's life.
>
> The story of Mira's mergence in to the Krishna Murti is one that marks the ultimate negation of worldly relations. It is also an annihilation of self. It is in fact a negation of the very basis of bhakti. Bhakti demands a social relationship. This requires that the two within the relationship remain separate beings in order

> to experience the presence of the other. Bhakti does not require that the bhakta blots herself out in the other. The bhakta strives to sing of the glories in order to demonstrate and act out a love for god in association with other bhaktas. The bhakta seeks opportunities to demonstrate a love through bhakti. A flight from this –to a mergence with the Ultimate—is a flight away from acting out this relationship.
>
> It is significant that the bhajans do not attribute to Mira a glorious, sudden death. For the bhajniks, glory belongs to Mira for living out a relationship with Krishna in the teeth of opposition—forging, within this process, other bonds in society too. It is not in fact the bhajniks described in Part II of this work who place such fervent faith in Mira's mergence into the Krishna murti. Those who do this come from a different strata of society. They are those privileged for whom securing a life after death is instrumentally important—rather than a securing of a better form of relationships.[43]

It is clear from Mira's life and the attitude of the Rajputs, especially the Sisodiya dynasty, that the bhakti of Mira was not only her solace but also an ideological instrument to demolish the Rajput values and authority. Even after the British conquered India and subjugated the feudal princes, Mira remained an enemy of the Rajput clan. That is why, as explained earlier, Mira was so much maligned as a person that even her name, till Mahatma Gandhi's time, was considered anathema in Rajasthan. No respectable girl was given the name 'Mira' even much after she was sought and resurrected by the Mahatma who affectionately called one of his disciples '*Mirabehn*'. Even now, she is respected only as a saint devotee and not a rebel who fought the *status quo*.

Mukta gives her book on Mira the meaningful title *Upholding the Common Life*, and that was the essence of the saint's life and works. Mukta concludes her story as follows:

> Do we want our historical figures to die before their time so that their integrity is saved from decay by a glorious end (Warner, 1983:27)? Is it necessary that our symbols of liberty become martyrs? I have had to struggle long with this question, and at last I leave Mira alive amidst the bhajniks, unviolated by self or the enemy, traveling, singing, in a community drawn from those

on the fringes of society. It is a resilient community, which has provided shelter and refuge to all those rejected by dominant society.

There is evidence of an underground passage from within the temple of Dwaraka to the outside. It would not have been difficult for Mira to slip away when faced with the Rana's emissaries, and later join up with groups of itinerant singers. So Mira travels on, with her ektara in her hand, embracing her liberties and inspiring others. Her songs continue to reach those scarred and humiliated and who grasp from these songs a message of emancipation.[44]

17

Surdas: The Blind Singer

Surdas, born blind, was a great Krishna devotee, composer and singer in the late middle age in north India. His language was Braja Bhasha, a dialect of Hindi, spoken in the areas which covered Delhi, Agra and Mathura. The western part of this area was Vrindavan, consisting of Krishna's birthplace and where his childhood 'pranks' and '*leelas*' and valiance with the milkmaids and Gopis are highly popular lores.

Though Surdas was blind, his other senses were always alert and sharp. It is said that he could recognise the voice of a person even many years after he heard it. With these faculties, blindness was hardly a major handicap for him. He grew up in the Braj country extending from Mathurapuri to Delhi, listening to the lores of Krishna. Surdas was a contemporary of another great singer, Tanzen, who was the court singer of the Emperor Akbar. Tanzen had belonged to the so-called 'Navaratna Sabha' (the circle of nine gems) of Akbar's court. Akbar himself was a great admirer of Surdas and it is recorded that he used to meet and interact with him. Though people in general considered both of them as equally great singers, Tanzen never envied Surdas's reputation. Instead, he admired him and was reputed to have written in praise of Surdas, whom he considered greater than himself. Following are the stanzas as composed by Tanzen on Surdas:

Kindhaun sur ko sar lagyo
Kindhaun sur ki pir

Kindhaun sur ko pada lagyo
Bedhyaun sakal sarir

Life and Times

Surdas' songs are still popular and even the illiterate goes about reciting and chanting them even after centuries. The details of his life are not known. One important source of such details is a calligraphic collection of biographies written by Bhav Prakash in 1689 CE. He wrote his book not much after than the demise of Surdas. Therefore, he must have been aware of some authentic facts about Surdas. Prakash's book is called *Chaurasi Vaisnav Ki Vartha,* which means 'Information about 84 Vaishnavas'. Another source of Surdas's life history is *Vallabha Digvijaya* written by Yadunath in 1601 CE. This book is about the Vaishnava saint Vallabhacharya who was Surdas's Guru.

Surdas was born to Saraswat Brahmin parents in 1478 CE in a village called Sihi near Delhi. He is supposed to have lived a long life and died in 1585 CE. As we have alredy noted, he left his house and lived near a pond not very far away from his birth place. At the age of 18, he moved to Gujarat where he met his chosen guru, Vallabhacharya. Till he was 31, he continued to live in Gujarat. By then, due to his oracular powers and musical proficiency, he had gathered around him a number of followers. His compositions are also known as *pada*s. He spent the rest of his life in Braja area. He died in Parasoli, in the presence of Vithalnath, son and successor to Vallabhacharya.

Vallabhacharya

In the Krishna Bhakti movement, Vallabhacharya was equal to if not higher than Ramanujacharya. Both of them had accepted the *Bhagavata Purana* as the basic text. However, there was also a difference. Ramanuja adumbrated *Dvaita Vedantha* while Vallabhacharya advocated *Pushti Marga*. Vallabhacharya converted Surdas to his *Pushti Marga*. Bhav Prakash describes their first meeting as follows:

> Once Shri Acharya, the Great Master (Vallabhacharya) came to Braj from Arail. Surdas was living at Gaughat. Surdas was an ascetic, in service of the Lord, and sang very beautifully. Many

people were his disciples. So when Shri Acharaya descended at Gaughat, Surdas' followers, having seen him, went to Surdas and said, Today the Acharya has come, the Great One who has conquered the South and defeated all its great pundits. Then Surdas came, from his place, to pay homage. The Acharya Mahaprabhu said, Surdas, come and please be seated. Then Surdas paid homage to him and sat down. Shri Acharya said, Surdas, sing some of the praise of the Lord. Surdas replied, Whatever you command, and then sang a pada.

O lord,
I am the crown amongst the sinners.
The others are just the beginners
I have been born a crook.
To Ajamil, the hunter, and to the whore
even to poison-breasted Putana
you granted salvation.
You have shown favors to all
but me.
This hurts.
I claim, emphatically, confidently
that nobdy else
is as capable of sinning
as I have been.
Still amidst the sinners,
and crooks,
I; Sur, die of shame.
for not having had
your favor.
Who else, deserves your grace
More than I?[45]

In Puranic lore, Krishna was many things to many people. He was Arjuna's charioteer, guide and guru. Before the beginning of the Kurukshetra war, he played the role of a statesman and a diplomat. He tried to mediate between the Kauravas and Pandavas to avoid bloodshed. To Radha and the gopis of Vrindavan, he was the ultimate lover. He was a child full of pranks to his mother and other elders. However, to his cruel uncle Kamsa, he was an equally deadly foe. In the *Bhagavat Gita* which constitutes his advice to Arjuna who was very reluctant to fight the Kauravas in whose ranks were his cousins, uncles, gurus like Bhishma, Drona, et cetera, Krishna rises above as a great philosopher. But Vallabhacharya was devoted to Krishna, as a flute-player, shepherd and the lover of Radha and other gopis. Even the senseless pranks of Krishna and the *Ras-Lila* were celebrated by Vallabhacharya. Surdas, as a disciple of Vallabhacharya, looked up to Krishna in the same way. J.R. Verma gives a beautiful and brief description of Surdas's perspective on Krishna:

> In the depiction of Radha, Surdas has scored over other writers on the subject, like Vidyapati and Chandidas in making her more vibrant, more profoundly attractive and more intensely youthful and by lending her greater depth and appeal. She longs for complete identification with the Lord, burns in the seething flames of separation, but has no complaint; her renunciation is lofty as the Himalayas, but is tempered with humility; her sense of duty is harder than flint, but her heart is tender as the morning dew. Being Krishna's childhood involvement, her love has grown with the years, and after separation from Krishna, she attains a quiet, spiritual dignity. She is in fact the Lord's own inner, inseparable, self-identifying power. Gopis are not represented as individuals, they are a composite entity, a multiple personality of Radha. In their anxious longing for full identification with the Lord, they attain the highest reaches of self-dedication. They accompany Him in the celebrations of Vasant (Spring) and Holi festivals and during Ras-Lila which brings about the socialization of their individual relations. Ras-Lila is Surdas's distinct artistic achievement. Under the magic spell of the music of the flute and dance, stones melted, the Yamuna ceased to flow and the moon stopped her onward journey in the sky! Ras Lila is raised to a spiritual level where love between the lover and the beloved is transformed into a mystical devotion. Gopis' love is ideal, it is not a sudden burst of passion. While ecstatically forgetful in His company, they are heart-broken in separation. In their pathetic plight, they despise the counsel of yoga from Uddhava, Krishna's courier. They provide the element of tragic pathos in the entire chronicle. Surdas has achieved great success in analyzing the emotion of the heart and stands on a high pedestal as a poet of pure emotions.[46]

18

Ramananda and the Ramanandis

In the medieval Indian, especially north Indian Bhakti movement, Swami Ramananda's name is an outstanding one. The fact that Ramananda is generally considered the preceptor of Tulsidas, Kabir and Ravidas adds to his stature. However, these three bhaktas grew to a higher stature and renown and even obscured their preceptor. This phenomenon occasionally tend some scholars to deny even the existencc of Ramananda, and to argue that his name was conjured up by the later sects known as Ramanandis to provide themselves legitimacy by claiming to belong to his tradition. However, Ramananda cannot be so lightly wiped off from history. Ramanandis continue to be a major presence in north India conducting conventions and debates on their *sampradaya*. There are both radicals and conservatives among them. William R. Pinch and other scholars have made detailed study on the movement.

Before probing further into Ramananda's life and teaching, it would be useful to explain a few technical words which are to appear often in our discussion. *Saguna* and *Nirguna* are two schools of bhakti. In Saguna bhakti, the deity or the object of worship has attributes. It is contrary in the case of Nirguna. Defining an object as a sum total of attributes would make the object itself non-existant. How this 'technological' problem is to be solved is a difficult question. However, nirguna bhakti could be said to be more radical in implication than the more conservative *saguna* proposition.

Another term which needs elucidation is *sant.* Sometimes the terms sant and saint are used as synonyms. Some use 'swami' as an epithet. But Bhakti scholars point out a difference in their respective meanings and etymologies. In English transliteration, some use sant and other santa; we prefer sant. However, in the following quotation we may use it as in original. Dr Darshan Singh explains as follows:

> The Santa Prampara or the nirguna sampradaya are names given to the religious movement which is represented by Kabir, Ravidasa and other bhaktas, and which flourishes in the later medieval centuries in Northern India. Two possible derivations of the term santa have been suggested. Either it is derived from the Pali word Santa which means quietist or it is the plural form of word sat which in Hindi is used in the singular sense meaning 'one who believes in the Truth', i.e. the perfected or the realised person. The term in the present context is used in the latter sense—the perfect or ideal person, which the seekers of this religious movement aim at becoming.[47]

Life and Times

Authentic writings on Ramananda's life are not available. The only relatively contemporary sources are Nabhadas's *Bhaktimal* (*Garland of Devotees*) written in the seventeenth century. He was himself a Ramanandi and naturally his account is more of a hagiography. Yet, from this and the casual references in other contemporary writings, it is possible to make out some outlines of his early life and activities. There is no doubt that he was a Brahmin, well-versed in Sanskrit and Brahmanic knowledge. The scholars have come to a consensus that Ramananda was born into a well-to-do Brahmin family in Prayag where the Yamuna joins the Ganga near present-day Allahabad, around 1300 AD. A brilliant student, he had learned all that his Prayag teachers could teach by the age of 12. He rejected the suggestion to take up priesthood or other Brahmin duties. Then his parents sent him to Kashi (Varanasi) where he could continue his studies further. Varanasi was even in those days a great centre of learning where scholars and students from all over India would gather for learning the ancient Indian lore and wisdom. Varanasi in those days was famous for its *gurukulas*, seminars and dispensations, mainly based on Brahmanic knowledge. Amongst many systems of Indian thought he tried to master, the twelfth century philosopher, Ramanujacharya, struck deep roots in his mind and heart. After a study of the relevant literature, he decided to go south to meet the followers of Ramanuja and learn more about his *visishtadwaita* and the Sreevaishnava cult.

Though Ramanada was very much attracted to Ramanuja, his faith in *advaita* lingered in his thoughts. It was Raghavanda, a follower of Ramanuja who converted Ramananda to *visishtadvaita*. However, there were regular debates between the preceptor and his disciples. Though Ramananda was a disciple of Raghavanand, he had his own followers and disciples. Among them were people from all castes and communities, even Muslims and women. Ramanuja's 'thirty doors' to self-realisation only admitted the 'twice-born' or '*Dwijas*'—Brahmins, Kshatriyas and Vaisyas who had the right to wear the sacred thread after the Upanayana ceremony. That means many of Ramananda's followers would not be entitled for self-realisation. Besides, the liberal views of Ramananda could not tolerate the peculiar dietary prescriptions of the visishtadwaitis. For these reasons, Ramananda broke with Raghavananda and other visishtadwait fraternies. Having parted with Ramanuja's Shri Vaishnavism, he founded his own sect and theology called *Ramavata*. The difference between the two in the object of worship was minimal—Shreevaishnavas worshipped Vishnu and his Avatar (incarnation) Krishna whereas Ramanandis worshipped Sree Ram of Ayodhya, another incarnation of Vishnu himself. However, as we have seen, they were sharply opposed to each other in social and other ritualistic aspects. It is with this newly found freedom and self confidence gained from the south that Ramananda went north and launched his mission which resulted in glorious results of historical significance.

William R. Pinch writes about Ramanandis of the twentieth century:

The belief in a glorious past in which persecutions by both Muslims and Dasnamis were overcome, the devotion to the central figure of Ramanand (and through him Ramchandra) unfettered by an association with the south Indian Brahman Ramanuja, and the dedication to an egalitarian social order that invited the participation of elite, shudra, and untouchable alike—these constituted the core reference points for a radical Ramanandi after 1921. The following poem by Ramavatar Yadav, entitled *Yatindra-stav* (Hymn to a Great Sadhu) and featured prominently in a 1935-1936 publication honoring the reinvigorated conception of Ramanand, brought these three elements together to glorify the living past of the sampradaya:

Though Hindu jati was lost in a fog of ignorance,
you shined a light on the right path.
Though we endured many blows at every step,
you nourished us with great support and wisdom.
Though some fled the battleground of their fate,
you injected vitality back in to their veins.
You cleansed the holy ground once again,
and showed the world the one-ness of Vishnu.
Who could have exposed the fallacy of high and low
if such a sadhu had not entered the world?
Who else could have inspired the notion that no one is
impure amid the tranquility of God's realm?
Who else could have drawn so many across the ocean
of existence in the sparkling moment of Ram-mantra?
Who else could have inspired Kabir and Ravidas to
liberate the oppressed with but a bit of verse?
Who else could have comforted the fallen souls who flocked
to them beneath a shower of resplendent love?
Who else could have banished the evil notion that
'he who can be cut and wounded must not be Hindu?'
Who else could have shown such valor destroying the
monolith of sin and expelling narrow-mindedness?
Surrounded by enemies everywhere, who would have preserved
the name 'Hindu' had such a sadhu not arrived.[48]

Kabir

Among the saint-poets of India, Kabir is perhaps the most famous and beloved. His *dohas* (poetic aphorism of two lines) are sung by even illiterates. People accept and recite dohas as a guide in their day to day life. There is a considerable following of people called *Kabirpanths*—people accepting the Kabir path. Prominent poets like Ravindranath Tagore have translated Kabir's dohas into their own languages. Dohas are generally in Hindi but are often coalesced with literary Urdu traditions. In the struggle for secularism as against communal and other divisive forces, Kabir's dohas are a source of great inspiration to modern India. However, in spite of all these fame and popularity, the details of his birth and life are still obscure. His parentage and family life still are shrouded in controversy. Whether he was married or not is also a matter of debate.

One version of his birth says he was born of a 'virgin' Brahmin widow. The legend has it that it was as a result of the famous saint Ramananda's blessing that she conceived and gave birth to Kabir. Blessing him, Ramananda predicted that her son would become a great man and popular preacher. Any way there is no doubt that among Ramananda's disciples the most outstanding were Kabir the weaver and Ravidas the cobbler.

According to a legend, Kabir was born as an illicit child. He was given up by his mother. A Muslim weaver Niru and his wife Nima brought him up and taught their trade in the sacred city of Varanasi on the banks of the Ganga. The general consensus is that Kabir was born in 1398 CE and died in 1518 CE. The legends, of course, say that he lived a long life of 120 years. The story goes that both Musilims and Hindus claimed Kabir as their own and they quarreled for the possession of his dead body.

There is a Kabirchaura in the Varanasi coast of Ganga where a tomb was also built in 1567 by a Mughal officer. Kabir counted himself as Ramananda's disciple and he was a monotheist opposed to idol-worship. One of Kabir's dohas declares that if by worshipping a piece of stone, one could attain salvation, he would worship a mountain itself. He was claimed by Ramananda as a disciple. He is popularly acclaimed as Kabir's guru but certainly the disciple surpassed the guru in many respects.

Kabir was a great scholar, a talented poet and a prophet of reform. Yet, interestingly, he was an illiterate. His bhakti was of the *nirguna* school. That is the object of worship is devoid of any attribute. But who was his deity? Unlike many other bhakti poets he was neither Vaishnavite nor Saivaite. He did not even worship Sri Rama who was the favorite deity of Ramananda, his guru. Sometimes his concept of god or *parabrahma* verged on a sort of atheism. For him, there was no creator without creation. The creator merged into creation. That means his omnipresence and omniscient super power is nature itself. In the following dohas, this idea comes into bold relief.

R.P. Tiwari summarizes the essence of Kabir's world outlook as follows:

> ...He was a seeker of Truth and we may have an idea of What he tried to teach from his writings. However, one may safely assert that belief in a Supreme Being is the foundation of his teaching but it is very difficult to define that Supreme Being. The Lord is beyond speech and sight and therefore to describe him is to attempt to achieve the impossible. In the words of Kabir;
>
> *jas kahiye tas hote nahin, jas hai taisa soyi*
>
> (what you speak of Him, that he is not. He is what He is (*Kabir Granthavali*, p. 310). And elsewhere again he says, none knows Thee as Thou art, what people speak of Thee does not conform to it (*Kabir Granthavali*, p. 103, 147). But Kabir had realized that the one Lord exists and anything else beside Him is nothing but the outcome of illusion and is artificial as the reflection in a mirror. For Kabir, God is not only the overlord but also all-pervading. He permeates the whole universe even as butter permeates milk.
>
> *gheeve doodh mein rami raha byapak sab hi thaur*
>
> The absolute reality is beyond our comprehension and the speech makes a futile attempt to express it. The one Lord who pervades all is indivisible, indestructible. He has got no colour, no body and cannot be measured by time and space (*Kabir Granthavali*, p. 102).
>
> *Abaran akal aik avinashi ghat ghat aap rahai*
>
> But Kabir does not like even to describe Him as one. He says:
>
> *aik kahoon to hai nahin, doyai kahoon to gaari*
> *Hai jaisaa taisan rahai, kahat Kabir bichari bichari*
>
> [If I say He is one, it is false and if I attribute duality to Him it is an abuse. Kabir after full reflecting over it declares let Him be what He is].
>
> Kabir has called Him Rama, but his Rama is not an incarnation of Vishnu. For Kabir, the implication of Rama is other than what the three worlds say.

Dasarath sut tihon lok bakhana
Ram nam ka maran na jana

Kabir has sung the glory of Krishna, Narasimha and other *avatara*s of the Hindus but denied that God incarnated in these *avatara*s because Brahman is beyond birth and death. Kabir says that He, the *Niranjan,* is beyond all (*Kabir Granthavali,* p. 227). For Kabir truth in respect of God is beyond *Saguna* and *Nirguna*.

Kabir holds that God is all-pervading. He is present everywhere as a whole and yet is beyond everything. This pervasiveness is so complete that Kabir asks:

sunu sakhi piu mahi jiu bassai,
jiu mahi basai ki piu.

So far as Kabir is concerned, he has no doubt that the Creator is in the universe and the universe in the Creator and therefore wherever he sees, he sees Him alone. Thus every insignificant little creature has its share of the Infinity of the Absolute in itself. Therefore, apart from God, the world, animate or inanimate, has no separate existence or reality of its own.

Man is oblivious of his reality due to Maya-deception of appearances and his own elusive nature. Once he frees himself from this Maya he realizes that he is in all and all are in him and there is none else but he. Kabir declares that it is only after this realization of his identity that he himself called himself Kabir and that he himself revealed himself.

hamhin aap Kabir kahava;
hamhin apana aap lakhava

This is the blending of the drop with the ocean and the ocean blending with the drop:

heart, heart hai sakhi rahya Kabir hiraayi
boond samani samand main so kat herya jaayi
heart heart hai sakhi rahya Kabir hiraayi,
samand samana boond main so kat herya jaayi

But this identity cannot be established by reasoning. Kabir says philosophy cannot attain to Him. God can be realized; identity can be established only when one takes recourse to sahaj and transcends the coarse mental processes. This sahaj has been defined by Kabir as the diverting of the five senses from the morbidities of a sensual life and diverting them to the Lord and consequently to attain to Him. Dadu, another saint of the period, has to say the following as regards the sahaj:

Dadu sarvar sahaj ka, tamain prem tarang
tahan man jhoolay atma, apane sayin sang

[In the lake of Sahaj there are the waves of love. The soul sports with the Lord].

Kabir and other saint-poets of the period believe that good deeds or acquisition of knowledge, though laudable in themselves, will not go a long way in gaining salvation. It is only possible through **Bhakti**, the love for the Lord. Kabir says 'The lock of error shuts the gate, open it with the key of love'. For Kabir it is love which has opened the portals into divinity and given him the vision of the Lord. It is love which has raised him from the pettiness of I and **mine**.

Sabda or word occupies the most important place in the doctrine of Kabir. For those who wish to know the truth will have to investigate the sabda. Kabir says that the world is born of the omkar and is destroyed by vicar (disintegration).

Omkarai jag upjai, vikarai jag jaye[49]

Kabir rejected all types of superstitions handed down from generation to generation. Many people believe that if one dies in Kashi one will go to heaven straightaway. Kabir did not subscribe to such beliefs. So when he became old and infirm and thought that death was imminent, he shifted his residence from Kasi to Maghahar where he died in 1518 and a tomb was erected there later.

Ravidas, the Chamar Saint

Ravidas (also called Raidas with a few other variations in spelling) was a contemporary of Kabir. Like Kabir he, too, was initiated to the path of bhakti by Ramananda. As in the case of many other saints and poets of ancient and medieval India, the dates of birth and death of Ravidas, too, are matters of dispute among followers and scholars. However, most of them have accepted c.1450–1520 CE as his life period.

The earliest sources on Ravidas's life and career are available in *Bhaktamal* by Nabhadas and *Bhaktavijaya* by Mahipathi. Ananthdas and Priyadas wrote commentaries on them because *Bhaktamal* (a garland of the stories of bhaktas) is a highly compressed account almost unintelligible without a commentary. All these accounts assert that Ravidas belonged to the *Chamar* community, an 'untouchable' caste of cobblers.

Chamar is the designated caste for those who bury carcasses from which they peel skins to make footwear for the higher castes. Besides the accounts and legends, the fact that Chamars consider Ravidas as their predecessor and hero also confirms the origins of the saint-poet. V.I. Lenin once wrote of the fate of revolutionaries after their death: 'People who malign and persecute them when they are alive and active make them harmless icons of admiration after their death. Sometimes they even absorb them into their own ranks as respectable luminaries.' We have seen this strange behaviour in the case of many Bhakti poets. Ravidas also was a victim of this strategy of the upper caste, especially the Brahmins. They claimed that actually Ravidas was a Brahmin in the previous birth who was born to Chamar parents to fulfill some duties. There are many other stories and legends invented by the higher caste to appropriate the saints born to other castes to their own 'holy ranks'.

However, Ravidas did not fall a prey to such subterfuges. He frankly and with pride occasionally declared himself as a Chamar. He sang:

O! People of the city!
my notorious caste is chamar!
In my heart in the essence
of all good qualities
Ram-Govind.

He means that purity is not a gift of birth, but that of bhakti which purifies the heart. Ravidas makes this point more explicit in another poem:

In whatever family a good Vaishna is found
Whether they be high caste or out caste
lord or pauper
The world will know one by his
faultless fragrance
Whether one's heart is Brahmana or Vaishya,
Sundra or kshatriya, Don, Chandala
or Mlecha
Through the worship of the Lord
one becomes pure
And liberates the self and both family lives.

Where was Ravidas born and when did he live? There are many claimants to that honour. Many places in north India are associated with his name; there are many places where there are still his devotees with temples built to honour him. All these places are asserted as his birth places by different groups of devotees. We may quote Dr Darshan Singh who wrote a study of him. The listing of these different places with which Ravidas was associated also will help us to understand the wide range of his activities and peregrinations. Dr Singh narrates:

> Claims also have been made by his followers in Rajasthan and Gujarat that Ravidasa is born in their respective states. But their argument on the basis of a large following of Ravidasa in those states and his association with some of the places there, such as Ravidasa Ki **Chattri** near Kumbhanasyama temple in Chittor and **Ravidasa Kund** (tank) and **kuti** (hut) at Madogarha in Dhara State of Rajasthan is weak in comparison with the above accounts based on the verses of Ravidasa and the early tradition. The **chattri**, the **kuti** and the **kund** may have been built in order to perpetuate the memory of his visits to these places. So it seems likely that Banarasa is his place of birth.
>
> In Banaras itself there are two big and old colonies inhabited by the **sudras** which are claimed as the birth place of the saint. The first of these two is Seeta Goverdhanapura, situated close to Banarasa Hindu University. According to tradition, an old tree at this place, whose trunk still stands there, is associated with Ravidasa. Now the late Santa Haridasaji of Ballan village in Jullundur district of Punjab has built there a four-storey temple in memory of Ravidasa.
>
> Another place which is claimed as the birth place of the saint is Madhuadih. This place is situated on the G.T. Road some one and a half miles to the west of Banarasa Cantonment. This village is comparatively larger and older than to Seer Goverdhanpura. It is still inhabited by **sudras (Harijanas).** Lahartara, the place associated with Bhakta Kabira, is part of this village. There was an old tank and a temple believed to be built by Ravidasa, but now they have been destroyed and only a raised mound can be seen. Every year in the month of Magha a big fair is held at this place to celebrate the birthday of Ravidasa.
>
> As far as the strong local tradition and the view of **Ravidasa Ramayana** is concerned, Maduadih is his birthplace. However, in the absence of some strong historical evidence, this assumption cannot be insisted upon. Seera Goverdhanpura may also be one

> of the many places associated with Ravidasa daghata, Maidagina Chauk, Guru Bagha, Lotan Bira, Visvanatha Mandira and Kabira Chaura.[50]

Though a Chamar, Ravidas's father had made enough money to be considered a wealthy man in his caste. He wanted his son, Ravidas, also to participate in the household business. However, his son's inclination was more on the other-worldly and less of the humdrum life of this world. So the father thought a way-out: to get him married. Ravidas married and became a family man. Yet, the father's plan did not work. Though Ravidas used to occasionally help his father reluctantly, his heart was elsewhere. Bhakti, an irrepressible yearning for union with god had begun as a passion for him. It is not known when exactly he met Swami Ramanand. However, it was their meeting that changed Ravidas' life.

Finding Ravidas and his wife not being of any help to run his business, Ravidas' father turned them out of his house. As he had nowhere to go, Ravidas and his wife began to live in a hut they built behind his father's house. For livelihood he took up his caste profession, that of a cobbler. However, he never gave up his impecunious ways. After saving a small part of his meagre earnings the balance was donated to the saints and bhaktas he happened to come across. It is said that whenever he met a saint or bhakta without footwear, he used to donate shoes free of cost.

Ravidas did not have any formal education. His hymns and songs were later recorded by his disciples from their memory. Owing to this, many scholars consider them mixed with interpolations and variations. Lack of formal or religious education hardly worried him. He believed and declared in his poems that knowledge was not inherited by high birth or learned from sacred texts. It was gained through association with saints and from the words of guru. Ravidas' guru, of course, was Ramananda, and as we have noted earlier, there were many saints whom he propitiated.

In Ravidas' early days, many, especially those of the upper castes, used to ridicule his bhakti and hymns. When he built a temple devoted to Vishnu and installed himself as the chief priest, his detractors not only scoffed at this but even complained to the king about this 'sacrilege'. The king summoned him and questioned him about the unauthorized action. Ravidas explained his position that god belonged to all, irrespective of caste or class and recited some of his poems to that effect. The king was satisfied and gladly acquitted him—so goes the story.

Ravidas' fame spread far and wide. Ravidas took long journeys in north India, from Kashi to Dwaraka to preach his gospel and the teachings of his guru, Ramananda. His following increased and disciples thronged around him. He realized this transformation and accepted it humbly as a gift from god. He sang heartily:

> *Who but Thee, my Jewel, could do such a thing?*
> *Cherisher of the poor, Lord of the earth;*
> *Thou hast put over my head the umbrella*
> *of spiritual sovereignty.*
> *Thou relentest towards him whose touch defileth the world;*
> *The lowly dost Thou exalt, my God, and none dost Thou fear.*
> *Namdev, Kabir, Trilochan, Sadhna and Sain were saved.*
> *Saith, Ravidasa hear, saints through God everything is done.*

During his travels in Rajasthan, Jhali Bai, the queen of Chittor, made her obeisance to the saint and became his disciple. Along with the queen, many among the royalty and commoners accepted the saint as guru. Even now there are many places of worship in Chittor which are associated with Ravidas's name. Dr Singh summarises his legacy as he concludes his account of Ravidas:

> His approach was realistic and practical. It convinced the Sudras of the purity and dignity of their caste and profession. His efforts gave altogether a new outlook and attitude to the people of India towards the so called low castes and disgraceful profession. In this he emphasized the purity of labour. It was in the vision of Santa Ravidasa that downtrodden classes found their social and religious freedom. Because of these reforms he has been regarded as the messiah of the sudra class. Soon after his passing away, he came to be identified with the liberation of the low castes: and till today the very name of Santa Ravidasa is the light that guides them out of slavery and suffering to the attainment of liberation and Immortality both religious and social.[51]

19

Varkaries, Vithoba and Pandharpur

The Bhakti movement of Maharashtra comes to an end with the passing away of Shivaji and his guru, Ramadas, in 1680 and 1681 respectively. As a matter of fact, Shivaji's rise to power and the establishment of his empire is closely related to the rise of the Bhakti movement, the most important protagonist of bhakti being Ramdas. If the Bhakti movement in Maharashtra is to be taken as one launched by Jnaneswar with his commentary on the *Bhagavat Gita* in 1290, it is almost the same time that Basava began his Veerasaiva movement in Karnataka. Most importantly, quite in line with the Bhakti movement elsewhere, in Maharastra too it was largely composed of persons from lower castes and even Muslims were attracted to it. Says Prabhakar Machwe;

> In this first wave of Bhakti poetry, there were Visoba Khechar, a grocer; Janabai, a maid-servant; Savanta, a gardener; Goroba, a potter; Chokha, a sweeper; Kanhopatra, a dancing girl; Narhari, a goldsmith. This wave also attracted Muslims: Shaha Muntoji Brahmani alias Mrintunjaya, who wrote Siddhasanketa Prabandh, Anubhavasara and many Abhangas in the fifteenth century.[52]

The Mahanubhavas

At the turn of the first millennium CE the main political formation in Maharashtra was the Yadava kingdom. Yadavas claim Vishnu's incarnation of Shri Krishna as their ancestry. Since Dwaraka on the Gujarat sea coast is supposed by tradition to be Krishna's capital and his final resting place, the Yadava

Kingdom had extended to Gujarat also. Yadava period was not very remarkable for either literary achievement or religious innovations. The closing years of their reign had witnessed the birth of a new sect, said to be the forerunners of the later Bhakti movement and literary efflorescence.

The founder of the Mahanubhava sect was Shri Chakradhara of the thirteenth century. Hailing from Gujarat, he was the only son of Vasudev, the minister of Trimala Dev, the King of Gujarat. Originally known as Harpal, he was fond of dice and gambling. This wasteful hobby caused him to lose all his money and ancestral wealth. Desolate and poor, he decided to go on a pilgrimage during which he came into contact with a spiritual person, Govindprabhu. Falling under his spell, he became his disciple to turn a new leaf in his life. Govindprabhu changed Harpal's name into Shri Chakradhara.

Chakradhara became a sanyasi in 1267 and founded his own sect called the Mahanubhavas. Chakradhara, in contrast to his earlier life of profligacy began an extremely ascetic life of a mendicant and wandering minstrel. He traveled across Maharashtra which he loved with all his heart. He began to gather around him many devoted followers and Nagdeva, Mahimbhatta, and Nathoba among them later became famous as Mahanubhava writers. There were women, too, among his followers. One of them, Nagambika, is considered the first Marathi poetess.

Chakradhara spoke to his followers not only on philosophical and religious issues but on day-to-day life, its problems and solutions. This added to his popular esteem and affection. The Mahanubhavas worshipped Sri Krishna and the sect's founder Chakradhara. They left an enduring store of prose and poetry which enriched Marathi literature and led to its development. They consciously avoided Sanskrit since their message was for the poor and lowly. There is a well-known story on this tradition. When Keshavadas wanted to write out the messages, parables and stories the master used to deliver among his followers in Sanskrit, another important disciple, Nagdeva, admonished him as follows:

> Do not do so, O! Keshav, the common devotees of the master will be deprived of his teachings if you put these into elite language.

Chakradhara never seemed to have written anything himself and his communication was only through the oral method. However, his discourses made in simple and elegant Marathi enriched by stories, parables and humour touched the hearts of his audience. Both of the two most prominent of the many holy Mahanubhava texts—*Leelacharitra* and *Govinda Prabhucharitra*—were written in verse by Mahimbhatta around 1298. The former was about Chakradhara and the latter on his preceptor, Govindaprabhu.

Kusumavati Deshpande and M.V. Rajadhyaksha summarise the contribution of the Mahanubhavas to the Marathi language and religion:

> The last years of the Yadava period were of great prosperity on the one hand, but of social and religious decadence on the other. The upper classes led lazy, luxurious lives, ritualism under the garb of religion playing an important part in them. Orthodoxy ruled supreme. The Pundits considered it their sacred duty to hold aloof from the lower classes for fear of contamination. Their knowledge of the Shastras was directed solely towards depriving the masses of spiritual enlightenment. The Mahanubhavas represent one kind of reaction against this social atmosphere. Their sect broke through the barriers of the caste system. It treated men and women alike, and granted the right of sanyas to all. These breaches were like gall to the orthodox and led to severe persecution of the Mahanubhavas. In their early days during the regime of the Yadava kings, they had won some royal patronage. Perhaps it was because the Mahanubhavas were devout worshippers of Lord Krishna, and the Yadava kings considered themselves to be the direct descendants of Krishna. But their unorthodox creed (which rejected the authority of the Vedas and the caste-system), their strange black garments, so different from the saffron of the other sanyasis, and other oddities of behaviour made them very unpopular. The secret code in which their religious texts were written isolated them from the general stream of literature too. Mahahubhava literature, therefore, had little influence on contemporary or subsequent trends in Marathi literature.[53]

Secular Reading of the Puranas

The itihasas, Ramayana and Mahabharat, ascribed to Valmiki and Vyasa respectively or the *Purana*s like the *Bhagavatha* are generally considered extensions of the holy texts like the *Veda*s. In these *itihasas* and *Purana*s, it is openly admitted that they were designed to convey the Vedic messages to common people, not well-versed in the ancient lore. This task was accomplished through stories and legends on the day-to-day life of people and their emotions. There is ample scope for reading these stories beyond their primary texts and their authors. Along with the religious and ethical poems, hymns and other literary pieces, a group of writers like Mukteswara transcreated and adapted such stories on a secular rather than religious and philosophical context. Their aim was not just to enlighten but to entertain as well. People fed up with repeated loads of heavy doses of philosophy and literature and those who were indifferent to the religion, took to these lighter works.

Muktheswara was only the leading figure in this category. There were many others like Vishnudas Mudgal who wrote secular poetry basing on the *Purana*s. His *Rama Yudha Kanda* was a very popular poem especially during Shivaji's wars to establish the Maratha kingdom and dynasty. As said earlier Shivaji's rise to power was a political continuation and fulfillment of this ideological and literary resurgence in Maharashtra. Having prepared the ground for the new resurgence by the Mahanubhavas and others, the time was ripe for the most glorious period in the history of Maharashtra, its literature, culture, politics and forms of worship. The creator of this glorious era was Jnaneswar, who is also called Jnanadev. He was followed by a series of outstanding philosophers and bhakti poets like Namdev, Tukaram, Eknath, Ramadas and Chokhamela to mention only the most prominent among them. Their cult and activities were centered round the folk god, Vithala or Vithoba, at the shrine of Pandharpur. Worshippers and pilgrims to Pandharpur are known as *Varkaris*. It is said that this nomenclature began with the first visit of Jnaneswar to Pandharpur.

Jnaneswar and the Varkaris

Jnaneswar's life and activities are written in many narratives in Marathi and other languages. The popular eighteenth century biography of Indian saints by Mahipati—*Bhakta Vijaya*—gives many facets of Jnaneswar's life. Though it contains hearsays, legends, miracles, et cetera, of doubtful credibility, there is no doubt that his life was brilliant, faithful, short and tragic too.

Religion and Politics

Jnaneswar was born in a period when Muslim power was rising in many parts of India including Maharashtra. Turks, Afghans and Mughals were spreading their tentacles. Maharashtra was no exception. It was Shivaji in the seventeenth century who retrieved Maharashtra from alien domination. Shivaji's efforts and his rise to power were closely related to the new awakening heralded by Jnaneswar and his followers. So it was but natural that Jnaneswar's movement had a Hindu revivalist character. It also had to fight the fading remnants of Jainism. At the same time, Jnaneswar too had to fight the orthodoxy of the Yadava society. However, he did not try to establish his own sect as his aim was to revive the Bhagavat Dharma, that is, the Hindu dharma itself. The change he brought about was regarding the nature of Bhagavat dharma. Least caring for the elaborate Brahminic rituals, he had adopted the Bhaktimarga, the simple worship of one's favourite God. He was a Vaishnavite philosophically and that was why he committed himself to the study, commentary and elucidation of the holy Vaishnavite text, the *Bhagavat Gita*. However, his favorite pilgrimage had been to Vithala of Pandharpur where he began the *Varkari* movement which it must be stressed, was not a sect.

Jnaneswar's Life

Jnaneswar was born to Brahmin parents in 1275 and died at the age of 21. By the time his life's mission was admirably conducted he went into *Samadhi* as the traditional accounts say. His main work *Jnaneswari*, an interpretation of *Bhagavat Gita* is said to have been finished at the age of 16. He had also written several other shorter works in his short life. His most important disciple was said to be Namdev. On the basis of linguistic evidence, scholars like R.G. Bhandarkar do not agree that Namdev was a contemporary of Jnanedev. Acording to Bhandarkar, there was an interval of a century between their lives. However, the widely trusted tradition is that both were contemporaries and had a preceptor-disciple relation between them.

Jnaneswar's trials and tribulations began with his birth itself. His father was Vithalpant Kulkarni, a village accountant and his mother, Rukminidevi. Vithalpant was spiritually inclined from boyhood. Though married, he abandoned his wife later to become a *sanyasi* as initiated by a guru. They were all based in modern Paithan. The guru, though a sanyasi himself, was a kind man, very considerate to those who were suffering due to caste restrictions, gender or poverty. On one of his travels, the guru met Jnaneswar's abandoned mother Rukminidevi who was as orphaned and desolate as a widow. The guru's heart melted for her and he advised his disciple to return home and take care of his abandoned wife. Vithalpant obeyed the guru and his *sanyasa* came to an end as he became a householder, again. A sanyasi giving up his *Sanyasasrama* (chosen path of sanyasa) was considered a deadly sin by the orthodoxy. Vithalpant and his family were declared outcastes. He went on pleading with the authorities to relieve him from this punishment by purificatory rituals and payment of fines. However, they insisted that the fit atonement of sin was death.

It is from this wedlock that Jnaneswar was born as the second child among the four. Nivrithinath was his elder brother whom Jnaneswara accepted as his guru. His younger brother was Sopandev and his only sister, Muktabai, was a poet of distinction. The orthodox custodians of society did not allow Vithalpant's son to conduct the Brahmins' traditional sacred thread ceremony (Upanayana) and they grew up as outcastes. The entire family went on a long pilgrimage to sacred places, worshipped in atonement of their 'sins'. However, the orthodoxy was adamant. Finally, Vithalpant and Rukminidevi left their children to their own fate and embarked on their final pilgrimage. They jumped into Prayag, a sacred place where the Yamuna and the Ganga confluenced and committed suicide.

Some traditions say they went to the Himalayas to visit the pilgrim centres and never returned.

Though their parents were gone forever, their children still went on to plead their case and placate the Brahmans of Paithan. They, too, did not succeed. The only means to which Jnaneswera could resort was to challenge the Brahmin orthodoxy. It is said that Jnaneswar, by his miraculous powers, made a water buffalo recite some Vedic verses to prove that the right to recite the Vedas was not the monopoly of Brahmins. The story may be apocryphal but the very fact that such legends suvive even today shows that Jnaneswara, from the beginning, was forced to denounce Brahmin orthodoxy. It is very clear that Jananeswar was a Vaishnavite who was later known as a devotee of Vithala at Pandharpur. It is from his pilgrimage to Vithala at Pandharpur that the Varkari movement began. The varkari devotees make regular pilgrimages to temple at Pandharpur. There is another closely associated movement called Palkhi. Palkhi is defined by some scholars as a palanquin bearing silver-plated clogs that represent Saint Dhyaneshwar in the annual pilgrimage in the month of Ashad to Pandharpur. It also often signifies as a movement synecdoche of the entire pilgrim procession that accompanies it. A history of Marathi literature gives the following description of a Jnanadev pilgrimage to Pandharpur.

> The pilgrimage of Jnanadev to Pandharpur, and thence to the shrines of the north in the company of Namdev, laid the foundation of the Varkari Panth. The shrine at Pandharpur had already become a centre for devotees of all castes: Gora, a potter; Sawata, a market-gardener; Chokha, a Mahar; Narhari, a goldsmith; Sena, a barber. Theirs was a simple unsophisticated devotion. When Jnanadev visited Pandharpur, this simple devotion was strengthened by Advaitavad. Namdev, a tailor, became the chief discriple of Jnanadev and also the true founder and propagator of the Varkari Panth. He has celebrated the life of Jnanadev in a work of three chapters in the ovee metre, called the Adi, Teerthavali and Samadhi. His devotional abhangas have an urgent poignancy and a simple lovingness. The miraculous life of Jnanadev embodied the ideal of 'Sainthood'. The life of Namdev was nearer that of the simple, common man and his abhangas

express the intense yearning of the common man for the god of his heart. The cult of Vitthalbhakti became widespread. Namdev traveled widely in Gujarat and the North, especially in the Punjab. He also wrote a number of songs in Hindi. Some of these have been incorporated in the sacred book of the Sikhs as "Namdevi di Mukhbani. Namdev is thus the first biographer in Marathi poetry, one of the greatest devotional poets and a propagator of the Warkari panth. He, more than anyone else, introduced the Bhakti-Marga of Maharashtra to the people of the North.[54]

Vithoba, the Mysterious God

Jnaneswari, written before Jnaneswar visited Pandharpur does not make any mention of the god Vithoba. Some other minor works attributed to Jnaneswar duly contain reference to Vithoba. But it is not clear that Vithoba was a synonym or incarnation of other Hindu gods like Vishnu, Krishna, Shiva or others. All we can surmise is that Vithoba is a local deity or a folk-god. His origins have to be sought in non-Hindu tribal tradition. The very style of Vithoba's icon and posture are quite unusual and unique as Eleanor Zelliot a modern authority on Dalit and Maharashtra traditions writes:

> The word Pandharpur has come to represent the long tradition of Maharashtrian culture. Note, not the god Vithoba, but the town, temple, and idea of Pandharpur, the center of the streams of pilgrims. Curiously enough, Vithoba is an almost quality-less god. There is the story of the god standing forever on a brick in Pandharpur in tribute of Pundalik's devotion to his patents, but there are no complex myths about Vithoba! Or rather there are many stories, but all telling of the god in some disguise or other, that of a Mahar Untouchable or a Brahman beggar, coming down to help a devotee. True, Vithoba is not an avatar of Vishnu; he is a 'natural' Vishnu. Some say that Vithoba is the same god as Vishnu, or Krishna, or, a few have said, Buddha; clearly he is associated with Shiva. But none of the complex mythology of most of the Hindu gods or the Buddha has rubbed off on Vithoba. And the iconography of Vitthal is different from any of these. He is shown standing on a brick—that brick thrown him by Pundalik to keep the god's feet from the mud while Pundalik continued his loving care of his parents. John M. Stanley has called this brick Vithoba's vahan or Vehicle, just as the bull Nandi is Shiva's Vehicle; but the

> brick makes vithoba a static god, transfixed by human devotion. Vithoba's arms are akimbo, hands on hips. He is dark, often black, often a naked young boy. On his head is a curious hat, high and conical, a symbol of Shiva, so that the image represents both Vishnu and Shiva, say some.[55]

Durga Bhagavat was not a believer in the ordinary sense of the term. She was a sociologist, essayist and a socialist. She was amongst the very few bold intellectuals who opposed Prime Minister Indira Gandhi's *Emergency* regime (1975–7) and underwent imprisonment for it. She even refused to accept government honors like the Padmasree. However, even a person like her appeared enamoured and even baffled by the phenomenon of the Vithoba cult. In an essay on Vithoba she describes the deity as the 'Blackish manifestation of Brahman'. To quote her fully:

> 'The Vithoba of Pandharpur' expresses the larger cultural meaning of Pandharpur and also refers to Vithoba as a 'blackish manifestation of Brahman' symbol of the quality of the Absolute.
>
> **
>
> Somewhere there exists some inner link between Pandhari (Pandharpur) and every Maharashtrian. Because Pandhari is said to be the home of the blackish manifestation of Brahman. Whether or not one has faith, one not only sympathises with but feels strongly attached to the principle of equality of the Varkari Panth. The kind of innate attachment one has for one's family and ancestors one feels also for Pandharpur.[56]

When we take all these into consideration, there is no wonder that Vithoba of Pandharpur was the center (it continues to be so) of the Maratha Bhakti movement and the medieval renaissance.

Namdev, The Second in Command

As we have mentioned, there is dispute as to whether Namdev was a contemporary of Jnaneswar though it was believed so by a majority. There are other controversial observations also regarding Namdev's life. Though he is believed to have belonged to a tailor caste, there is also a belief that he was a highway robber and that he reformed himself after seeing the inconsolable grief of a woman after her husband was killed by robbers. After repenting for his life as a robber, Namdev became a devotee of Vithoba. During the life of Jnaneswar, Namdev was his constant companion. After Jnandev's premature death, Namdev traveled widely to propagate his message. He went to north Gujarat, Rajasthan and Punjab. Guru Nanak had heard about Namdev and read his prayers and soliloquies and included some of his poems written in *Abhang* style in the *Guru Granth Sahib*. The Abhang was a popular poetic style adopted by Jnaneswar, Namdev, Eknath and Tukaram. In order to demonstrate some of Namdev's self-questioning doubts and prayers, an English translation of his work is given as follows:

From Vedic students first the truth I sought,
And found them full of "Thou Shalt, Thou shalt not"
Never shall they possess tranquility,
For mighty in them is the power of "me".

From Scripture scholars sought I once again
The form divine, but found them rent in twain
Not one agrees with what the others say,
But pride and error lead them all astray.

Next in Purana I sought that form so fair
But still, alas, no place of rest was there.
The preachers preach of Brahma but set their mind
On lust, and so true peace they never find.

Ask of the Haridas the way devout;
You will find in him no faith at all but doubt
He tells in words the Name's high excellence,
While all the time engrossed with things of sense.

Weary with seeking, here are last am I,
Low at thy feet, O Pandurang I lie
My worldly life is full of tears, but thou
(Tis Nama cries), O save me now.

Ekanath and Contemporaries

Among the immediate followers of Jnaneswar was Ekanath, a Brahmin who was deeply influenced by *Jnaneswari*. By the time Ekanath flourished about a hundred years after Jnaneswar, he found that the original text of *Jnaneswari* was widely corrupted. He undertook a close study of the text and eliminated the obvious errors and mistakes committed by copyists. So much so that the present *Jnaneswari* text is the one which was corrected and edited by Ekanath. He completed his critical edition of *Jnaneswari* in 1584 CE.

Besides preparing the critical text of *Jnaneswari*, Ekanath has left us a wide variety of literary production. They include commentaries on ancient and modern works, folksongs, *Abhangas*. His rendering of folksongs is known as '*Gaulans*': His chief work is a commentary on the eleventh Skanda of *Bhagavat* written during 1570–3 while staying at Varanasi. Besides being a worshipper of Vithoba, Ekanath was very much attracted to Vaishnavism and Krishna cult. Much fond of the Bhagavath Purana, he re-wrote it in Marathi with detailed commentaries. The Sanskrit pundits in Varanasi had severely criticized him for transcribing and transcreating the holy texts in the revered language Sanskrit to the 'vulgar' language of the common people. Ekanath resisted them and stuck on to his own mother tongue and continued to write in popular Marathi. Ekanath did not restrict the Bhakti movement to the worship of chosen deities and debate over philosophical issues. For him, religion was a matter concerned with the good conduct of the common men and women. The practical aspects of the entire life were concerned with Bhakti. Therefore, his method of discourse was simpler than those of Jnaneswar and Namdev. Besides his devotional work, Ekanath also wrote or re-wrote in Marathi some of the stories in the *Purana*s. Among them, *Rukmini Swayamvara* and *Bhavaratha Ramayana* are important. Ekanath was not a great genius like Jnaneswar. But his capacity for propagating the message of bhakti and simplifying the intricacies of the scholarly debate was remarkable. Perhaps that is why he is also called the founder of *Madhura-Bhakti* (sweet-devotion).

Dasopant

Dasopant was a talented poet of Ekanath's time. Other important poets who contributed to the development of Marathi literature during the time of Ekanath and Dasopant were Rama Janardhan, Ravi Janardhan and Vitha Janardhan, who were together known as '*Nathpanchayatan*'.

Earlier, we characterized the new resurgence which began with Jnaneswar had a Hindu revivalist character. Nevertheless, it was an ideological resistance as well to the Muslim and Mughal onslaught in Maharashtra. However, it is typical of the composite culture of India that there were Muslim writers too, who contributed to the development of Marathi literature. The writings were not necessarily on Islamic tenets like those of Sufis. They promoted religious tolerance and harmony.

It is also interesting to note that Christianity also began to make inroads in Maharashtra after the arrival of Vasco-da-Gama in 1498 CE and their establishment of Goa as their centre of Portuguese operation. In order to propagate their religion Christian missionaries began to study the local language and wrote their messages and scriptures in it. Later, they introduced the printing press in India. In order to suit Indian alphabets to the movable type, some reforms were necessary in the Indian alphabets. They were mainly designed for handwriting and calligraphy. Christians had pioneered this task too. In the sixteenth century another noteworthy work was brought out by Father Stephens (1549-1610) which is called *Christ Purana*.

Tukaram

After Jnaneswar, Namdev and Eknath, the Bhakti movement was without a prominent promoter for about three centuries. It doesn't mean the Varkari practices and Vithoba worship had disappeared or declined. However, there was no new breakthrough in the development of bhakti. The thread of bhakti left by Ekanath was taken up by Tukaram (1608–50) in the seventeenth century. Although considered the carrier of the heritage left by Jnaneswar, Namdev and Ekanath, Thukaram's life and career were turbulent and tragic.

Tukaram was born in Dehi, a small village in Pune, on the coast of the river Indrayani. He belonged to a Vaisya family whose livelihood was from usury, trade and agriculture. As a non-Brahmin, he sometimes referred to himself as a Sudra. His parents were Bolhoba and Kankai. He was the second child and had four siblings. Though from the childhood itself he was interested in the ancient wisdom and scriptures, he took up the family jobs in trade and agriculture after a normal schooling. Married at the age of 17, his first wife was afflicted by asthma and he was married again to Jijabai. He had a son by his first wife. His elder brother Saoji became a religious mendicant and left home. Therefore, the family's responsibilities fell on the shoulders of Tukaram. He carried out his responsibilities fairly well and his trade prospered until a devastating famine gripped the entire Deccan.

The great famine of the Deccan (1630–31) threw the life of the peninsular region thoroughly out of gear. The rains failed for two years consecutively. The rivers of Narmada, Tapti and Godavari and the tributaries of Krishna and Kaveri dried up and looked like broad sandy highways. Humans and beasts died in thousands. Even the birds in the sky began to disappear. Absence of transport systems prevented import of food from neighboring areas in such large quantities as was required. The pack animals died in thousands to add to this malady. The land around Thukaram's village on the border of Bijapur and thc Mugal dominions had already been reduced to wilderness. Wild beasts grew in number and began to prowl at the deserted villages in search of prey—both living and the dead. Close on the heels of these events cholera and other epidemics began to take their toll without distinguishing between the rich and poor. Some took to robbing and looting the very few well-to-do people and the law of the jungle prevailed.

Tukaram was shattered. His business was lost for ever, and his livelihood was precarious. His mental tranquility was upset as famine and starvation deaths had sneaked into his own household.

Modern biographers write of Tukaram's state of business, family and mind after the terrible reign of drought and death:

> The famine has come to an end. His business stopped. His only son died of starvation. He faced the crisis of his life. At thirteen he had entered business; at seventeen his parents died. And soon his elder brother's wife died as a consequence of which his brother became a mendicant; and now at the age of twenty one he found

> himself bankrupt. He had no face to show the people owing to bankruptcy.
>
> His father- in-law came to his help and lent to him some money to pull on and even that was lost again. He had to support a large family and the sight of crying babies and pale faces must have destroyed his faith in the very concept of life. It is in this period that his first wife Rukma died of starvation crying in her death-bed food, food as Tukaram recorded later on repentantly. His eldest son Sanru also died soon.
>
> Tukaram was too sensitive a man to take this devastation philosophically. In just four years he saw several deaths in the family; and bankruptcy poverty, dishonor and humiliation, destroyed the security for ever.[57]

Tukaram died in 1650 at the early age of 42. He could survive the ravages of famine for 18 years. The deep wounds it left in his mind and soul had never cured. His *Abhanga*s were scarred by these wounds. His deep devotion to his god was thinly veiled by pessimism and irony in his songs.

After the famine, Tukaram had begun to look after and revive his business and fulfill his responsibilities to the family. But a clear lack of keenness was evident in him. His heart and mind was away from all those and were engaged in contemplating the deeper problems of life and his own varied experiences. The following stanzas of his *Abhangas* will prove it.

I am scorched by the fires of Sansar,
While serving the household
And remember your feat, God,
Come to me, my Master.

Tukaram did not feel at home even in his own birth place. He felt like an alien there:

This is not my country,
By chance came to wade here;
What can I claim as mine?
...I am a stranger here!

All great thinkers and innovators are devoted to unravel the complex problems of the day so that the humankind could enjoy a better and nobler life. They are all beset by the travails of self-doubt and agonizing introspection. They search here, there and even in very unlikely nook and corner for the answers. Tukaram had more than a usual share of such worries and queries as we saw in the above narrative. His unusually chequered career and experiences also added to this burden. He had deeply imbibed the teachings of his Marathi predecessors, Jnanadev, Namdev, Eknath and others and wrote in their praise. Jnaneswar's *Janaeswari*, a study of *Bhagavat Gita* had influenced him very much. However, his restless mind in search of truth was not satisfied. He wanted to write his own translation of the sacred book. He did and called it the *Maratha Gita.* Tukaram got some consolation from his regular pilgrimages to Pandharpur as a Varkari to worship Krishna and Vithoba. The traditional cult of his family was known as 'Gosai'. Then at the age 32 in 1640, he found solace in a new faith, the Chaitanya cult (not to be confused with the Bengali Chaitanya). Tukaram was initiated into this revolutionary cult by Babaji Chaitanya. How Tukaram's life and spiritual career were metamorphosed is hinted in his following *Abhangas* lines:

Tuka says, my tie is broken
By the great Guru Babaji

Chaitanya was a famous cult in the heart land of Deccan from the fifteenth to the eighteenth centuries. It was a radical variety of Bhakti movement without the usual worship of deities like Vishnu, Krishna, Siva or such other traditional gods. It was purely a this-worldly cult similar to the Naths and Siddhas. They accepted in their ranks both Hindus and Muslims and all castes and both genders. Having originated in Sourashtra it had spread to Maharashtra and finally to Telegana region in Andhra. Most of Telengana in those days had consisted of Gulbarga. The Gulbarga Kings had a soft corner for Chaitanyas—some say they accepted the cult as a state religion. Raghava Chaitanya's shrine in Gulbarga is even now visited for worship by both Muslims and Hindus. One of Raghava Chaitanya's chief disciples, Keshav Chaitanya had belonged to Tukaram's village or region. Babaji Chaitanya, whom we have mentioned as the person who converted Tukaram to this cult, was a follower of Keshav Chaitanya. Besides Tukaram, there were several Marathi poets of the seventeenth century attached to this cult. Some of the Chaitanyas were very much influenced by the Mahanubhavas of Maharashtra. Babaji is said to have suddenly disappeared one day never to be seen again. There are several legends about his mystic or mysterious disappearance. It has an interesting similarity with Tukaram, who too mysteriously disappeared in 1650. No one heard or saw him since.

Social Rebel

Tukaram was a fierce opponent of Brahmanic orthodoxy, caste system, untouchability and all types of social inequality. His attacks both in prose and poetry of the caste system and untouchability and Brahmanical prerogatives, bristle with brimstone and fire. Nemede gives us a few examples in translation:

A Brahman who gets angry over
teaching a Mahar is not a Brahman,
Suicide is the only expiation for such a Brahman.

The Brahmins retaliated by humiliating and out-casting Tukaram. However, he did not retreat or relent. He fought back giving instances of many low caste devotees who became the heralds of a new humanistic and egalitarian India. He wrote and sang:

Holy is the family, holy is the country, where servants of God are born,
Is there any man who was purified by the pride of caste?
—Let me know.
The untouchable castes have crossed Samsar by means of Bhakti,
And even the Puranas sign their praise;
....Gora, the potter; Ravidas, the cobbler;
Dabir, the Momin; Latif, the Musalman; Sena, the barber
— were all devotees of Vishnu.
Kanhopatra, the Carver, Chokha Mela and Vanka Were Mahars;
Jant, the maid-servant of Namdev—how great was her
faith that Vitthal would eat with her!
Caste does not exist for the devotees of Vishnu,
This is the judgment of the Vedas.

20

Chokhamela: The Untouchable Saint

Chokhamela, the untouchable saint poet of Maharashtra's *Varkari* tradition had belonged to the lowest of lower caste, the Mahars and lived in late thirteenth and early fourteenth centuries. He had accepted Namdev as his guru who was very fond of Chokha. It is interesting that in one aspect the guru and disciple had close resemblance. The family members of both were a collective of *bhakti* poets. Namdev's was a large family of fourteen including a servant-maid who was considered as a member of the family. She was an untouchable: Chokha's was a smaller family of wife, son, sister and brother-in-law. Namdev's wife, son, daughter and even the servant-maid were worshippers of Vithoba and left us some poems written by them in praise of the 'Black Deity':

Chokhamela's wife Soyrabai, sister Nirmala, son Karmamela and brother-in-law Bhanga were all devotees of Vithoba and had written *Abhangas* dedicated to Vithoba. The Varkari pilgrimage to Pandharpur was opened to all castes and classes of people. Some of the occupation and class-status of the important Varkari personnel are given in the following poem by Chokha himself:

The savior of his devotees
who never turns away;
hurries to help them with their chores.
He dusts and cleans, and fetches water;
the upholder of dharma;

saves from the searing flames of nirvana.
He keeps the cows at the milkman's house
and happily with others
breaks the pot of curds.
He pulled a wall for
Dhyaneshwar; made Changdev
famous; weeded the beds
for Saavata the gardener,
and fired pots for Gora.
He loves more than his own self
goldsmith, cobbler and Namdev the tailor.
He grinds the grain
at Jani's home sweeps the dirt
and brings the cow dung in.
Says Chokha, he is so tender:
his devotees know him
as a fond mother![58]

Chokhamela does identify the people he hinted at. They are:

> Jnaneshwar the rebel Brahmin, Changdev the yogi turned saint, Namdev the tailor, Gora the potter, Savata the gardener, Chokha the mahar, Janabai the servant/nurse at Namdev's house, Joga the oilman, Narahari the goldsmith, Sena the barber, Kanhopatra the courtesan and later after a couple of centuries there is Eknath the liberal Brahmin scholar saint and then the flower of the Warkari movement Tukaram who was a peasant, a lower caste kunbi: these are the saint poets.[59]

Thus, although the Varkaris were comprised of all caste and classes including untouchables, the latter could not enter the temple's 'sanctum sanctorum'. They had to keep themselves away from the main entrance. Many of Chokhamela's poems state this discrimination but only obliquely. Here is an example:

They thrash me, Vithu,
now don't walk so slow.
The pandits whip,
some crime,
don't know what:
How did Vithob's necklace come round your throat?
They curse and strike

and say I polluted you.
Do not send the cur at your door
away,
Give of everything.
You,
Chakrapani,
yours is the deed.
With folded hands,
Chokha begs.
I revealed our secret,
don't turn away.[60]

Even after Chokha became well known as a Varkari and a poet, he was still working to earn his livelihood and support his family. It was during such physical labour that he met his end in the town of Mangalavedha. He died when a wall of the house he was building collapsed on him. Though this is the official version of his death, obviously propagated by the upper castes, many of his contemporaries and admirers believed that he was killed by the upper caste owners of the said house.

Soyrabai and Nirmala

We have already said that Chokha's wife Soyrabai and his sister Nirmala were also poets of distinction. Soyrabai lived in Pandharpur and Nirmala in Mehunpuri near Aurangabad. Nirmala was married to Bhanga who was Soyrabai's brother. Though both of them were very fond of and respected Chokha, they did not hesitate to criticize him for his indifference to the family. It is said that Chokha was indifferent even to the birth of his son Karmamela. Even when his wife was writhing in labour pain, Chokhamela was nowhere near to console her. Soyrabai wrote an *Abhanga* on this. The regard and affection with which they held Chokha is proved by the fact that in their *Abhanga*s they always called themselves Chokha's Mahari (Mahari is the woman-Mahar or Mahar woman) and that Soyrabai occasionally rose to the heights or descends into the depths of mysticisms is evident in the following *Abhanga*.

House and home are meaningless; samsara is meaningless,
the corporeal body is meaningless.

Your name is meaningful, all else is meaningless;
if people don't drown, it is only because of the Name.
All things are meaningless.
Ideas are meaningless.
Great wisdom is meaningless. Who cares?
The science of words is meaningless.
Words themselves are meaningless.
Knowledge is meaningless.
Why speak of these things?
If your mind is not steady, that's also meaningless,
and then how will you come to Hari?
Till then, there's no meaning in speaking speech
says Chokha's Mahari.[61]

However, Nirmala does not wander into the other worldly thoughts and worries. An example of her *Abhangas*:

I am certain of you; I surrender to your feet.
Now, do what you think is right; I have put down my burden.
I have put my head in your lap, knowing what the future holds.
Nirmala says, Save me or kill me; now the burden is yours.[62]

Here is yet another example:

People say you should gain the ultimate goal, but they don't have the skill at all.
Pure bhakti feeling, meditation on the Name—this is the source of spirituality.
Censure, fault finding, praise, honour, dishonour—treat all these as vomit!
In spirituality, others' food, others' money, others' women should be considered polluting.
Nirmala says, This is the way to the ultimate goal: the companionship of the saints night and day.[63]

Though Bhanga was also a devotee and poet, Nirmala did not refer to him. She refers mainly to her brother Chokha. However, Nirmala, whose main concerns were devotion to Vithoba and self-realisation, was also concerned with the common miseries of people and when she spoke of them, she did not even spare her beloved brother, whose indifference to the family sometimes were just akin to culpable misdemeanour. She sings as follows:

Conscious of the threat of samsara,
Chokha went to Mehunpuri.

Seeing him, Nirmala was joyous,
And ran to embrace his feet.

She sat near him, asked him how he was,
if his wife was well.

Nirmala said, 'Tell me what to do now'.

Listening to her, Chokha said,
'She is nine months pregnant.

There is no provision for this in the house,
she told me.

To find out what to do in this great difficulty,
I have come quickly to your place.'

Nirmala said, 'What can I say to you?
You are at fault.

Tell me, elder brother,
how could you act so thoughtlessly?

How could you come running here without asking her?
My sister-in-law will cry wildly.'

Chokha said, 'Vithu will take care of everything.
I have put my burden on him.'

Nirmala said, 'It is not fair to give Vithoba
such trouble.'

But he stayed there happily for one month,
his mind entangled in Pandurang.

Night and day, his only passion was the Name of Vitthal.
There was no thought of samsara in his mind.

After dinner, he sat alone.
Nirmala said to him

'Many days have passed. I remember the king of
Pandhari and I feel sad.

Nothing tastes sweet to me. When will I place my head on His feet?'
Nirmala said, 'O King of Gods, meet me soon.'

Chokha said to Nirmala, "Sing the Name day and night.
That makes samsara happy, truly, both here and in the other world.

This is the great way: peace, pardon, and mercy will dwell in you.'

Nirmala heard this joyously and embraced his feet.[64]

21

Tulsidas and Rama Bhakti

Goswami Tulsidas is one of the greatest poets in Hindi literature. A contemporary of Kabir, he wrote 31 books of poems of which only 12 survive. His magnum opus, *Ramacharitramanas,* a classic in Hindi is the story of Rama, the King of Ayodhya. The original story of Rama is narrated in Valmiki's *Ramayana*, reputed to be the *Adikavya* (the first book of poetry) in Sanskrit.

Valmiki's *Ramamyana* does not attribute any divine qualities to Rama. However, Tulsi does and goes further to describe him as god, an incarnation of Vishnu. It is a fact that there are about hundreds of versions of the Rama story in India and south-east Asia. Tulsi was not a devotee of Rama or any other deity to begin with. His early poems confirm it. They are mostly on carnal love or sensuous experiences and longing. This is how this transformation came about in his life.

Tulsidas was born in a Brahmin family in 1532 CE (d.1623) at Rajapur, in present-day, Uttar Pradesh. After this traditional Brahminic education in Sanskrit, a real guru came along and initiated him into Ram Bhakti. He had high regard for him. However, Tulsi does not mention his name in his poems. Some people speculate that the guru was Ramananda. Ramananda, too, was a worshipper of Ram and this speculation cannot be easily brushed away. Ramananda's views on many issues except the worship of Ram differed widely from Tulsi's, as we shall shortly see. One difference in the views of Ramananda and Tulsi was about caste. While Tulsi believed in it, Ramananda did not.

However, Ramananda did not care. Says R.L. Handa:

> The wave of the **bhakti** movement spear-headed in the North by Ramananda may have also provided a helpful clue to Tulsidas. To Ramananda it was not very relevant to lay stress on the **Nirguna** or **Saguna** aspect of Rama **bhakti**. As long as people could be drawn towards his preaching's and share his religious fervour, he felt fully satisfied. His disciples were free to interpret Rama in any manner they liked so long as they felt drawn towards Him as an object of worship and devotion. Kabir and his associates and followers, as we have seen, conceived Rama as a formless God whereas for Tulsidas and his followers, the various qualities and achievements of Rama were symbolic of divinity and they worshipped Rama as Saguna God.[65]

Tulsi had a very intimate married life. He was so deeply in love with his wife that he could never suffer any separation from her. It was this love that prompted him to write his early poems devoted to beautiful women, their love and his intense attachment to them. Once, his wife went to visit her father. She went alone without taking her husband along. At about midnight, she was surprised to see her husband in her room. The room was on the first floor of her father's house. In the dead of night she saw her husband crawling through the window from outside. The surprised wife asked him how he could climb up to the window. He said there was a rope hanging on the branch of the tree which was above the window. And hanging on to the rope he climbed up. Some legends suggest that when she peeped out of the window she saw a big python hanging on to the branch of the tree and there was no rope to be seen. That means Tulsi climbed up hanging on to the python. The story of the python may be an exaggeration or apocryphal. However, it proves the dispassionate love and pain at the separation from his woman. She then responded to him thus: "It you are devoted to Rama with half as much fervour as you are devoted to me, you will be rewarded with salvation and eternal bliss".

This comment set Tulsi thinking which proved a turning point in his life, according to a popular legend.

Tulsi's *Ramacharitramanas* is not only the story of Rama as a god or as an incarnation of Lord Vishnu but also a political and social testament, when Tulsi describes Rama as a brave warrior an ideal ruler, a dutiful son and an affectionate brother. He had to deal with politics, society, war and family relations. Tulsi goes into all these and presents his own views on Rama as ideal.

Savitri Chandra Shobha elaborates Tulsi's ideas on politics and rulership as under:

> Tulsi supports and upholds the institution of rulership on both religio-phiosophical and practical grounds. For Tulsi the ideal ruler is Rama, who himself is God and assumed human form in order to redeem the earth (**bhumi**) from evil, and in particular his devotees and the **brahmans**. This does not, however, mean that Tulsi attributes divine qualities to all rulers or even to good rulers. Apart from Rama, the good rulers mentioned by Tulsi in **Manasa**, are Satyaketu, (Ravana in his previous birth), Pratapbhanu, Raja Janaka, Raja Dasharath and his son, Bharata. While these rulers have all the moral, material and spiritual attributes of a good ruler, divine qualities are not specifically attributed to them anywhere. However, from an analysis of Tulsi's works it is interesting to note that Tulsi frequently uses the word "**sahib**" for Rama and even for Hanuman, whom he places on a high pedestal. In fact, he uses the word "**sahibi**" for kingly authority. Since the word "**sahib**" was used in medieval Persian literature for persons in authority, including the ruler, the use by Tulsi of the same word for Rama suggests that he associates divine qualities with a ruler- as was the popular concept.
>
> Tulsi's main argument for the need of a ruler is the social necessity, an idea which he shared with most of his contemporaries, Hindu or Muslim. A strong ruler and firm state policies are essential to curb the evil propensities of the evil elements in society who form the overwhelming majority. Tulsi illustrates his concept with a telling simile. He compares the ruler to a goldsmith who fashions beautiful jewels from metal by constant hammering (i.e., by punishment). On account of the stern orders and sound policies of the ruler, even the good people are afraid. He goes on to say that a period (**kal**) is called good or bad according to the qualities of the ruler. A second cause for social disorder, according to Tulsi, is the encroachment of the members of one caste (**varna**) on the functions of another. **Varna-sankar** according to Tulsi leads to sorrow, want, and crime in society. In fact, these are the specific features of **Kali-Yuga**, according to Tulsi.[66]

It would be wrong to expect modern democratic ideals from a

medieval thinker or poet. Even after making an allowance for these limitations, Tulsi's ideas were very different from those of his contemporaries like Kabir. It is well known and evident from the account on saints, that the bhakti poets of Tulsidas's days sharply criticised and rejected the caste discrimination and untouchability. However, Tulsi did not accept such ideas of protest. Savitri Chandra Shobha explains it further as follows:

> Tulsi adopts a dual approach to society. On the one hand, he classifies society on the basis of the essential qualities of individuals, and on the other, he appears to conform to the traditional concept of **Varnashram**. However, primarily he divides society into three categories—**uttam**, **madhyam** and **adham** or **neech**, or high, medium and low. A forth category of khal or dusta, i.e., the wicked or the vile is sometimes added to the above. Tulsi makes an interesting suggestion regarding the proportion of these categories in society. He says that the **uttam**, **madhyam**, **adham** and **khal** increase in proportion of one to ten. It would imply that persons of high and medium categories comprised a very small fraction of society—about one percent if taken literally. This understanding forms the essential basis of Tulsi's attitude towards society and the state. If the evil, the wicked and the low constitute the overwhelming majority of the total population in society, social controls become necessary for keeping their evil propensities in check. As shall be argued later, this provided a basis for the entry of the concept of caste from the back door. It also provides a justification for the institution of monarchy.
>
> Tulsi describes in detail the essential qualities pertaining to the different categories of people, according to his classification. To the **uttam** or the first category of people, Tulsi ascribes ethical, spiritual and social qualities. The ethical and the spiritual qualities are to some extent traditional. They include humility (**vinaya**), absence of arrogance (**nirabhimana**), straightforwardness, equanimity (**samata**), lack of attachment to worldly things (**anasakti**), and above all, a sense of discrimination or understanding of good and bad (**vivek**). Tulsi includes the saints in this category, laying considerable emphasis on their ethical and spiritual qualities. But the saints alone do not comprise the category **uttam**. Other elements are also included, but one of their basic virtues seems to be their being not opposed to the saints.[67]

22

Guru Nanak and the Sikhs

Among the saints of the Bhakti movement, Guru Nanak (1469–1538) has a special place of importance. He tried to synthesise all the best in Indian religious tradition and the diversities of the Bhakti movement. He did not establish a special sect or religion on his own. However, as it happens often in history, religion grew up around him, making use of his words and teachings which have been summarized in the *Guru Granth Sahib*. It is a compendium of Nanak's teachings and extracts from many scriptures of religions that prevailed at the time. He wrote in Punjabi which was not a developed language then. The *Guru Granth Sahib* may be said to have given Punjabi its present form, including its alphabets.

Nanak was born in a village called Nankana Sahib near Lahore, now in Pakistan. Earlier, this place was known as Talwardi Rai Bhoe located south-west about 65 Kilometer from Lahore. His parents were traditional Hindus—his father was Kalu Mehta, a village record keeper and mother Tripta. His primary education was carried out with the help of a tutor. However, his father considered him not inclined much to studies. So his father entrusted him to tend cattle. From childhood owards, Nanak showed signs of spiritual inclination and a meditative mood.

Leaving the cattle to graze or wander, Nanak used to take rest and even sleep till sunset under the shade of trees. He was indifferent to caste and religious distinctions and customs like untouchability which were associated with them. He refused to wear the sacred thread. His parents were in a fix. Even at a young age, Nanak showed his inclination of mind. When the family priest, Har Dayal, raised questions to him he gave metaphorical explanations and stood firm. Finally, his parents prevailed upon him to take business as a source of livelihood. However, this new endeavour also did not succeed because he distributed whatever he earned among the *sadhus*, the poor and the needy. His father again found this difficult to bear and punished the son. Needless to say, the punishment did not deter Nanak from his faith in generosity and sympathy for the poor and the *sadhus*. The story goes that when he was returning after his bath in the village tank, he gave a brass jug and gold ring to a mendicant who asked for alms. Nanak's father, Mehta, got fed up with his son's behaviour and turned him out of his house. Nanak left his parents and began to live with his sister, Nanki, His sister was married to Lala Jairam who was Diwan to Daulat Khan Lodi of Sultanpur. There is a story that Nanak became a pupil of Syed Hussein, a courtier of Lodi though the official accounts by Sikhs do not accord with this. However, they admit that Nanak had an association with Syed Hussein from whom he learned much about the doctrines and practices of Islam. Nanak lived in Sultanpur with his sister for the next ten years or so. Nanak was a great traveler, fond of visiting pilgrim centers and other important places. He took the opportunity of staying in Sultanpur with his sister, Nanki, who had connections with the high and mighty through her marriage. His travels were not confined to the Indian subcontinent as he visited many places in Persia (present-day Iran) and West Asia up to Saudi Arabia and Jerusalem near the Mediterranean coast. M.A. Karandikar draws an account of places Nanak visited:

> He traveled via Goindwal near Amritsar. The Dukhbhanjani Sahib and the Ber Sahib testify to this halt. At Amenabad he met Lalo the carpenter. He paid a visit to Talwandi, met his parents, relatives and Rai Bular too. Then he visited Lahore and Sialkot. In this journey he also met Sajjan, the Thug, who later became Nanak's disciple. The first Udasi or holy journey seems to have begun in AD 1505. The travels took Nanak to Kurukshetra, Karnal,

> Panipat, Hardwar, Delhi, Mathura-Brindabun, Nankmatta (in Pillibhit district), Ayodhya, Lucknow, Kashi, Patna, Gaya, Raj Mahal, Malder, Dacca, Dhanpur, Kamrup, Dhubri, Chittagong and Jagannath Puri. He returned through the Vindhya region, Madhya Bharat and Rajasthan. The second Udasi to the south was undertaken in AD 1506 and the stages included Sirsa, Bikaner, Ajmer, Pushkar, Abu, Ujjain, Bedar, Pongal, Madras, Nagapattinam and Ceylon. The return journey took him through Rameshwaram via Malabar Coast, Sudamapuri, Dwaraka, Sindh, the modern Montagomery (at Satghar), then back to Lahore through Talwandi. The third Udasi began about AD 1514 and covered Mansarovar, Tibet, across the Kaliash mountains and (through Ladakh) Kashmir, Riasi and Jammu. The fourth journey took place between AD 1518 and 1522 when Guru Nanak visited Mecca, Medina, Jerusalem, Damascus, Aleppo and Baghdad and returned via Persia, Turkestan, Kabul and Peshawar.[68]

Nanak was married in 1488 at the age of 18. He had two sons—Srichand and Lakmidas. A person of independent perspectives, Srichand founded a sub-sect of the Sikh religion called *Udasi*. The Udasis were like the 'Gnana Marga' monks among Hindus. They concentrated on studying the scriptures and gaining knowledge. They refrained from wearing the traditional Sikh attire. This helped them from being persecuted by Mughal rulers like Aurangazeb who ascended the throne in 1617. Nanak's second son, Lakmidas's descendants were known as *Bedi Sahib Sadamars*. Being descendants of Guru Nanak, they are held in high esteem by the Sikhs.

The Adi Granth

Guru Nanak's teachings are contained in the *Adi Granth* (Primal Scripture). It is more known by the name *Sri Guru Granth Sahib*. It contains the guru's words, both spoken and written as well as the interpretations and elaborations by his disciples of more than one generation. As a matter of fact, it evolved through centuries to reach the final form. This process of evolution is narrated by G.S. Talib;

> The Principal source of **Bani** included in the holy Granth Sahib were the **Pothis** aforementioned, found in Goindwal. These were scribed from Samvat 1627 to 1629 (1570–72) by Baba Sahas Ram,

> son of Baba Mohan and grandson of Guru Amar Das. These two volumes between them consist of 300 and 224 leaves respectively, making a total of 1048 pages, all written in one hand, except two hymns, presumably in Guru Ram Das's hand, prior to his assumption Guruship. Some pages are left blank. On page 94 of Volume II is written, 'Ghulam Mastan Jeth Chand'—Jeth Chand being Guru Ram Das's original name. So this is in the authentic hand of Guru Ram Das.
>
> In these Pothis are included 15 ragas out of the 30 that found place in the Volume as finalized under the guidance of Guru Arjan Dev. The 31st raga, Jaijawanti was the mould of some hymns of Guru Teg Bahadur, and was added when under the command of Guru Gobind Singh the Volume as it now stands, was completed. In the Pothis the order of the ragas and of the hymns of the Gurus is not the same as in the extant canon of Guru Granth Sahib. In volume I of the Pothis the following eleven ragas are included: Suhi, Prabhati, Dhanasari, Basant, Telang, Gujari, Bilawal, Bhairon, Maru and Kedara. In Volume II, 4 ragas appear: Ramkali, Sorath, Malar, Sarang. Thus a total of 15 ragas appear in these Pothis. To these however, additions were made when the Scripture was finalized.
>
> Some additions were made to the pre-existing Banis, when final form was given by Guru Arjan Dev to the holy Granth Sahib, e.g. in the Pothis **Anandu** contains 38 pauris, and **Siddha-Goshti** 72 pauris. Besides these, **Vars** and much other Bani was added. Guru Angad Dev's Slokas were procured from some other source. On the margin of P.216 of Vol.II is written: '**Guru Angad Gurmukhi akkhar banae. Babe de aggie Shabad bhet kita'** Guru Angad formulated the Gurmukhi Script. He presented the collection of hymns to the holy Guru Nanak.[69]

In every Gurudwara (Sikh place of worship), a copy of *Adi Granth* is kept open in a ceremonial manner. Since Sikhs do not worship idols and are monotheists, it would seem that the *Granth* itself is the object of worship rather than just a scripture to be read and get enlightened from. The entry to the Gurudwara, participation in congregational prayer and common dining are all open to everyone, whatever their caste or religion or faith. The common dining is also part of the congregational reading of the *Granth* and prayer.

Gurmukhi is the language of *Adi Granth*. Its final version

was completed by the additions from Guru Arjan Dev and the Gurmukhi script was designed by Guru Angad Dev. Arjan Singh later explained why the Granth was written in Gurmukhi rather than Sanskrit and gave the credit to Nanak himself. Arjan Dev's explanation in verse is translated into English by Talib as follows:

> *The Guru, perfectly-endowed, withdrew into solitude,*
> *And called Gurdas to his presence.*
> *Seating him by his side, to him he revealed his purpose thus:*
> *Listen, brother! To my wish.*
> *Make the Granth into an ample volume,*
> *And write it out in the Gurumukhi Characters.*
> *In the Patti devised by Guru Nanak,*
> *Are included thirty-five letters.*
> *In these letters record the entire Bani of the Gurus,*
> *Which all may be able to study with ease,*
> *Those that are greatly endowed with understanding,*
> *Should study it more amply through their learning.*
> *After a study and contemplation of many years,*
> *May alone its essence be ralized.*
> *Such essence too in Gurumukhi should they express with hearts full of reverence,*
> *In language that may be easy to follow,*
> *Those endowed with learning express themselves*
> *In Sanskrit and the Mohammadan tongues:*
> *Over all such writing shall it spread soon,*
> *As oily substance poured over water.*
> *Householders engaged in daily labour, who have little learning,*
> *Yet seek knowledge, may study it with ease.*
> *By it shall be indicated a broad card-road on which those traversing, shall nowise stray.*
> *Therefore, write you down the Gurmukhi letters,*
> *That these over the wide world may get known.*
> *Let those with faith read these with ease—*
> *Thereby shall they learn contemplation of God, giver of liberation.*
> *Great is the merit of those letters,*
> *That the world over shall be known as Gurmukhi.*
> *These shall mankind see, read, write and offer to these reverence;*
> *And to annual their sins shall to these be devoted.*[70]

A Compendium

The greatness and uniqueness of Nanak's teachings and the *Granth* lie in the fact that both the guru and the book liberally accept and quote from many other scriptures and saints. Some were added by Nanak's followers after his death and also by many saint-poets from all over India. Talib's analysis and classification of the verses in the *Granth* are given below:

Guru Nanak Dev	947	
Guru Angad Dev	63	
Guru Amar Das	869	
Guru Ram Das	638	
Guru Arjan Dev	2312	
Guru Tegh Bahadur	115	
Guru Gobind Singh	1 (Sloka)	
Baba Sundar	6	
The Bards Satta and Balvand	8	
The Bhaktas: Sadhna	1	
Surdas	2	(Of one hymn only 1 line in Raga Sarang)
Sain	1	
Kabir	534	
Jaidev	2	
Trilochan	5	
Dhanna	4	
Namdev	62	
Parmanand	1	
Pipa	1	
Shaikh Farid	123	
Beni	3	
The Bhatts, authors of Swaiyyas	123	
Bhikhan	2	
Mardana	3	
Ravi Das	40	
Ramanand	2	
Total	5751	Verse-Units

The second half of this list almost looks like a roll-call of the stalwarts of the Bhakti movement in medieval India. This proves the catholicity and universality of Guru Nanak's thought and teachings.

Nanak's Politics

Being an apostle of unity and compassion, Nanak was always opposed to dictatorial rulers and oppressive regimes. He was against the conquests of other countries and aggrandisement of ruling dynasties. He was a bitter critique of Babar's invasion and occupation of India. At the same time, he supported the Lodi dynasty. He was an eye-witness of the first Battle of Panipat (1526) in which the Lodis were ousted from power by the invading Zahir ud-Din Muhammed Babar to establish the Mughal throne in Delhi. When Nanak was living in Delhi with his sister whose husband was the Minister (Diwan) of the Lodi feudal chief Daulat Khan Lodi, Nanak, too, served in the government of Delhi Sultan Ibrahim Lodi. Nanak was employed as a *modi,* that is, one in-charge of the state granary. Nanak was critical of the Sultan for not protecting his subjects against Babar's invasions. Its morals and consequences are as follows according to Professor Shahabuddin Iraqi:

> 'Babur ruled over Khurasan and terrified Hindustan. The creator takes no blame to Himself; it was death disguised as a Mughal who made war on us.' 'Bringing a bridal procession of sin, Babar hastened from Kabul and demanded (by force) the wealth (of India) as his bride... They (the people) sing the paeans of murder and smear themselves with the saffron of blood.' Referring to the consequences of Babur's invasion, Nanak says, 'If a tyrant slay a tyrant, there is no grievance; but if a ferocious lion falls upon a herd (of cattle), the master of the herd is accountable.' This is evidently in the context of Ibrahim Lodi's defeat at the battle of Panipat in 1526, for Nanak the latter is 'master of the herd' who did not protect his subjects. 'The dogs of (Ibrahim) Lodi have spoiled the priceless inheritance; when they are dead, no one will remember them'.[71]

Nanak gives a graphic account of the Battle of Panipat and the atrocities and looting by the Mughals. He laments:

> *Where are those sports, those stables and those horses?*
> *Where are those bugles and clarions?*
> *Where are those who buckled under swords and might*
> *in the battles?*
> *Where are those scarlet in uniforms?*

Nanak not only condemned the Emperor and their conquests, but he was also very critical, like Kabir and Surdas, of government officials such as local tax collectors, court officials and army personnel who made the life of the poor miserable. However, some changes in his attitude towards the Mughals were discernible with the ascent of Akbar the Great (1540–1605) who was third in line of the dynasty founded by Babar. Besides, Nanak, four of his followers who later became prominent Sikh gurus—Angad Dev, Amar Das, Ram Das, Arjan Dev—were Akbar's contemporaries. Akbar, who had strongly promoted Hindu-Muslim unity and general harmony among all sections of his subjects was very much impressed by the Sikh religion which also advocated unity of all faiths. Akbar found in their teachings elements of his own religious belief. Akbar despised fundamentalism and had attempted to found a new religion, '*Din Ilahi*'. Nanak and his followers mentioned above kept good relations with Akbar. Akbar gave them grants to establish Gurudwaras and also the right to collect taxes from villages. He also encouraged the attempts of Sikhs to organise themselves to promote their religion first in Amritsar and gradually to other centers. Akbar gave as a marriage gift the rights to collect taxes in a few villages to the daughter of Amar Das. By giving it, Akbar sought the blessings of Das in the war against Chittor in 1597. When many conservative and traditional religious teachers and Pundits complained about Sikh activities as being harmful and unethical, Akbar praised the social services rendered by the Sikhs.

After Akbar's death, the relations between the Mughals and the Sikhs began to sore. The change came with Akbar's son Jahangir's ascent to throne. The Sikhs, too, were responsible for this souring of relations. It was set off by some action of Guru Arjan Dev to reorganise and strengthen the hold of Sikhs among the people. He promoted the conversion of Hindus and Muslims into the Sikh religion. He began to collect taxes also from the areas inhabited by the Sikhs. The Sikhs used to give money, commodities and other valuable things as offerings to the Gurudwaras. The offerings were entirely voluntary. It was from those offerings that the Gurudwaras were run and their functions were conducted. There is no wonder that the Mughal administration looked upon the compulsory taxation by Arjan Dev as an attempt to usurp the authority of the state and organise a parallel administration. Emperor Jahangir ordered the arrest and trial of Arjan Dev. He was found guilty of high treason. The judgment was to give Arjan capital punishment. However, his son, Guru Har Gobind, appealed for mercy and capital punishment was reduced to imprisonment in Lahore prison. Though the capital punishment was commuted, Arjan was tortured and persecuted in prison by the officials and security personnel.

Arjan Dev's son and successor Guru Har Gobind (1606–44) did not take his father's sufferings at the hands of the Mughal officers lightly. He resorted to the option of resistance to the oppressive regime. He organised an army and adopted a militant line with its headquarters at Ramdarpur (now Amritsar). The Sikh documents give us detailed information about hundreds of horses and elephants and the arms collected by Har Gobind. Jahangir's army attacked Hargobind's headquarters but was defeated. When Jahangir died and his son Shajahan acceded the throne the relation between Har Gobind and the Sikhs on the one hand and the Mughal administration on the other began to improve. However, Har Gobind's militancy and the parallel army could not sit smoothly with the emperor. Relations became worse when Aurangazeb ascended the throne by ousting his rival claimant and elder brother Dara Sikoh. Aurangazeb suspected that during his struggle for the throne, the Sikhs were conspiring with his rivals. This suspicion and his fanaticism led to the complete collapse of the mutually cordial relationship, leading to an all-out war between the Sikhs and the Mughals. Eventually, a Sikh kingdom came into being under Ranjit Singh.

Bhakti and Political Power

Though the Bhakti movement certainly had a pan-Indian character, it assumed vastly diverse forms in different parts of the subcontinent during its course. The movement in South India led by the Alvars and Nayanars was also associated with the different ruling dynasties like Pandya, Chola and Chera. Among these dynasties, some individuals opposed bhakti while others promoted it. Various forms of the movement like *saguna* and *nirguna*, and the *Vaishnava* and Shaiva had fundamental differences with each other. The Bhakti movement under the leadership of the Varkari saints in Maharashtra had paved the way for the rise of Shivaji. However, the movement initiated by Guru Nanak was quite different from all these. Though Nanak's teachings and the *Guru Granth Sahib* contain many noble ideas like opposition to oppression by the rich and the powerful, promotion of equality and fraternity and criticism of the iniquitous system of caste and untouchability, years of persecution by the Mughals gradually made the Sikhs, too, to resort to militarism. It was soon to become a militant sect with armies, armaments and even the state. The state power of the Sikhs was similar to that of any other state. The contemporary Mughal state was an instrument of violence, exploitation and extortion and alien to the humane teachings of Guru Nanak. However, Sikh gurus like Har Gobind, his son Guru Tegh Bahadur, and much later, his son, Guru Gobind Singh, nurtured militarism and political ambitions. Guru Tegh Bahadur was assasinated under the orders of Aurangzeb.

It was his son, Guru Gobind Singh, who devised a soldier's uniform to be compulsorily worn always by all Sikhs, which included the five articles of faith called 'Five Ks'—Kesh (uncut hair), Kangha (comb worn in the hair), Kirpan (sword), Kachcha (fighting shorts) and Kara (steel bracelet). The idea was to convert the entire community, including the old and the young into a special army, the Khalsa. Guru Gobind's launch of the 'Khalsa' was significant in the history of Sikhs as many ordinary Sikhs were apprehensive of taking up arms to fight the mighty Mughals. Answering a call given by Guru Gobind Singh, five brave and dedicated Sikhs came forward to take up arms first and sacrifice their lives to save their faith. All this was in the name of their venerable founder Guru Nanak. It was also true that Gobind Singh had tried to meet Aurangazeb and make peace. However, Aurangzeb avoided meeting him under one pretext or other. In the meanwhile, a Pathan assassinated Guru

Gobind Singh on 7th October 1708. This marked the end of the Sikh's guru tradition as Gobind was the tenth and last Sikh Guru. Thereafter, the privilege and authority of the gurus were vested on the 'Khalsa' and the holy book, the *Guru Granth Sahib*.

Sikhism

Sikh community's militarism was essentially a response and resistance to Mughal persecution which were inspired by Guru Nanak's endeavors that roused the community's self-respect and its will to fight wrong-doings. However, long years of struggle had made militarism and politics come to dominate the community's core. This, in turn, led to the complete marginalisation of tenets like love and compassion which were fundamental to Nanak's tachings. This was the case not only of Nanak. Many saints of bhakti also had the same experience. Their followers worshipped the saints but did not imbibe their teachings or live according to their prescription. Let us see a summarised and truthful version of Nanak's teachings given by Shahabuddin Iraqi.

> Like Kabir, Nanak was a monotheist and monist, believing in that God is one, without attributes and everywhere manifest. 'There is but one God whose name is true, the Creator....immortal, unborn, self-existent. He also said, 'Millions of men give millions upon millions of descriptions of Him, but they fail to describe Him'.
>
> Nanak did not believe in the **avatar** theory and he rejected the idol worship which was the outcome of the concept of God taking physical form: 'My brethren, you worship goddesses and gods; what can you ask them? And what can they give you? Even if a stone be washed with water, it will again sink in it.'
>
> Nanak had no faith in Heaven or Hell as reward or punishment after death but he believed in attaining salvation within one's lifetime (**Jiwan mukti**). The condition laid down by Nanak for a man to reach such a state of mind is strict, and the devotee who qualifies becomes a 'perfect man' close to divinity. 'Joy and sorrow are the same to him. He is ever is bliss and never in woe...Honour and dishonour affect him not. A king and a beggar are alike to him. Whatever is the will of God is the best to him. Such a man, says Nanak, may be said to have attained salvation.'
>
> Nanak enjoins upon his followers to live as ideal men, not as

ascetics but as householders depending on their own labour. While narrating the ten stages of human life, he says that 'in the seventh he collects things for a house to live in'. 'He alone, O Nanak, knows the (right) way, who eats the fruit of his earnings and shares it with others.'

Within the cult, was required hard work and honest dealings in the professions which included not only trade but also agriculture. But at the same time, Nanak was also against the accumulation of wealth 'Nanak says, man must depart; why amass property and wealth?' Every Sikh was expected to voluntarily contribute to the common fund at the disposal of the guru or the local **sangats**. This contribution was made by rich and poor at the rate of one-tenth of their income, though an individual might willingly contribute more.

The institutions of **sangat** and **pangat** (i.e. mixed congregations and inter-dinning) started by Nanak and continued by his successors not only had a wholesome effect on the lives of the Sikhs but also presented a new social structure based on liberal and secular values. The system was a direct incentive to the promotion of social solidarity. Besides, it was Nanak's clear directive to adopt social service for all without discrimination. The **Guru Granth** suggests three **marga** (ways) of pious life—remembering **Name** (God), **kirtan**, and social service, of which the last was the most important. The spirit behind it was not less than what was maintained by the Muslim mystics.

Nanak refused to recognize any restriction based on birth. He asserts that every man, irrespective of his position in the caste hierarchy, was eligible for salvation. Those who took shelter in God were equals: 'Perceive (in all men) the light (of God). Do not ask (a man's) caste for, in the hereafter, there is no caste; caste and status are futile, for the one (God) watches over all.' And also 'we having taken shelter in God are neither high, low, nor in between. We all are God's servants.'

Nanak rejected outright the very idea of impurity attached to any human being and refused to admit anyone being untouchable: 'Nanak is with those who are low-born among the lowly; Nay, who are lowest of the low; how can he rival the great.'

Defining the conduct of Brahmans and Kshatriyas, Nanak says that while the Brahman is one who knows the transcendent lord, performs deeds of devotion, penance, self-restraint and humility, the quality of a Kshatriya is to have bravery and charity.

Here Nanak redefines varnas as something related not to birth but to worth. He says, 'As a man soweth so shall he reap; as he earneth so shall he eat... Men are judged according to their acts.'

Nanak and other Sikh gurus did not accept the scriptural authority of the Vedas and Puranas. The **Guru Granth** alone has been regarded and maintained as religious scripture in the Sikh cult. However, Nanak's own opinion about the authority of early scriptures is indicated in the following declaration: 'Some read the Vedas, some the Puranas... (but) I know not and never know anything than thy name (O, God)'.[72]

23

Sufism and Bhakti

Sufism is an off-shoot or a sect within the Islamic tradition which began in Arabia after the death of Prophet Mohammed (570–632 CE). It was an attempt to re-establish and assert the teachings of the Prophet which suffered a process of dilution after his death. The Sufis were the reformers who sought to retrieve Islam from the creeping decay. Such developments are not unique to Islam. Buddhism, Christianity and various other sects within Hinduism also had the experience of deviating from the teachings and practices of their founders. It is then that the reformers who seek to re-establish the pristine purity of the teachings of the founders appear on the historical scene. Often such attempts result in the split of the original religious community. The Mahayanas and Hinayanas in Buddhism, Catholics and Protestants in Christianity, the Sunnis and Shias in Islam are examples of such splits. Then, again, there may appear further splits within the splinter groups.

The Sufis actually did not leave the Islamic community, but worked within it as a catalytic agent. India's Bhakti movement is in many ways similar to Sufism. The Bhakti movement, as we have seen, was an attempt to reform the Hindu society and save it from Brahminic orthodoxy, the iniquitous caste system, the irrelevant ritualistic practices whose original meanings were forgotten. The Islamic situation was different from the Hindu experience. The Brahminical authority was supported and promoted by the Hindu kings and states. However, it was never the state itself. On account of many historical reasons, Mohammed had to function as not only a founder of the religion, but as a statesman who had to take up power. After the death of Mohammed, the struggle for succession by his followers created many problems and complexities. The Sufi movement was the product of these conflicts. Since Islam became a state structure too, wealth, worldly ambitions, pursuit of power, luxurious lifestyle, et cetera became attractions for those in political and religious authority. Sufis called for a rejection of the crassly materialistic tendencies and stood for an ascetic life marked by simplicity, morals, prayer and truthfullness. However, such a life was not so much a passive submission to the status quo as it was a way of protest and a quest for an alternative. This protest aspect was evident in the activities of the Shia sect as against the status-quoist Sunnis.

Says the South Lebanon-born historian Mahmoud M. Ayoub who was Director of Islamic Studies in Temple University, Philadelphia:

> ...Shiaism and Sufism may be regarded as the two most important protest movements against the despotic authority, wealth, and worldliness of the rapidly expanding and powerful Muslim empire which followed the death of the Prophet Muhammad. While the Shia protest was political, and often revolutionary, that of Sufism expressed itself, at least in the formative stages of Sufi history, in an ascetic rejection of the world with all its wealth and pleasures. Hence the perfect leader or shaykh is not a good and just ruler, but an anonymous perfect man. He is an intimate friend (wali) of God, the grace, or blessing (barakah) of whose presence in the world is necessary for its well-being. The imams likewise, are the proofs (hujaj) of God over His creation. They are the pillars or supports (arkan) of the earth, without whom it would quake and melt away.[73]

Sufism, as we have seen, appeared in India not very long after the Prophet's time. It came in the early centuries of the second millennium CE. It was also a time when the Turks and Afghans had conquered north-west India and established the Delhi Sultanate in the early thirteenth century. They were the pioneers of Sufism in India. Shahabuddin Iraqi gives us the following account:

> In India, Sufism was introduced and popularized by two 11th century Sufis, Shaikh Ali Hujwiri of Ghazna and Shaikh Safiuddin Gazruni. The former settled in Lahore where he composed his famous, Kashaf-ul Mahjub, the first treatise on Sufism in Persian. The latter lived in Uchh in South Punjab. His dargah became a place of pilgrimage, but the Gazruni Silsilah could not gain popularity. By the 12th century, the Sufis organized themselves into silsilahs (fraternities or orders), each called after a great Sufi Shaikh to whom the followers traced their spiritual descent. Two of the silsilahs introduced in India just after the formation of the Delhi sultanate in the beginning of the thirteenth century were the Chishti and the Suhrawardi.
>
> The Chishti silsilah was founded by Khwaja Abu Ishaq Shami (AD 940) in Chisht, a village near Herat. It was brought to India by Khwaja Muinuddin Chisti who established a Chishti mystic centre in Ajmer even before the Turkish conquest of India. Under his able successors, such as Shaikh and Shaikh Nizamuddin Auliya, the silsilah spread far and many Chishti mystic centres were established in northern India. On the other hand, the Suhrawardi silsilah was founded by Shaikh Najibuddin Abdul Qahir Suhrawardi (d. AD 1169) in Suhraward (a town in Jibal), but was developed by his nephew, Shaikh Shihabuddin Suhrawardi (d.AD 1234).[74]

The word 'Sufi' is derived from the woolen clothes they usually wore. This woolen dress worn in the summers and winters was not only a resistance to the cold climate, but also as a mark of their identity and rejection of luxury and extravagance. In a valuable collection of papers on 'Sufism' presented in an international seminar, its editor, Hamid Hussain, explains the lifestyle and ideals of the Sufis. In his introduction, he says:

> Sufi and Bhakti philosophies, though often quoted and talked about, are rarely understood in their correct perspectives. Sufism basically connotes renunciation of worldly pleasures, complete devotion of God and healing of human hearts and sufferings through spiritualism and service towards humanity. It is a way to reach God through the rigorous practices of **salat** (prayer), **faqr** (poverty), **zikr** (remembrance of God), **fana** (anhilation) and **safa** (purity of body and soul). Important components of these practices are **tauba** (repentance), **zuhud** (asceticism), **tawakkul** (trust in God), reza (satisfaction) et cetera. In this pursuit a Sufi moves

through different stations of mystic experiences. Bhakti movement is also a mystic movement, an offshoot of Hinduism, but a reaction to its ritualism, casetism and social stratification.

Sufism became an important institution during the medieval period with great moral sway over the State as well as the populace at the hands of Shaikh Moin al-Din Chishti, Shaikh Qutub al-Din Bakhtiyar Kaki, Shaikh Farid al-Din Ganji Shakr, Shaikh Nizam al-Din Auliya and Shaikh Nasir al-Din Chiragh-I Delhi of the Chishti order. Notable Sufis of other orders, especially Shaikh Rukn al-Din, Shaikh Sadr al-Din and Shaikh Sama al-Din of Suhrawardi **silsilah** also left deep impact on the Sultanate. Similarly, simultaneously, rather subsequently, emerged Bhakti movement in the fertile soil of Indian spititualism. The brightest stars among them were Kabir, Tulsidas, Meera Bai, Nanak, Chaitanya, Namdev et cetera. They were for egalitarian society, not exactly in terms of Marxist form of classless society, but a society in which there are respect and concern towards each other, human dignity and feeling of fraternity.[75]

Institutionalisation of Sufi

As it always happens in the history of religious and reform movements, its popularity and spread had led to the institutionalisation of the Sufi sect. Institutionalisation naturally leads to the reversal of the processes of reform and the purity of the original movement. In the place of an original dynamic character it tends to assume the preserves of the status quo. Sufism, too, was not an exception to this mode of evolution.

Owing to the widespread expansion, Sufism had different centres of activity from where they guided their followers. As the Sufis had tried to keep away from power-politics, the State did not come into conflict with them. Often the state patronized Sufi centres with land and money. The devotees also contributed to the upkeep of these centres. Thus Sufi centres became rich and accumulated gold, cash and land. Originally when the head of the centre passed away the senior most Sufi used to be appointed in his place as routine. However, as time passed succession became hereditary and hence the quality of the heads of the centres deteriorated perceptibly. Iraqi describes these centres as follows:

"The establishment of **Khanqahs** was an integral part of the Sufi **silsilahs**. Having been effectively organized on a large scale, they became centres of mystic activity and forums for the regulation of the corporate life of the Sufis. Hence, the formation of such training centres had to be based on certain principles, even if the **Khanqahs** of different orders were organized on different patterns. Shaikh Shihabuddin Suhrawardi in his **Awarif-ul Ma'arif** gives seven basic principles for **Khanqah** organization. The Shaikh (spiritual teacher) was the central figure and ultimate authority of the **Khanqah**, responsible not only for the entire administration of the centre, but also for affiliated branches across the country. He was, therefore, highly respected, and was called with the title of **Shaikh-ul-Islam** to denote his spiritual position and power.

The Shaikh was required to possess the requisite qualities and qualifications. Shaikh Nizamuddin Auliya used to tell his disciples that a Shaikh must be acquainted with Islamic sciences and a knowledge of the Quran, **hadis** (prophetic traditions) and fiqh (jurisprudence) was necessary. Any instruction given by the Shaikh that was inconsistent with the Quranic injunction could be turned down by the **murid**. It may be noticed that these were the qualifications to be possessed by the ulama also.

In order to maintain their spiritual identity, Shaikhs would adopt some special articles of daily use, the Khirqah (patched frock), the sajjadah (prayer-carpet), the nalain-ichubin (wooden sandals), the tasbih (rosary) or the asa (wooden stick) as mystic insignia, and whomever was entrusted with these articles at the time of the Shaikh's demise came to be regarded as the spiritual successor. Previously, the appointment of chief successor was made from amongst senior and highly qualified disciples, but later, as pointed out by Mohammad Habib, some Shaikhs began to appoint 'their own sons as their successors, and thus mysticism ceased to be a spiritual urge and degenerated into a comfortable and recognized hereditary trade or profession, which catered to the needs of the ignorant and the credulous'.

In the Suhrawardi silsilah the hereditary succession had become an accepted tradition. The founder of the order, Shaikh Najibuddin Abdul Qahir, had appointed his nephew, Shaikh Shihabuddin, his chief khalifa and Sajjadah-nashin. Shaikh Bahauddin Zakariya's son, Shaikh Sadruddin Arif (d. AD 1285), succeeded him as his chief successor in Multan, though his disciple, Jalaluddin Surkh Bukhari (d. AD 1291), founded a separate Suhrawardi centre at Uchch. Shaikh Sadruddin too was succeeded by his son, Shaikh Ruknuddin Abul Fath (d. AD 1335). As Shaikh Ruknuddin had no son, after his death a struggle for succession began between a grandson of the Shaikh's brother and a nephew. The problem became so serious that the matter was referred to Muhammad bin Tughluq for arbitration. Both parties went to Daulatabad to argue their claims. The Sultan decided in favour of Shaikh Hud who was sent back to Multan with state honours to take charge.[76]

Sufism and Sikhism

The Sikh religion based on the teachings of Guru Nanak has later taken many forms in religion, politics and the internal military form of organisation as we have seen. However, it certainly was originally a product of the Bhakti movement. The celebrated scripture of the Sikhs *Guru Granth Sahib* is almost a comprehensive compendium of Indian Bhakti literature. This compendium contains many extracts from different religious scriptures including those of the Sufis. Among the Sufis, the *Guru Granth Sahib* gives a pride of place to Baba Farid a great humanist of all time and the Sufi Saint of distinction. Hamid Hussain writes on the impact of Sufism on Sikhism.

> Bhakti movement generated clearly due to the Sufi influence. Since Sikhism is the outcome of Bhakti movement; there is an inherent linkage of Sufism and Sikhism. It was Punjab where initially they came. Here Sufism flourished to an unprecedented extent. Also here was born, probably, chronologically the youngest religion of the world, 'Sikhism'. The advent of Islam and Sufism in Punjab led to cultural and linguistic interaction between the two civilizations. The influence on each other was immense. Persian and Arabic vocabulary was imbibed by the Punjabi language. On the other hand, cultural tenets of Islam also received fulsome impact of local dialects and culture. The most important and interesting outcome of the said intercourse was on the metaphysical thought and practices. Shaikh Farid al-Din Ganj-i-Shakr, popularly known as Baba Farid played an important role in transforming the religious, linguistic and cultural ethos of the land. Two centuries later Guru Nanak was born when a new composite culture and vitally transformed language had evolved in the soil. Hence the impact of the Arabic-Persian culture and Islam, especially through the Sufis on Punjabi language, culture

> and on the socio-religious ethos of Punjab and more so on Sikhism needs no emphasis.[77]

Baba Farid though fervently had believed in all the teachings of Koran (Quran), created the impression that he even went beyond the Sharia which prescribed the dictum—*'An Eye for an Eye'* and *'A Tooth for a Tooth'* which was seen a just punishment for a culprit. This meant if somebody caused injury to the eye of a person the culprit could legally be deprived of his own eyes. However, Farid did not approve of such procedures and called upon the victim to pardon the culprit. The following verse reflects the concept of tolerance and non-violence as propounded by Farid.

> *Faride Jo tein marain Mukkian tinhan na marain ghumm*
> *As panre ghar jaiya, pair tinhan de chumm. Do not strike when struck on the face, you will rather go back home after kissing their feet.*[78]

Sufis and Lower Castes

Many historians are of the opinion that the spread of Islam in India was due to the Islamist concept of equality which attracted many who suffered the inequalities of caste hierarchy in Hindu society. However, some historians like Irfan Habib do not agree with this. He says that Islam came to India as the religion of the ruling class and were not specially enamoured by the lower caste among Hindus. They concentrated in winning over the upper-class Hindus to the Islamist fold, though some Hindus of lower caste directly serving the rich upper caste might have been drawn towards the new religion.

This situation changed with the growth and spread of Sufi influence. Shahabuddin Iraqi, while generally agreeing with Habib, said that many Indian Sufis took pride in being Indians. He described how the Sufis had earnestly tried to integrate themselves to Indian mores and traditions. He says:

> Hindus belonging to the lower strata of society were particularly influenced by the simple and straightforward religious and social precepts of Islam. Many weavers, oil-pressers, water-carriers, leather-workers and sweepers embraced Islam. This was the case

particularly in Bengal, Uttar Pradesh, Punjab and western India. In the later sixteenth century in north-eastern Bengal many regarded as outcastes, became Muslims. But the hopes and aspirations of the lower-class converts for equality of status in Muslim society were not fulfilled. Muslim orthodoxy did not accord them this—they continued to remain in the same inferior status. Thus, they naturally were caught in a dilemma. But to say that in the medieval period there were attempts at re-conversion is a misconception: re-conversion to Hinduism was not possible in the medieval period. Brahmanical orthodoxy and formalism could hardly meet such a challenge. But in the course of Bhakti movement there was already a suggestion of the possibility of transcending the caste system.

However, many converts retained 'their skilled or non-skilled ancestral professions and this brought into Islam some vague features of caste distinctions. In rural areas most of them continued to live with the Hindus of their caste and to observe Hindu rites and customs, as also to have Hindu wives. Nanak's remark in the **Guru Granth** is important: 'You wear a **dhoti** and a mark, and carry a rosary, yet you eat the bread of **mlechhas** (i.e.Muslims). You perform the Hindu ceremony at home, read the Koran in public and associate with (or act like) the Mohammedans. So in most of the cases converts were neither fully Hindu nor completely Muslim.

The Sufi attitude towards the Hindus and Hinduism was based on understanding and adjustment, because it was believed that all religions were different roads leading to the same destination. Believing in **ahimsa**, living as vegetarians, and giving equal status to all, was bound to increase the scope of their contact with Hindus. Shaikh Muinuddin Chishti took two wives, and one of them was the daughter of a Hindu Raja of Ajmer. Shaikh Hamiduddin Nagori (d.1276) was proud of being born in India.[78]

Like the Bhakti movement, the Sufis also contributed to the development of the newly evolving Indian languages and literatures. In certain respects, the Sufi contribution was even more in absorbing Persian and Arabic vocabulary and idioms. This also had finally resulted in the birth and growth of a new Indian language which we now call Urdu. Specially suited for lyricism and melody, Urdu certainly gave a new dimension to Sufi poetry. Along with this, a new musical tradition too came into being. Hindustani music tradition is largely indebted to Sufi Music.

What we have discussed above amply proves that the Sufi and Bhakti movements interacted with and borrowed many ideas and practices from each other. However, it would be wrong to assume that they synthesized with each other. The Sufis never tried to deviate from Koran consciously, though one could agree they unconsciously tried to re-interpret or revise some Koranic injunction. Iraqi concludes:

> ...though the Sufi doctrine of **Wahdat-ul Wajud** was very close to the Upanishadic Advaita, the quest of God the theory of incarnation was opposed to the Islamic and Sufi concept of strict monotheism. Similarly, the Sufis never subscribed to the Vaishnava faith of **avagaman** or transmigration of the soul. Besides, while the Sufis believed in **Wahdat-ul Adyan** or unity of religions, the Nirguna bhaktas challenged the institutional form of all religions. The essentials of the mystic thought of the **sants** were indigenous, and Sufism offered only an atmosphere of spiritual stimulus.[79]

24

Bhakti and Fanaticism in Kashmir

The breathtakingly beautiful Jammu and Kashmir (J and K) in the extreme north-west of India, with international borders with Pakistan and China, is now a region of conflict, bloodshed and terrorism. Conflicts and civil strife are not new in Kashmir's history, as perhaps in the case of most countries. Nevertheless, a long period of peaceful cultural advance and achievement had offset such conflicts as incidental and far between. A narration of the long history from the time of Emperor Asoka, who introduced Buddhism (which still survives in some parts of Jammu and Kashmir like Ladakh), is an interesting exercise. However, for the present purpose we are concerned only with the Bhakti movement of the medieval times,

Jammu and Kashmir nestles in the lap of the mighty Himalayas, with its glistening snow heights reaching out to embrace the blue skies. The Himalayas are not a long and high stretch of snow and rocks, resembling the Great Wall of China. They are a complex of hills, valleys and mountain ranges. Often glaciers come down rolling, destroying everything in their way and growing in weight and shape. The lower reaches of the mountain ranges are rich in thick vegetation, wild animals and flowers of exquisite beauty, colour and fragrance.

Culturally, Kashmir has always been an integral part of the Indian subcontinent. The Mughals annexed it politically to make it a part of their Indian empire. In peaceful times, the region was their summer retreat to help them escape the scorching heat of Delhi. Mughal Emperor Jahangir, who built the famous Shalimar Garden in the precincts of Sringar, wrote in his memoir, *Tuzuki-Jahangir;*

> If one were to take to praise Kashmir, whole books would have to be written....Kashmir is a garden of eternal spring, or an iron fort to a palace of Kings—a delightful flower bed, and a heart-expanding heritage for dervishes. Its pleasant meads and enchanting cascades are beyond all description. There are running streams and fountains beyond count. Wherever the eye reaches, there are verdure and running water. The red rose, the violet and the narcissus grow of themselves; in the fields, there are all kinds of flowers and all sorts of sweet-scented herbs more than can be calculated. In the soul-enchanting spring the hills and plains are filled with blossoms; the gates, the walls, the courts, the roofs are lighted up by the torches of the banquet-adoring tulips.[80]

The actual population of present-day Jammu and Kashmir State is difficult to be estimated because its frontiers are still in dispute. The north-east portion is supposed to be an independent republic called 'Azad Kashmir' which in reality is a colony of Pakistan. It was carved out from J and K by tribal hordes from Pakistan after the partition of the country in 1947 according to the Mountbatten plan. The northern strip of the state called Aksai Chin was occupied by China in what was considered by India as an act of aggression. There are now three major areas, Kashmir Valley in the south-central part, Jammu to the east and Ladakh in the extreme north-east, bordering Tibet. The north-west part, comprising Gilgit and Punch, is not considered part of the Valley, but is part of J and K State. The largest part is the Kashmir valley of which 70 per cent of population is Muslim. Jammu has a majority of Hindus, known as Pundits. Jawaharlal Nehru, whose ancestors hailed from there, bore the epithet 'Pundit', which of course he gave up later in life. The majority of the population in Ladakh is Buddhist. As per the latest census, the population is estimated as more than ten million.

Religion and Culture

There is a story that Emperor Asoka, in the fourth century BCE, had deputed his missionaries to Kashmir to propagate

Buddhism. Modern historians are of the opinion that Buddhism became a popular religion only in the fifth century CE, or almost at the time China accepted that religion. Before that, various forms of Hinduism might have prevailed in the valley. The decay and decline of Buddhism paved the way for a resurgence of Hinduism, heralded by Adi Sankara who is reputed to have visited Kashmir in the ninth century CE during his *Digvijaya* and perhaps established a *math* (monastery) there. Sankara and his *Advaita Vedanta* left deep imprints on Kashmir's resurgent Hinduism, which is known as Kashmir's Saivism.

Kashmir Saivism has many features in common with the Tamil Saivism of Nayanar and Basava's Veerasaivism of Karnataka. However, along with these, there were important variations too. Kashmir's Saivism is known as 'Trikha Saivism,' which, as we have indicated, has many elements borrowed from Sankara's Advaita Vedanta. However, it did not accept Sankara's theories of *maya* and the illusion of the material world.

Dr Pranabananda Jash, who was a professor in Tagore's Viswa Bharati, may guide us through the medley of these intricate doctrinal differences. He explains:

> The singular importance of Kasmira in the field of religious history lies in the fact that it was the home of a separate school of Saivism having a philosophy similar to that of **Advaita** as developed by Samkara. It is called Kasmira Saivism, because the originators and the writers who revealed it and enriched its literature belonged to and flourished in Kasmira. It is otherwise known as **Trika-sastra** or **Trika-sasana** or simply **Trika** and more rarely, also as **Rahasya-sampradaya** and **Tryambaka-sampradaya**. The word '**Trika**' implies its acceptance of a trinity or triad, whether it be the **Siddha**, **Namaka** and **Malini** of the ninety two **Agamas** recognised by it, or the trinity consisting of **Siva**, **Sakti** and **Anu**; or **Pati**, **Pasa** and **Pasu**; or, again, of **Siva**, **Sakti** and **Nara** or lastly, of the goddesses **Para**, **Apara** and **Paratpara**; or because it explains the three modes of knowledge of Reality, viz., non-dual (**abheda**), dual (**bheda**) and dual-cum-non-dual (**bhedabheda**).
>
> It is to be noted in this connection that although the Trika system of Saivism seems to have made its first appearance in Kasmira at the beginning of the ninth century A.D., **Saivasasana** or **Saivagama**, i.e., Saivism as such, can be traced back to earlier period. It is, however, difficult to determine how and when this

Trika system first appeared. There are common elements in the dogma of Kasmira Saivism and that of the South Indian Saivism. Yet, in their philosophy they differ perceptibly, the Kasmira School being idealist and the South Indian pluralist in its metaphysics. The mention of the Brahmanas from Kasmira in South Indian inscriptions may lead to the inference that South Indian Saivism is to some extent influenced by the Kasmira Brahmanas. J.N. Farquhar, on the other hand, thinks that the teaching of Sankara during his controversial tours must have influenced the Saiva leaders of this state and this ultimately led to the writing of the **Siva-sutras** and the movement which followed it.

There is no denying the fact that it has much in consonance with the **Advaita Vedanta** especially as regards the nature of the ultimate cause of the universe. "Both hold it to be not only all-inclusive but also all-controlling. But, it must also be borne in mind that Kasmira Saivism has also fundamental differences with **Vedanta** as preached by Samkaracarya. It does not, for instance, emphasise either the infallibility or the eternity of the **Vedas** and **Upanisads**, nor does it deny the reality of the world. Abhinavagupta boldly asserts that he must give first place to facts of experience, second to reason and only third place to the scriptures. This attitude towards the **Vedas** may be explained by the fact that Kasmira Saivism has absorbed many philosophical influences from the Samkhya and Buddhist schools. The former is semi-heterodox, being atheistic and the second undoubtedly heterodox. Cosmopolitan in outlook, it encourages even a Sudra to follow the path of liberation (**moksa**). This is undoubtedly the influence of the heterodox philosophies, particularly of Buddhism. Eliot further points out that "in Kashmir it was chiefly philosophic, in the Dravidian countries chiefly religious. In the South it calls on God to help the sinner out of the mire,. Whereas the school of Kashmir, especially in its later developments resembles the doctrine of Sankara, though its terminology is its own....The essential similarity of all Saivite schools is so great that coincidences even in details do not prove descent or borrowing and the special terms of Kashmirian Philosophy, such as Spanda and Pratyabhijna, seem not to be used in the south.[81]

Arrival of Islam

Muslim rule was finally and firmly established in Kashmir by Shah Mir by deposing the last Hindu ruler, Kota Rani (1338–9).

She was the widow of the last Hindu King of Kashmir, Udayana Deva (1323–38). Muslim missionaries were attracted, to the change of regime and came from abroad to propagate their faith and proselytise people. Pressure, patronage and even bribes were resorted to by the new rulers to convert people into Islam. However, the early Muslim missionaries who came before Shah Mir's regime were, Sufis. As is well-known, Sufi was a peaceful sect, preaching tolerance of different faiths. They were a parallel stream of the Bhakti movement of the Hindus, helping and cooperating with each other: while Turks, and Afghans came with swords and cavalries to conquer India with blood and iron, the Sufis came with their songs of peace and devotion to God, to 'conquer' minds and hearts. In the process, they left an indelible imprint on the history and culture of India and Sufis like Chishti and Nizamuddin Aulia are now authentic saints of India, adored and worshipped by both Hindus and Muslims.

The Sufis from West Asia first began to migrate to India to escape from the terror and persecution of tyrants like Timur. To escape from this terror-ridden regime, seven hundred followers of the Sufi saint, Sayyid Ali Handani, left Persia and migrated to Kashmir. These gentle and meditative people even joined the Hindus and Buddhists in common prayer. The hosts were delighted and they knew the Sufis were not to be feared but admired and loved. They taught the universality of all religions and devotion to the compassionate God, which of course led to hostility from the conservatives. The Sufis did not compel or even persuade the Hindus to accept their tenets or Islamic dogmas. By their simple life, ardent devotion and songs, people were attracted to their creed.

A Sufi saint from Turkeystan came to the Valley in the first half of the fourteenth century. His name was Sayyid Bilal Shah. He was an engaging and charming personality who could win over people easily. He made many converts—the most important of them being a feudal chieftain, Rinchin by name, whose territory extended up to the north, beyond the Valley. The new energy and moral strength he gained by the new faith did not make him a peaceful princeling, but a conqueror himself. He conquered the Valley in 1320 CE and became the first Muslim ruler of Kashmir before Shah Mir deposed Kota Rani, the last Hindu ruler, in 1339.

Till now we were discussing the amiable and tolerant face of Islam as revealed mainly through the peaceful and meditative sect of the Sufis. However, the period also witnessed petty narrow-minded rulers as well. One example among many is the case of an early Sultan, Sikandar (1389–1413). Bhattacharjea condemns him in the following sharp words:

> In fact, one of the early Sultans, Sikandar (1389-1413), equaled the most bloodthirsty and iconoclastic Muslim conquerers anywhere in his zeal to obliterate all traces of the Hindu religion and convert its followers to Islam on pain of death. Temples were leveled and some of the grandest monuments of old damaged and disfigured. Archaeologists agree that the scale of destruction wreaked on the monumental structures at Martand and Avantipura suggest the use of gunpowder. Thousands of Hindus escaped across the borders of Kashmir; others were massacred...
>
> Sikandar is still known in the valley as 'Butshikan' (idol-breaker). That this title is reserved for him, however, suggests that his Muslim predecessors and successors did not fully share his iconoclastic zeal, although some like Mirza Haider Dughlat, Yaqub Shah Chak, some Mughal Governors and the Afghan rulers were also religious zealots.[82]

Apostle of Peace and Harmony

In this period of storm, turmoil and intolerance, a woman saint-poet appeared in Kashmir to preach and sing the glory of god and the bliss of peace and harmony. She was in the line of other famous women Bhakti saint-poets like Andal of Tamilnadu, Akka Mahadevi of Karnataka, and Mira Bai of Rajasthan. She endeared herself to both Muslims and Hindus. As in the case of Kabir Das, upon her death, her Hindu and Muslim admirers claimed the body for the right to conduct the funeral rites according to their respective rituals and customs. Even her name was altered to suit the tastes of each community. The name her parents gave her was Padmavathi. However, after she left her parent's home to be a wandering minstrel and apostle, Hindus called her Lalleswary and Muslims addressed her as Lalla Arifa. In due course, all her admirers and worshippers affectionately called her Lal Ded—meaning 'Lal the Mother'. She had many followers and disciples, some of whom were as famous as she was. They belonged to all communities, religions, groups and castes. Her most outstanding disciple, who may be considered her chosen successor, was a Muslim divine, Shaikh Noor-ud-Din, who came to be known as Nurud Rishi. He was born in 1377 into a distinguished orthodox Muslim family. From boyhood itself he was averse to traditional formal schooling in Madrasas where the Mullas and Maulavis taught the *Koran* by rote, not understanding its essence. Thoughtful and given to contemplation, this led Noor-ud-Din to self-doubt and restlessness. It was at this crucial juncture in life that he saw the wandering saint Lal Ded. Often he joined her train of followers. She gave him self-confidence and solace. She advised him to have faith in himself and in his destiny, and not to depend on higher powers, human or divine, whom the Mullas and priests advised to rely upon. Regaining his self-confidence, Sheikh Noor-ud-Din became a new man, sure of his mission in life. The legends in the valley aver that Nurud Rishi as an infant sucked at Lal Ded's breast and imbibed her mysticism and ideas of religious harmony. So Sheikh Noor-ud-Din, both in his name and teaching, personifies his mentor Lal Ded. Nurud Rishi was also influenced by Sufis. He blended Sufism with Lal Ded's teachings founded a new order of Sufis known as Sufi Rishis, which was a vital and popular force in Kashmir for many years to come.

Lal Ded's Formative Years

As is the case with any of India's ancient saints and poets, Lal Ded's life and career are also wrapped in legends, myths and miracles. It is from an analysis of these materials that we have to reconstruct their lives. Too many of the details are matters of controversy.

The general consensus is that she was born about 1335 CE. The earliest known historical account of Lal Ded is found in Azam Dedamari's *Waqiat-i-Kashmir* (1730 CE) written more than three centuries after her demise. The author had gathered material from the legends prevailing in the Valley. She was born into a well-to-do family of Pundits in Pandrethan about 65 km south east of Srinagar. Their family priest, Shri Siddha Mo, was a scholar and devotee of Trika Saivism. Lal Ded was initially attracted to Trika Saivism through the priest. She was married at the early age of 12, as was usual in Pundit communities to a groom belonging to a very rich family. They renamed her as Padmavathi, as was the custom for married girls in the Pundit community. She was not happy in the husband's family as she was treated very harshly and with disdain. Her mother-in-law was very unhappy with the bride who, instead of being 'modest and submissive', chose a trenchant path for independence in her behaivour and views. The mother-in-law even accused the bride of infidelity to her husband. In spite of all these unhappy experiences, she took special care to fulfill her duties as a daughter-in-law and did whatever she was asked to do.

This did not deter her in-laws from persecuting and harassing her. Finally, unable to bear it any more, she bade farewell to her home without even caring to take with her clothes, ornaments and other personal belongings. Thus, she lived in the jungles infested with wild animals and on street pavements with beggars and other mendicants. She went about in rags, and some say naked as did Akka Mahadevi of Karnataka, who went about the streets naked with her long luxuriant hair to hide her nudity. She sang and wandered as a mendicant. Gradually, a team of followers started accompanying her and soon they swelled in numbers. Among them were Hindus and Muslims. The most important disciple and successor was Nurud Rishi, of whom we have discussed in detail.

Lal Ded's Teachings

There are many similarities in the lives of women saints like Lal Ded, Andal, Akka Mahadevi and Mira Bai. However, in one respect, Lal Ded was different from others. The others sang the glory of their beloved deity and their intense passion for unison with their chosen gods, namely, Krishna, Shiva or Vishnu. Though these devotional songs contained social messages, they were essentially spontaneous outpourings of

Bhakti. Lal Ded's poems by contrast were didactic and messages for peace and harmony among the people who were driven by religious and casteist strife.

It is very difficult to translate her poems because of their colloquial language and the intensity of devotion. Bhattacharjea reluctantly attempts to translate a few passages as follows:

The lover is he who burns with love,
Whose self doth shine like gold;
When man's heart lights up with the flame of love,
Then shall he reach the infinite.

***

Sow thou the seed of friendship for me everywhere,
And slay not even my enemies.

Nurud Rishi, chief disciple of Lal Ded was more explicit:

Thy rosary is like a snake;
Thou bendest it on seeing the disciples;
Thou hast eaten six platefuls, one like another;
If thou art a priest, then who are the robbers?

And he advised his disciples:

Do not go to the sheikh and priest and mullah;
Do not feed the cattle on anchor leaves;
Do not shut thyself up in mosques or forests;
Enter thine own body with breath controlled in communion with God.

Nurud Rishi sang of his mentor as follows:

That Lalla of Padmapore, she drank,
her fill of divine amrita and found
her seat in the lap of Lord O, God,
grant me the same blessed wish![83]

So Lal Ded's teachings were simple and meant for even illiterate people. She also rose occasionally to deeper questions of philosophy and metaphysics. J.L. Kaul summaries this idea and ideology as follows:

> In a picturesque succession of metaphors like the ones above, she tells us how on her spiritual path she has had to undergo all the

painful processes that a newly-picked cotton pod undergoes form the moment when the cleaner and the carder kick it to the time when spun into "gossammar yarn" and woven into cloth and then dashed on the washing stone, the tailor eventually works his scissors on it. There are continuous references in her verses to the hard disciplines she practiced, mainly the awakening of the Kundalini by means of mastering her vital airs, **prana** and **apana**. These, for instance:

1. *I worked and worked at the bellow-pipe*
   till the light flared forth and I saw the true Self.
   till the light shone within and spread without.
2. *The steed of mind speedeth over the sky*
   and a lakh leagues traverseth he in the twinkling of the eye.
   Yet a man of true intelligence can rein in the curvetting steed,
   And on the wheels of ***prana*** *and* ***apana*** *guide his chariot aright.*
3. *I closed the doors and windows of my body's mansion,*
   and caught my life-breath as a thief within;
   I bound him fast in the cell of my heart and with the stinging whip of ***OM*** *I flayed him there.*
4. *Searching and seeking Him. I, Lalla, wearied myself, and even beyond my strength I strove.*
   Looking for Him. I found his door's bolted and barred;
   this deepened my longing and stiffened my resolve;
   and I would not move but stood where I was,
   full of longing and love, to gaze on Him
5. *Mastering my vita airs, I cut my way*
   though Forests Six, when the mystic Moon awoke for me
   and the world of ***Prakriti*** *dried up.*
   Thus came I to where I found the Lord.

Lal Ded impresses upon us the truth that mere ritual, pilgrimage or formal worship will not do. 'An idol is but a stone and a temple is but stone'. She declaims, and it is the height of folly to 'offer a living sheep to a lifeless stone'.[84]

25

Assam and Sankara Deva's Vaishnavite Reforms

The Vaishnavite Bhakti Movement took a long step forward in North East India in the fifteenth and sixteenth centuries CE. North-east India comprised of Assam, Bengal and Orissa, now fragmented into many more states. The most important stalwarts and pioneers of this resurgence were Sankara Deva in Assam and Chaitanya in Bengal with their contemporaries and followers. Chaitanya was about forty years younger than Sankara Deva.

When Sankara Deva was born in 1449 (August-September), Assam's social and religious life had presented a bleak and bizarre picture. Maheswar Neog, Professor of Guwahati University and an authority on Sankara Deva gives us a succinct description of this in the following words:

> If the political scene of Kamarupa was full of turmoil, the social conditions were far worse. The country was disunited through various jarring religious sects, heterogeneous faiths and practices. The land had from the earliest times been the home of various Tibeto-Burman tribes, who had their own religious beliefs and rites, which came slowly to be influenced by different forms of Hindu religion and also in their turn influenced them. In the Sakta work, **Yoginitantra**, the admission is frankly made that in the domain of Kamakhya, religion was of Kirata birth. The earliest Hindu faith to have had a place in Assam was Saivism, which when later heavily encroached upon by Saktism went underground and found a fertile soil among the Kacharis, who

called Lord Siva by a new name, Bathau. He is still worshipped among different tribes as Budha, the old god, or Baliyababa, the mad god.

Saktism or the worship of goddess 'of many names and forms, who is adored with sexual rites and the sacrifice of animals, or when the law permits, of men', became the biggest religion of Kamarupa by the beginning of the second millennium of the Christian era. The Nilachala hill near Guwahati with the **yoni-pitha** of Kamakhya became the centre of this religion. Both the chief scriptures of Assam Saktism, the **Kalika-purana** and the **Yogini-tantra**, belong to the left-hand or extremist school of Saktism, and enjoin blood sacrifices (the offering of one's own flesh and blood 'nearest to the heart' to the deity) and various other esoteric rites. The ritual consisting of the partaking of the five elements, better known as **pancha-makara**, form a prominent feature. Another form of ritual was virgin-worship, in which a girl is considered as representing the Devi and the procreant principle of life. Blood sacrifice was, and still is, a constant part of Sakta rituals, and a great number of animals was daily and occasionally slaughtered in propitiation of the goddess. The slaughter of men, perhaps in no way connected with what is known as head-hunting ritual of some of the Assam tribes, had got its canonical sanction in the **Kalika-purana**, and was occasionally performed particularly in the Bhairavi temple on the Nilachala and Tamresvari temple near Sadiya, now in the Lohit district of the NEFA. Then again, there was the **sabarotsava**, the festival of the Sabaras (a tribe), the very description of which reeks of frank sensuality.

There were the many excesses of a very debased form of Buddhism, known as Vajrayana, 'a queer mixture of monistic philosophy, magic and erotics, with a small admixture of Buddhist ideas'. Kamakhya or Kamarupa and Sirihatta of this region were of special significance to the Vajrayanists, who held **pancha-makara** as indispensable to the votary and enjoined the enjoyment of **prajnaparamita** or perfect truth residing in every woman. In the writings of the Vaishnavas there are references to the Vajrayanist religion as **vamanaya** or **pashandanaya** (left-hand or heterodox way) and to its adherents as Buddhist magicians, who exploited people with secret doctrines and the show of funny idols.

The followers of Nathism and worshippers of Dharma, the tortoise-god, perhaps with some Austric origin, of Manasa, the serpent goddess, and of Sitala or Ai, the smallpox goddess, and other minor deities were also many. **Sanyasis** or mendicants roamed about the towns and villages, and some of them were only cheats or robbers in the guise of the religions. Men were heathens, and worshipped clouds and rivers, barns or hay-lofts. Animistic beliefs and usages were rife not only among the tribesmen but also among the uneducated general populace. Spells and incantations found a good market. An atmosphere of mystery shrouded the whole country inasmuch as Kamarupa became known to the outside world as a land of black art and necromancy, by which one could take and give others any form one liked. Superstitions held the uncouth in very firm grip and made them easy victims of malicious gods and rapacious magic-men.[85]

[pancha-'ma'kara means the five concepts which begin with the alphabet 'Ma'. They are Malsya, Meat, Madya (liquor) Mythuma (copulation) and Manthras (sacred hymns)].

Birth and Boyhood

Sankara was born in a Kayastha family in the village Nowgong on the banks of the Brahmaputra, which is present-day Assam. His father, Kusumavara, was an overlord. Known those days as *Siromani,* an overlord could be called a feudal chieftain of minor feudatories. His mother was Satyasandha who died soon after Sankara's birth. He was brought by his grandmother Khersuti. She wielded a great deal of influence on the education and career of Sankara. The family belonged to the Sankara sect of Saivites. Sankara Deva was considered by his parents as a special blessing from Siva for he was born after their being childless for long and after years of worship at a neighboring temple. The grateful parents named the child Sankara, another name of Siva.

Sankara grew into a handsome and robust young man. He was pampered by his grandmother so much so that he did not take any interest in normal schooling. Besides the boyish pranks, Sankara was often fond of wrestling and fighting with his friends. He was also adept in swimming across the turbulent waters of the mighty Brahmaputra. For some years his grandmother tolerated all this, believing that in due course he would go to school. However, he did not. Once, sitting by his side she was serving meals to him with affection. Then she spoke to him, how great and scholarly were his ancestors. She said, all this was possible because they went to talented Pundits to be taught and became scholars themselves. It was the duty of Sankara to live up to their traditions. Sankara was quite struck by his loving grandmother's advice. It was decided that he would go to a proper teacher and so a competent teacher was found. He was the learned Brahmin, Mahendra Kandali, who ran a boarding school. Living at Kandali's school, Sankara began to read voraciously the books available there. Thus, at the age of 12, Sankara started schooling. However, he was not very much impressed by lectures or classes. Often, he used to take leave in order to skip classes. The story goes that in order to get his permission to leave the shool Sankara used to even bribe the teacher with money and clothes!

By the time he left the school at the age of 17 or 18, he had a thorough grounding in Sanskrit, the *Veda*s, *Upanishad*s and the *Purana*s. Among the *Purana*s he was highly impressed by the *Bhagavatha*—the great *Vaishnava Purana*. Sankara Deva also began to write poems and other narratives in Sanskrit. Many biographers ascribe *Hari Sankara-Upaghyana* to Sankara Deva having written it during his school days. Sankara's learning and diligence impressed his teacher so much that he suggested Sankara should be henceforth called Sankara Deva. The reading and study of the *Bhagavatha Purana* led to his rejection of Shakta-Saivism and the embrace of Vaishnavism as his life's philosophy.

After attaining adulthood, Sankara Deva left the school for good. On reaching home, his kith and kin and well-wishers asked him to take up the responsibility of *Siromani*. However, he was averse to such positions and responsibilities. He was inclined to lead the life of an intellectual and a devotee of Vishnu. His community—*Bhuyan*—was not a well-knit group and was further weakened by internal strife and conflict. The community expected that a scholar with sound education and popularity like Sankara Deva, in spite of his young age, could set matters right. *Ahom* tribe who occupied the neighbouring areas of the Bhuyans, were steadily rising in power and influence and posing a threat to the Bhuyans. Although Sankara Deva was not fascinated by self and power, ultimately he had to submit to the wishes of his people. They insisted on his marrying and leading a respectable householder's life. Still not beyond his teens, Sankara Deva thus came to be known as *Dekagiri*, the young master. He married a beautiful Kayastha girl, Suryavati. Unfortunately, she died soon after giving birth to a girl-child. Sankara Deva's new faith is reflected in the name he gave to his daughter—Manu or Haripriya. The untimely death of Suryavati inflicted a deep wound in his heart from which he never did recover. He was almost fed up with worldly pleasures and concerns and wanted to go on a long pilgrimage to recover himself from the desperate situation into which he had fallen. Sankara Deva assigned his duties as *Siromani* to his uncles and left on a pilgrimage in 1481, at the age of 32, with a retinue of seventeen followers including his teacher, Mahendra Kandali. By the time he left for his pilgrimage, his minor daughter was given in marriage to a cousin. His son-in-law was also entrusted with household duties. The pilgrimage took almost 12 years. He visited several places situated in present-day Uttar Pradesh (UP), Bihar and Orissa. Some people argue that he went to south India also. However, there is no clear evidence of such a sojourn to the south. In UP, he covered many places associated with Sri Krishna's childhood like Vrindavan. He also met Vrindavan Goswamis who were outstanding Vaishnavites and scholars of Sri Krishna lore. Sankara Deva had the benefit of detailed conversations with the Vaishnavacharyas. When he returned home at the age of 42, his grandmother was still alive.

The Mission and Conversions

Sankara Deva's Vaishnavism had his distinct personal stamp. He infused some of his Vedantic ideas into Vaishnavism. He propagated his cult by means of theoretical books, hymns and dramas. The manuscripts for his dramas were illustrated by himself and this proved his proficiency in calligraphy and painting as well. He convened congregations and held discourses on his faith. People attending them were given opportunities to raise questions and even dispute with him. Sankara patiently replied to them whether they were his followers or professed opponents.

Sankara Deva gained many followers in this way. Though many of them belonged to the middle rung of caste hierarchy, occasionally some Brahmin and rich merchants, too, joined him. One of them was Bhavananda who was very rich and had contributed liberally to Sankara Deva for his congregations and other missionary activities.

Sankara Deva's followers, with their own distinct faith and methods of worship, were fast becoming a new community or sect in the far-flung areas of Kamarupa, that is, a region which consists of present-day Assam, Meghalaya, Arunachal Pradesh and their neighbourhoods. Cooch Behar was an indented state then situated on the western border of Kamarupa. Sankara Deva guided this movement from his headquarters in the city of Patbausi in Cooch Behar. He was elated by the rising tide of Vaishnavism throughout the country. He encouraged the evolution of the Vaishnavite community as a distinct entity by accepting neophytes and converts. He personally guided the proselytising campaign with the assistance of his prominent disciples like Madhavadeva whom he nominated as his successor.

Sankara Deva did not frontally attack the system of caste, as was done by many bhakti saints like Ramananda, Kabir and Ravidasa. But by accepting outscastes, Muslims and others engaged in socially lower avocations, he revealed his mind on the issue. So also was his attitude to the bizarre customs, rites and worship explained at the beginning of this chapter.The rising popularity of his simple and moral Vaishnavite teachings gave a form to the unexpressed resentment of people against these rituals. Only the Brahmin priestly class, which had made their livelihood on these practices, was to defend them. They were biding their time to wreak vengeance upon the person who not only demeaned their faith but also in effect attacked their means of livelihood.

Trial and Acquittal

The old priestly class and the orthodoxy complained to the king with exaggerated and distorted versions of Sankara Deva's activities and teachings. The Buddhists, who had some hold in Kamarupa and Cooch Behar, also detested the saint reformer. The Buddists of those times were not followers of the original teachings of Gautama Buddha and they belonged to the Vajrayana sect that swore by Tantricism and animal sacrifice. They came into conflict with Sankara Deva's Vaishnavism, based on pure love and worship of god Vishnu. Sankara Deva had written a vitriolic attack on them called *Pashandamardana* (The Quelling of Heretics). All these show that along with the spread of Vaishnavism, the opposition to it also had made a strong but futile bid to resist it.

When the situation reached its boiling point, Sankara Deva resorted to a stratagem to silence his opponents intellectually. He arranged a conference of scholars to which the top Brahmin priests and Pundits were invited to debate the issues of dispute. They came fully armed with their ideas and reference tomes. It was such a comprehensive debate in which no issues, minor or major, were left out. The final outcome was a glorious victory for Sankara Deva. He had wisely based his arguments in favour of Vaishnavism based on traditional texts and other authorities. So the opponents found it hard to refute him.

However, it soon became evident that the Brahmin priests and scholars did not gracefully accept defeat. Pondering over the discomfiture suffered at the hands of the erudite Vaishnava saint, they sought a helping hand from the king of Ahoms, Suhummung (1497–1539), whose jurisdiction covered Sankara Deva's headquarters at Patbausi. Ahom rulers were neither Vaishnavites nor Saivites. They were followers of traditional faiths which were akin to tribal rites. So the Brahmin opponents of Vaishnavism could not persuade them on religious grounds. So they tried to persuade the king to act against Sankara, saying the activities of the rebel reformer could cause disaffection among people. This, of course, alarmed the king who was already in the shadow of tribal resistance and threats from neighbouring rulers bent on driving out the new Ahom conquerors. So King Suhummung decided to act expeditiously on the menace posed by Vaishnavism and its leader Sankara Deva.

The king summoned Sankara Deva to his court to face trial for his 'irreligious' activities which were said to be causing disaffection to the kingdom. He was also charged with being hand-in-glove with Buddhism, a heterodox faith with self-proclaimed atheism. Of course, the latter charge was totally baseless for he had fought Buddhists tooth and nail. The other charge of course was a matter of opinion and legitimately debated. The king himself had presided over the court of trial. Sankara Deva defended himself with his erudition and famous eloquence. The monarch was highly impressed by his honesty and devotion. To the chagrin of the plaintiffs, the king acquitted Sankara Deva ceremoniously. It is said that in delivering his verdict, the king exhibited anger at those who brought up trumped-up charges against a saintly person.

This was not the end of the attempts to punish and persecute Sankara Deva by his detractors. More serious attempts to arrest and persecute him and his disciples were in store, which will be discussed in due course.

Ahoms and Bhuyans

When Ahoms assumed the over-lordship of Bhuyan territory they gave them limited autonomy, took into confidence promising Bhuyan youths and entrusted them with administrative responsibilities. Some were honoured for distinctive qualities or achievements. Sankara Deva's cousin Jagatananda was honoured by the title Ramadeva for his religious fervour. Sankara Deva's son-in-law, Hari, was appointed to a high position in the army.

Along with the benefits, the state services also had its risks and hazards. Owing to inexperience and lack of expertise some elephants in the charge of Hari and Madhavadeva—Sankara's disciple escaped from the enclosure. This became a serious case of lack of vigilance and culpable negligence of duty by Hari and Madhavadeva. The case was tried and both of them were convicted. Though both of them were awarded capital punishment, it was executed only against Hari. Madhavadeva had appeared to executors as a mendicant and was set free on assurance of good conduct. As a surety for his assurance, his legs were bound by chains. Being humiliated and bound in chains, he wandered about the neighbouring villages and begged for his livelihood. Even in this pitiable condition, there were some senior officials and members of the royalty who knew Madhavdeva's proficiency in the ancient lore and devotion. They invited him to read sacred texts including the *Ramayana*. For this, he was paid handsomely with money and food. After six months, Madhavdeva was set free, with chains removed.

After release, Madhavdeva walked all the long way to Dhuwasat where his master Sankaradeva was staying and gave the news of his son-in-law, Hari's execution. Madhavadeva also told him about the humiliation and punishment he suffered. Certainly Sankara Deva was taken aback and came to the conclusion that life in Ahom country was no longer possible or desirable. When Sankara Deva was shifting his residences from place to place, important developments were taking place in Cooch Behar politics and administration. King Viswasimha of Cooch Behar had died in 1534 CE and his son, Malladeva, succeeded him to the throne. Ascending the throne, he adopted a new name, Naranarayana. Naranarayana declared his brother Sukaladeva as crown prince and entrusted him the second most powerful job in the kingdom, namely Commander-in-Chief of the Army. Both brothers had the best of education in Varanasi and could write poems and hymns in Sanskrit. The crown prince wrote a commentary on the famous *Gita Govinda* of Jayadeva. Both of them were great patrons of art and letters.

Besides being a man of letters, he was a warrior *par excellence*. He mobilized a considerable army and trained them and attacked the Ahom country, in order to fulfill the ambition of his father, Viswasimha. He almost decimated the entire Ahom army and its generals had to flee from the battle ground for life. Ahoms being defeated and their remnants finding asylums in marginal areas, the entire Kamarupa fell under the sway of Naranarayana and his brother. Sankara Deva was hughly impressed by the scholarship, literary acumen and military powers of the brothers. So he thought life under them would facilitate his missionary and literary activities or perhaps even encourage them. Thus Sankara Deva migrated to Kamarupa proper.

Persecution Again

Before settling down in Kamarupa, Sankara Deva made his last pilgrimage to Puri. Returning to his new residence in Kamarupa, Sankara Deva was earnestly engaged in his routine activities like writing books, composing hymns, performing plays and proselytising. He was hopeful that now under the liberal administration of Naranarayana, he could pursue his mission peacefully and effectively. However, this was not to be. His old foes of the priestly class and conservatives were not to give him peace and freedom. They complained in unison to the king about the possible disaffection and disturbance that might ensue from the activities and teachings of Sankara Deva. Contrary to expectation, the king took these misgivings seriously and decided to curb Sankara Deva's activities. His reaction was unusually harsh. He vowed even to kill Sankara Deva as a rebel, if necessary. Policemen were dispatched to apprehend the rebel and bring him in chains for trial.

Sankara Deva and his close associates got scent of the king's plan. He found time to escape from the wrath of the king and flee from his residence at Patbansi. This only enraged the king further. The police arrested Narayana Thakur and Gokulachand, two close associates and disciples of Sankara Deva. They were beaten up and tortured to extract the whereabouts of their master. The Kingdom of Bhutan nestling in the lap of Himalayas lies to the north-west of Kamarupa (Assam as it is called today). Traders from Bhutan used to travel through these hilly terrains on horses. Naranarayana bartered his two incalcitrant Vaishnava prisoners for horses from Bhutanese traders and washed his hands off the whole affair. Taking the Vaishnavas home, the Bhutanese found that they were hardly the stuff to be treated as commodities for sale or barter. The traders were so impressed by their character and godliness that they paid the requisite money to the policemen of the king to set them free. Finally, the policemen themselves became converts to Vaishnavism.

When it seemed that normalcy had been achieved, and peace was re-established, Sankara Deva emerged from underground to undertake his mission. He began his work and travels.

However, he soon found that apparent calm was but a mirage. He could move about freely for only about two months and a half. By this time, the Brahmin opponents got into action and again approached the King Naranarayana, with their charges against Sankara Deva. The king agreed to oblige them. However, his brother, who was the crown prince and Commander-in-Chief of the army, was not inclined to go the king's way. He finally believed Sankara Deva was innocent and was not doing anything illegal. Rajguru Krishnabhushananda and Sankara Deva's son, Ramananda, were his employees. They reported to their patron about the possibility of the imminent arrest of Sankara Deva. The crown prince took him in his care and moved him secretly to a safe place across a small river.

King Naranarayana knew about this. While his bother adopted such an attitude, how could he fulfill his assurance given to the Brahmins? Finally, he assured his brother that nothing arbitrary would be done to harm Sankara Deva and promised him that a fair trial would be arranged where he could defend himself freely. On the basis of this assurance, the king asked the prince to hand him over for trial. The trial took not only many days but assumed the form of a series of debates between the plaintiffs and defendant. Sankara Deva with his eloquence, reason and erudition won and the Brahmins, as once again, accepted defeat meekly and resentfully.

The Glory

Sankara Deva was growing old with its physical infirmities but his mind was always alert and fresh. He had the satisfaction of seeing the success and glory of his creed. He realised that his Assam no more resembled the one in which he was born, though remnants of old faiths and rites remained and the priestly class was very much reduced in number owing to the proselytising activities of the Vaishnavas. They submitted to the new spiritual and social order and the society was largely free from the shackles of superstitions and orthodox rituals. How did Vaishnavism and Sankara Deva achieve these goals and free the common folk from the dominance of Brahmin scholasticism and exploitation? Brahmins, and to an extent Kshatriyas, were a power in the state structure as advisers to the kings and army chiefs and big landholders and feudal chiefs as well. Loosening their grip on society and religion was also liberatory function. By rejecting the scholastic exercises, sacrifices and elaborate rituals, the simple devotion that bhakti preached appealed to people at large. All these ideas were couched in the native tongues of the people instead of the Brahminic Sanskrit which the ordinary folks could not understand. Adding to these simple and attractive ideas was the lyrical and mellifluous music of Sankara Deva's hymns and poems. Maheswar Neog has translated some such pieces.

> *Where there is **bhakti**, there is salvation:*
> *the **bhakta** alone knoweth this truth,*
> *as it is only the jeweller who*
> *knoweth the philosopher's stone and speaketh of its properties.*
> *Sankara, the servant of Krishna, sayeth this:*
> *Do thou offer thy love at the feet of Govinda,*
> *for he alone is a **pandita**, he alone is esteemed,*
> *who singeth the glory of Hari.*
> ....
> *O scholar, why does not thou*
> *perceive the straight path!*
> *A crore of rituals have been performed,*
> *Hari hath not been attained to,*
> *and thou hast time and again been falling*
> *upon the cycle of rebirth!*
>
> *Thou hast muttered spells, undergone austerities*
> *and visited holy places too,*
> *and hast spent thy years in Gaya and Kasi.*
> *Yoga and logic have been mastered by thee,*
> *yet clouded is thy mind,*
> *for without devotion there can be no salvation.*
> *All piety resideth in the name of Rama;*
> *this is the essential messages of all holy books.*
>
> *Hari-**nama** is the supreme religion of Kali Age:*
> *thou hast read of this,*
> *yet hast thou not grasped its meaning.*
> *This servant of Krishna sayeth:*

The body tarrieth but a moment,
human life then cannot be had once again,
setting aside the vanity about rituals
do thou apply all thy faculties
to meditate on the feet of Hari.[86]

Last Days

In the course of this rather long narrative on the Bhakti movement in the Indian subcontinent, we have acquainted ourselves with a number of outstanding bhakti poet-saints and social reformers. Very few careers, however match that of Sankara Deva, either in personal sufferings or in the sway he had over the cultural area of his activities. However, it is also true that he was able to overcome all such obstructions and persecutions and become a universally recognised saint and social reformer. He lived to witness this metamorphosis himself.

Even his erstwhile opponents and persecutors came round to accepting his faith and guidance. However, he was wary of accepting into his fold these dubious characters. It is said that even King Naranarayana, who made the saint's life miserable, approached Sankara Deva during his last days for admission into the Vaishnava or more correctly Neo-Vaishnava fold. However, Sankara Deva was reluctant to admit him, for he feared that practicing Brahmins and ruling kings could not be relied upon to be faithful to the tenets of Vaishnavism.

Sankara Deva was aware that his end was fast nearing. Being an intensely godly man, he was hardly worried. However, he was anxious about the future of his movement, though he had laid firm foundations for its functioning and continuity. A network of *satrams* (inns) or branch offices with chosen cadres in charge was built around the whole country. Yet, they must also have a chief, who would adorn that prestigious post of power and privilege. Many of his followers looked to his sons to take up that responsibility, but Sankaradeva chose his chief disciple, Madhavadeva as his successor.

Thus having made perfect arrangements for the smooth transition, the saint peacefully passed away in September 1560, leaving a rich legacy which continues to be a living tradition in modern Assam.

Madhava in Command

Madhavadeva began enthusiastically his work of holding up the torch handed to him by his master. He undertook a tour of the country visiting the satrams and putting things in order. He also wrote hymns in praise of Vishnu-Krishna and his major work, *Nada Goshala,* was completed. The basic Vaishnava texts such as the *Bhagavatha Purana* with the well-known commentary of Sreedharaswamy, the *Bhagavat Gita* and Sankaradeva's *Bhakti Ratnakara*, in Sanskrit, and explained in simple Assamese and the Assamese works of Sankara Deva were provided in the satrams with necessary commentaries for the neophytes. As we have seen, the philosophy of Vedanta had a profound impact on Sankara Deva's Vaishnavism. Besides the *Upanishads* and the *Bhagavat Gita*, Badarayana's *Brahmasutra* consisted the *Prasanthatraya* of Sankaracharya, who founded the Vedanta of the Advaita school. However, neither Sankara Deva nor his younger contemporary Chaitanya of Bengal considered it necessary to infuse the teaching of Sankaracharya in toto. Needless to say, Madhavadeva also proceeded on these lines.

Sankara Deva's charismatic personality no longer present, the old priestly class began to campaign against Vaishnavism. The opponents once again approached the king and judiciary by characterising Madhavadeva as a propagator of a corrupt religion. However, Madhavadeva was able to overcome these criticisms and convince the king and judiciary of the legitimacy of Vishnavism. He eloquently put up the defence of his master. Here is an instance:

> Handsome to look at, his whole physique is white and resplendent like the sun. His sight, pleasing to people in assemblies, can destroy sins. He is handsome without the aid of any ornaments; grave and majestic, and wise. His lotus-like eyes are large and extremely charming; and his complexion is like the light of the moon. His gait looks like the lovely pace of an elephant. His voice is deep like thunder.[87]

Vaishnavites had set in motion a new resurgence in the general philosophy, literature and art in Assam. As said before, Sankara Deva himself was not just the greatest poet of Assam but a musician and painter as well. Madhavadeva, during his visits to various santrams had encouraged followers to paint murals. These paintings were rather conventional and aimed at propagating the faith. However, the ultimate result was the encouragement received by the artists and painters.

As an effective means of propagating Vaishnavism even among the poor and illiterate, Sankara Deva used to write plays and also perform them occasionally. He used to act in plays besides directing them. Madhavadeva continued the tradition. He established temples as schools of drama for training and theatres for its performance.

Many new men of letters appeared in the wake of the advancement of Vaishnavism. Madhav Kandali, who translated the *Ramayana* with some modifications, was perhaps only person next to Sankara Deva in poetic talents.

Niyog concludes his assessment of the impact of Sankara Deva's Vaishnava Bhakti movement in Assam as follows:

> The great Sankaradeva movement thus brought about a new and comprehensive outlook on life and a distinctly healthy tone to social behaviour. It accelerated the pace of a renascence of literature and fine arts like music and painting. The dignity of the individual endeavour of man as a distinct religious being and not as 'the thrall of theological despotism' was declared. Assam discovered herself as an integral part of the holy land of Bharatavarsha, and gloried in the discovery. The holy books in Sanskrit, the litterae humaniores of India, could no longer be sealed to the common man's view by a rigid oligarchy. The use of the local language in expositions of theology and philosophy was in itself a challenge to the erstwhile guardians of secret doctrines who understood the significance of the challenge and 'protested very much'. The new humanism eyed askance at the numerous blood sacrifices, including the immolation of man, and the nice sacerdotalism that was the order of the day in Hindu society. The use of Assamese, an Indo-Aryan tongue, which formed but an island in a Tibeto-Burman ocean, as the medium for the propagation of the neo-Vaishnava faith led to its emergence as the language of all the people. The ancient kingdom of Kamarupa was now undergoing a huge change, and it was having almost a regeneration, political and social, which timed well with the cultural resurgence initiated by Sankaradeva; and the first possibilities of a unified and modern Assam were now in evidence.[88]

26

Chaitanya and Bengal Vaishnavism

In the Vaishnavite Bhakti movement of Indian subcontinent in general and Bengal in particular, Chaitanya's role is outstanding. Chaitanya more precisely Sri Krishna Chaitanya or Shri Chaitanya Maha Prabhu as he is known popularly was in many ways quite different from other Vaishnavite Saints. His medium of poems and writing was in the elite language, Sanskrit, unlike many other bhakti saints who deliberately rejected Sanskrit and chose the peoples' spoken language. Though, like Tulsidas, he did not defend the caste system as a natural order, he did not oppose it either unlike Jnaneswar, Kabir, Nanak, Ramanand, Ravidas and other bhakti stalwarts. Of course, the total impact of Chaitanya's Vaishnavism was a rejection of casteism. As a case in point, his biographers point out how he did personally officiate in burying the corpse of a Muslim according to Muslim rites.

Chaitanya was not the founder of Bengal Vaishnavism as he had predecessors whose torch he inherited; but he raised it higher to become the most outstanding figure of the movement.

Dr Sukumar Sen, an authority on the history of Bengal and Bengali literature, observes as follows:

> CHAITANYA brought together the people of Bengal and Orissa and also a large body of men from other parts of India who came in personal contract with him, on a common platform of emancipated religious thought and spiritual emotion, which gave a fillip to intellectual activity and created a new interest in life

> and a new literary and artistic urge. The common platform was open to all, high and low, rich and poor, Hindu and Muslim. Chaitanya did not try openly to do away with the caste system, but he indirectly attempted to undo its evil effects. He respected the casteism of the priesthood but did not himself hesitate to bury with his own hand the dead body of Haridas, a Muslim by birth, and observe his death ceremony ('urs'). This was the origin of the custom of the death ceremony ('Mahotasav') and its anniversary regularly observed by the mendicant Vaishnavs. Nityananda also did not encourage casteism and he treated all men as equal. Begal Vaishnavism did away with casteism to this extent that some of the non-brahman followers of Chaitanya became acknowledged gurus who had brahmans among their disciples. But this tendency of liberalism was checked by the imposition of the rigid rules of conduct laid down by the Brindavan School.
>
> As an advance towards social freedom this was a gain, no doubt, but not much. The psychological effect, however, was remarkable inasmuch as it brought about an atmosphere of relief and thankfulness; and thoughtful men found an outlet for their emotional upsurge—which invariably flowed into poetry and music. Chaitanya was a lover of the songs of Jayadeva, Vidyapati, Chandidas and other poets, and he imparted his love to some of his followers. This was the beginning of the lyric impulse that brought vitality into literature and music.
>
> Chaitanya was so magnetic and overwhelming a personality and his influence was so pervasive that he was even during his lifetime looked upon as an incarnation of God.[89]

Chaitanya not only had benefitted by the inspirations he drew from his predecessors, but in turn, he helped to propagate their works and perpetuate their names. Sukumar Sen, in his biography of Chandidas, writes as follows:

> It is generally accepted that much that is significant in the life and culture of the Bengali people is due to Chaitanya: his personality and his activities. He was indirectly responsible for the preservation of the name and fame of Chandidas from falling into the depth of oblivion. Krishnadas Kaviraj, the most dependable biographer of Chaitanya, a younger contemporary of the master, records that during his later years Chaitanya received emotional sustenance from the songs of Jayadeva (in Sanskrit), Vidyapati (in Maithili) and Chandidas (in Bengali). Jayadeva had an all-India vogue but the other two poets were known within limited areas.

> Vidyapati perhaps and Chandidas surely would have been entirely forgotten like many other good writers of lyrical songs but for the stamp of Chaitanya's appreciation pressed indelibly by his best biographer.[90]

It may be noted that Jayadeva wrote in Sanskrit, Vidyapati in Mythili and Chandidas in Bengali. All of them had penned their superb poems extolling the love of the Gopis of Vrindavan for Krishna and especially that of Radha. In their exotic raphsodies of Gopis and Krishna, they allowed themselves to depict the sensuous aspects more than bhakti. Or it could be said that bhakti itself was depicted as love with an overdose of *Sringara Rasa*. How these tendencies merged inside Chaitanya's poems and bhakti have to be explored.

Life of Chaitanya

Chaitanya was born in 1486 CE in Nabadwip in Nadia, West Bengal, then a centre of scholarship and Bhakti movement. Chaitanya was almost forty years younger to Sankara Deva who was the pioneer of Vaishnavism in the neighbouring cultural region of Assam. It is not unlikely that Sankara Deva's influence from the east was pervasive in Nabadwip.

Chaitanya's family was not a very well off. His father, Jagannatha Misra, was an adherent of Vaishnavism and mother, Sachidevi, was also an ardent religious woman. The name that the parents gave Chaitanya was Viswambhara. His elder brother Viswaroopan left home to lead an ascetic life. Viswambhara was fondly called by his pet-name Nimai. Nimai was not a quiet or submissive child. He was boisterous and mischievous. The boy's pranks were very much tolerated by his parents who pampered him in the absence of their elder son. He was given the traditional Brahmanic and Sanskrit education under two Pandits and later on after school-level teaching when Nimai showed great promise, he was sent to an institution for higher education. After completing his course in the institute, he left it to his parents to look after the household affairs. Though he gained some elementary knowledge of grammar, literature and proficiency in eloquence at the institute, it was doubtful whether he had attained in-depth understanding of any of the subjects taught there.

In the meanwhile, his father, Jagannatha Misra, passed away and the family responsibilities fell on his shoulders. He married Laxmi, daughter of a Pundit. His father-in-law was a scholar of some eminence. With his assistance, Viswambhara started his own Sanskrit school and began to receive pupils. Till this time, Viswambhara did not show any special interest in religious matters. He was not even sufficiently humble. People complained of his self-centred and boastful behaviour. However, the success of his school made him a notable personality in Nabadwip.

In order to run the school successfully and meet the expenses of his household, Chaitanya required assistance. For that, he undertook a tour of the eastern parts of Bengal. He expected that by meeting his students and other friendly persons, he might be able to get presents and contributions. Along with that, he could acquaint himself with many places and renew his friendships. Viswambhara's calculations did not fail. The tour was successful.

However, when he returned home to Nabadwip, sad tidings were awaiting him. His wife, whom he deeply loved, had died of Snakebite. This was a big blow to Viswambhara. His modern biographers like Dilip Kumar Mukherjee and A.K. Majumdar believe that his interest in worldly life began to ebb by this bereavement. His mother, Sachidevi, was very much worried about her son's predicament. She was afraid that Viswambhara might also leave the householder's life like his ascetic brother who went away as a mendicant. So without even consulting Viswambhara, she found out a beautiful and 'god-fearing' girl. She was Vishnupriya Devi, the daughter of a scholar named Sanatana Misra. Sachidevi did not consult her son about this proposal for a second marriage. The idea was brought to Viswambhara's attention only on the morning of the wedding day which Sachidevi decided on her own. Viswambhara was surprised and unhappy at this proposal. He first thought of rejecting it out of hand. However, on second thoughts, he felt that by doing so, he would be causing unhappiness to his loving mother. The mother being perhaps the only person whom Viswambara loved and trusted, he finally acceded to her wish.

In the history of Bengal Vaishnavism, Vishnupriya has been a highly respected and loved figure. Chaitanya had many contemporary biographers and hagiographers like Krishnadas Kaviraj, Vrindavandas and others. Many such biographers who personally knew Vishnupriya have written about her character, loyalty to her husband and godliness. Since Viswambhara took a new turn in his life, Vishnupriya was not able to enjoy family life for long. However, she continued to be loyal to her husband's ideals and faith till her end.

Viswambhara continued his work in his Sanskrit school for some time after his father's demise. His father's funeral rites were conducted according to tradition. As part of the funeral rites, he went to Gaya for a pilgrimage. It seems that in Gaya, Viswambhara had some kind of a mental shock or enlightenment as Gautama Buddha had had more than two thousand years earlier. Dilip Kumar Mukherjee says that Viswambhara was never able to explain what that was. Even in later years, Chaitanya used to weep and shiver and even fall unconscious when Gaya was mentioned. It is there that the 22 year-old Viswambhara met a great yogi called Eswarapuri. Viswambhara prostrated before him and accepted him as his guru. Eswarapuri recited to him the *Dasakshara Mantra* in praise of Lord Krishna. Dilip Kumar Mukherjee believes that this new enlightenment of Viswambhara was not a bolt from the blue. Actually, some sort of a mental transformation was taking place in Viswambhara for some time. The mystical atmosphere of Gaya with Eswarapuri's magic touch might have prompted Viswambhara's enlightenment.

Jayadeva

Of the many predecessors in the Vaishnava Bhakti movement, Chaitanya was especially influenced by Chandidas (Bengali), Vidyapathi (Mythili) and Jayadeva (Sanskrit). Of these, Jayadeva, the author of *Gita Govinda* assumes the first place. The ace linguist Suniti Kumar Chatterji calls this twelfth century Sanskrit poet 'the Last of the Ancients and the First of the Moderns in Indo-Aryan literature'. He explains the political and cultural situations in which Jayadeva flourished and assesses his significance in the history of Indian cultural growth. He writes:

> JAYADEVA, the author of the Gita-govinda, is pre-eminent among Sanskrit poets and is acknowledged universally to be the writer of the sweetest lyrics in the Sanskrit language. His name comes spontaneously at the end as the last great poet in an enumeration of the classic poets of Sanskrit—Aswaghosha, Bhasa, Kalidasa, Bhartrihari, Harshadeva, Bharavi, Bhavabhuti, Magha, Kshemendra, Somadeva, Bilhana, Sriharsha, Jayadeva. He is in fact the last of the classical poets of Sanskrit of pan-Indian celebrity, whose influence on the later poets and scholars all over India through his single work, the Gita-govinda, is almost comparable to that of the great Kalidasa himself. The tradition of verse-composition in Sanskrit remained unabated in India after the 12th century when Jayadeva flourished. But the coming of the Turks and the rise of the 'Vernaculars' (New Indo-Aryan as well as Middle Dravidian languages) restricted the patronage and popularity (though not the production) of poetical and other works in Sanskrit in the subsequent centuries. Great poets indeed arose in Muslim times, showing that the Hindu mind as it expressed itself in the classical language of India was still capable of rising very near to the highest level attained by it under more propitious conditions five hundred or a thousand years before. They were writers—prosateiurs and poets—whose works shed luster on both the Sanskrit scholarship and the poetic genius of India. They deserve to be resuscitated and critically studied, with almost as much care as the ancient. Unquestionably they too form some of the most brilliant manifestations of the Indian spirit during the last few centuries—e.g., Rupa Gosvami and Jiva Gosvami, Kavi Karnapura, Jagannatha Kavi and Nilakantha Dikshita. But the era of Classical Sanskrit Poetry closes with the 12th century. Jayadeva sang not only the swan-song of the age which was passing away, but he also sang in the advent of a new age in Indian literature—the 'Vernacular' Age.[91]

Jayadeva was the court poet of Lakshmanasena, the last Hindu king of Bengal. As in the case of most of the ancient Indian poets and sages, the dates of their lives are not accurately known. However, Jayadeva has mentioned his parents' names—Bhoja Deva and Rema Devi—in his *Gita Govinda*. Rema Devi was also known as Vamadevi and Radha Devi. His wife was Padmavathi, also known as Rohini. Jayadeva belonged to the village, Kenduli Sasan near Puri in present-day Khurda District of Odisha. According to another view, Jayadeva was born in Kendubilva in the Bhirbhum District of West Bengal. It is said that King Lakshmanasena conferred on Jayadeva, the title *Kavi-Raja*. The earliest available hagiography of Jayadeva is by Kavi Vanamalidas written in the first half of the seventeenth century called *Jayadeva Charitha*. It gives less facts and more legends and exaggerated accounts of his achievements. Jayadeva seems to have traveled to distant places and pilgrim centres. It must have been during these pilgrimages that he came to know about Pandharpur and its deity, Vithobha. It is quite likely that he wrote many other books also and deserved the honours conferred upon him by King Lakshmanasena. However, they have all gone into oblivion and only *Gita Govinda* remains popular even to this day.

As Chatterji correctly notes, *Gita Govinda* is perhaps one of the sweetest lyrics in the Sanskrit language. It often transgresses the wise limits poets usually adopt in their works and titillates the sensitivity of the readers and devotees by the erotic descriptions of the liaison between Radha and Krishna. However, their poetic excellence is never disputed.

About the quality, content and the style of *Gita Govinda*, Chatterji says:

> We are charmed by the Music of Jayadeva's verse, particularly of the 24 songs, and one feels tempted to try even the impossible—to make the reader have a taste of the quality of his verse. But, for the ordinary reader who has not immersed his mind in the atmosphere of orthodox Vaishnava ideas about the spiritual or divine character of these poems, he may not feel very happy with what may be described as frank and free, and full and detailed rendering, in terms of poetry, the erotic sculptures, crude and vigorous, but beautiful withal, of the Khajuraho temples, and of the sculptures in Orissa temples like those of Puri and Konarak. The translations will ordinarily fail to create a universal enthusiasm, as tastes are different in this matter.[92]

Without attempting to translate Jayadeva's stanzas in metric verses, which might not convey to the reader the essential charm of the original, Chatterji only gives us prose translation along with the Sanskrit origin.

Thou wearest ear-rings in Thy ears,
Thou wearest beautiful garlands of wild flowers:
Victory, Victory to Thee, Hari our Lord God (Refrain).

Thou art the Adornment of the orb of the Sun, the day's jewel,
Thou destroyest rebirth:
Thou art the Swan sporting in the lake of mind of the sages:

Thou didst quell the Poisonous Serpent Kaliya,
Thou makest people happy:
Thou art a veritable Sun, opening up the Lotus of the Yadu Clam:

Thou didst destroy the demons Madhu, Mura and Naraka:
Thou ridest on Garuda, the divine Eagle:
Thou art the reason why all the Gods find their joyous sport:

Thine eyes are like spotless petals of the lotus,
Thou freest souls from Being;
Thou art the Source of the Three Worlds:

Janaka's daughter's Adornment art Thou (as her husband):
Thou didst conquer the demon Dushana:
In battle Thou didst kill the Ten-headed Ravana:[93]

Vidyapati

Vidyapati Thakur belonged to the ancient Mithila region in north-east Bihar bordering West Bengal. His mother tongue was Mythili, which was until then only a spoken language. Vidyapati made Mythili his medium of worship and songs and thereby the language came to occupy a place of prestige within Hindi. His poetic skills earned him the sobriquet Mythili Kavi Kokil meaning the Poet Cuckoo of Mythili. The centre of this region was the ancient kingdom of Mithila, where Sita Devi the spouse of Sri Rama was said to have been born. Vidyapati was well-versed in Sanskrit and the *Ababrahmsa* form of Bengali, besides his own mother tongue. It is likely that he could handle Bengali also, though not as efficiently as his mother tongue. Vidyapati was born in the village of Bishphi of Darbhanga province under the Madhubani district of Bihar in the year 1350 CE. He lived during the period 1350–1460 CE according to one source.

Vidyapati's lifetime witnessed the mushrooming of a number of sects within Vaishnavisms. One was known as the Goswami sect and the other as the Sahaja sect. Goswamis had their abode in Vrindavan that is, present-day Uttar Pradesh and the Sahaja sect was mainly spread in eastern Bihar and western Bengal. The Goswamis were strong adherents of the *Vedas*. They deeply studied them and made it the basis of their faith. The Sahaja did not reject the *Vedas* altogether but they were very indifferent to its teachings. Their most important scripture was the *Bhagavata Purana* and especially its tenth canto. They also gave importance to the eleventh canto of the *Purana*.

Thus drawing inspiration from the stories of *Krishna Avatara* and *Krishna Leela*, the Sahajas believed the human body to be the sacred repository of all that is worth worshipping. It went to the extent of celebrating the union of the male and female as in the union of Krishna and Radha, as the accomplishment of liberation or *moksha*. This was the source of the growth and spread of the erotic art tradition in Vaishnavism. As Suniti Kumar Chatterji correctly pointed out, the famed erotic sculptures of Khajuraho and Konark in Odisha were the artistic expressions of this trend. The Sahajas accepted Vidyapati as one among them. The leading figures of Sahaja Bhakti belonged to a group called the seven *Rasika Bhaktas*. Vidyapati was one among them. Another member of this group was the famous sage Villwamangal who had intimate relations with a "prostitute" named Chinthamani.

Vidyapati is also said to have had illegitimate as well as legitimate relations with many women who provided inspiration for his poems and songs. For example, Vidyapati was so fascinated by Queen Lakhima of Sivasimha Maharaja to such an extent that he could compose good songs only in her presence.

Chandidas

Chandidas, the Vaishnavite Bhakti poet and singer of Bengal, was the favourite of Chaitanya. No doubt, they were all either predecessors or contemporaries of Chaitanya while he was young. Though scholars have worked hard to fix his birthplace and dates, they have not yet achieved much success in their endeavour. As Sukumar Sen testifies, had it not been for Chaitanya's admiration, Chandidas would have been forgotten. Such oblivion seems to have descended upon him during or immediately after Chaitanya's demise. For example, Vrindavandas, who wrote the biography of Chaitanya immediately after his demise, says that the best known poets of the time were Vidyapati, Jayadeva and Kalidasa. He leaves out Chandidas from the list of the best.

There is no doubt that Chandidas was born in early sixteenth century in north Bengal on the northern side of the river Ganga. The place was known as Northern Radha. There was a village called Ramkali. It was a Hindu suburb of the city of Gaur, the capital of the Muslim Sultans who ruled Bengal after Lakshmanasena, the region's last Hindu ruler. That the Sultans had respected Chandidas and loved his melodious songs in praise of Vishnu and Krishna and that unfortunately Chandidas had come to grief on account of this is another story. Circumstantial evidence confirm the surmise that Chandidas was born in Ramkali and his activities were confined to this part on the other side of the Ganga and outside the Sultan's domains.

Chandidas had to sow his seeds and poems not on barren land. This region was famous for Krishna Bhakti and puppet shows, dramatic performances and musical sessions. Many scenes from the *Purana*s and folklore were represented on temple walls and public places. Chandidas not only wrote poems for these performances, but recited, directed and participated in them as an actor-singer.

Besides being a composer and singer par excellence, Chandidas seems to have been a robust and handsome person. People were attracted to him by his talent and masculine prowess. Chandidas was a brilliant scholar. That did not prevent him from being a compulsive lover. Legends are many which describe his torrid love affairs and adventures. Some may be true, others apocryphal. Here is one among them.

Tara was a lovely girl. She did not belong to Chandidas's Brahmin caste. She used to help her poor family by washing clothes and had probably belonged to a family of washerfolk (dhobi). Chandidas fell in love with her. They used to meet secretly at appointed places to keep away from the prying eyes of relatives and strangers. Once, after he arrived at their decided place of rendezvous, Tara failed to show up. The sky was overcast and the night dark. To add to this, rain began to pour down heavily. Drenched in water and his wet clothes sticking to the skin, Chandidas decided to move to the doorsteps of his lover's house nearby. Even then, he did not give up his hope, and shivering in cold and drenched, he reached the house steps of Tara. Naturally, the entrance was closed and bolted from inside. He tried to make some noises to attract his girl who was inside the house. She was deeply in conversation with a friend and forgot all about the appointment with Chandidas. The legends, as given in the accounts, are rather equivocal on whether the friend was another paramour of Tara. Anyway, she opened the door and saw Chandidas all wet and shivering in the dark night. She had no kind words for Chandidas whom she scolded for coming to her house. She, in effect, turned him away in the rainy night. Having reached home, Chandidas could do only one thing in retribution: write a poem on his plight, which he did. However, in spite of the insult he suffered at the hands of his lover, he had no mind to rebuke her. The following is a weak translation in English of his heart-rending soliloquy:

Oh! Such a dark night, the sky over cast
How could the lover come far away (from house)
In a corner of the ground, my lover
is bearing the brunt of nature.
My heart sinks at the sight.

Among his love affairs there is a story of Chandidas living with a low-caste woman. Sukumar Sen says that there is not even an iota of evidence for the relationship. However, he admits that legends and hearsay evidence are so persistent that it would be too rash to reject them.

Chandidas apparently did not sing against the caste system. Yet, his life and affairs make it clear that he did not care for caste. He was a Brahmin by caste. That did not prevent him from loving or living with low-caste women or men. His love-life gave him poetic insights of love, which do not recognize social barriers. He often tends, though implicitly, to equate his lover to the divine love of Radha and Krishna. The following two verses stress that love, whether human or divine, is the only bond that binds—all others are hollow and futile. With love, strangers become friends; without it, friends and relatives become strangers. Let us quote Chandidas' love of Radha and Krishna, the overtones of which are more humane than divine.

My friends, who was it who told me the name of Shyam?
Getting into the ears it has pierced my heart; I feel disturbed.
Even then the sweetness of the name seems to be
inexhaustible and my tongue goes on repeating it.
As I mutter on I lose command over myself. How can
I meet him, my friend?
If his name is charged with so much potency, I wonder,
what would happen when I come in physical contact.
How can the girls of his neighbourhood hold themselves
when they have a look of him?
However I may try I cannot forget it. What can I do
to get it out of me?
Dvija Chandidas says: Girls leave their husbands and come freely to him.[94]

Chandidas, had personally experienced the torments of unrequited love. He transposes them onto a love-lorn Radha awaiting Krishna's embraces.

You are a master charmer, my love.
There is no one like you to steal the heart of a helpless girl.
My home is no longer a home to me; my home is away
from home.
A stranger is now my own man, and my own people
are strangers to me.
Night is but day to me day night.
Still, beloved, I fail to understand you.
An evil fate brought me in, a flotsam tuft of moss;
There is no one to collect me close and speak a few
charitable words.
My love, if you go on tormenting me,

> *You may better take your stands before me I'll immolate myself.*[95]

Chandidas was a deep scholar whatever be the legends about him like his indifference to studies during his boyhood et cetera. Nevertheless, he was a sensitive person given to fun and frolic, thoughtful but also emotional. No wonder he was not only a favourite of Chaitanya, but also of generations of Bengalis to this day.

The Career After Gaya

Till now we were discussing the three poets who attracted Chaitanya and became the sources of his inspiration. Now we pass on to the new life he adopted after his transformation at Gaya. Chaitanya returned home to Navadweep, an entirely changed man. He was no longer the old rash and haughty youngster. He became meditative and well-behaved. Often he used to shut himself up in a room and for hours after hours, sing the praises of Radha and Krishna and chant their names in meditation. Sometimes, overwhelmed by intense bhakti, he used to cry aloud, fall down on the floor lying unconscious. The people of the family and neighbourhood thought that he had become mad. As time passed, this strange behaviour became part of his spiritual life and people took it that way. However, his bhakti was so intense that it sought some way to break the seclusion of his subjectivity.

This was how the public mission of propagating his Neo-Vaishnavism began. He began to sing in public with his acolytes and march on the streets dancing and singing. As time passed, the crowds joined him, singing songs and the processions began to swell. Chaitanya was still continuing to run his school. There also he lectured on Radha and Krishna. Then, step by step, he came to a juncture when he had no subject to teach his students except Krishna and bhakti. Students and parents complained, but to no avail. One by one, the students began to leave and finally, Chaitanya was forced to close down the establishment.

The State and Religion

While the spread and popularity of Vaishnavism grew and a

new revival of Hinduism seemed imminent, the movement began to attract hostility from Muslim authorities. Bengal was then known as Gaid or Gardh. Hussain Shah of Sayyid heritage was Sultan of Gardh. The Muslim rulers and Sultans were promoting conversion to Islam, mainly for political advantage. Mosques, were being built everywhere under the Sultan's patronage. Hussain Shah's conversion policy naturally came into conflict with Chaitanya's Vaishnavite mission. Chaitanya and his followers had to face many hurdles in their missionary pursuits.

If we compare the fanatic Muslim rulers of India like Sikandar Lodi, Tuglak, Aurangazeb and others, Hussain Shah was tolerant, but by no means as secular as Akbar the Great. Hussain Shah's antipathy to idol worshippers as 'infidels' (kafir) also contributed to this harassment. Chaitanya's Vaishnavism is nowadays designated as Neo-vaishnavism because of the new alterations introduced by Chaitanya in the old cult.

Chaitanya's main medium of propagating his Vaishnavism was the group-singing and parade/procession conducted by him and his rising number of followers. Hussain Shah and his officers did not view this as harmless activities of a religious sect. They were afraid that in due course, these may pose a challenge to their authority. One of his senior officers in Nabadwip named Quasi went even further than his king. He actually issued an order banning such religious processions which he alleged would affect the law and order situation. Although by nature, tolerant and peaceful, Chaitanya could not succumb to this effrontery. He decided to defy Quasi's ban or was perhaps persuaded to do so by his devotees. Chaitanya took out a procession of singing and dancing along with the followers in the streets which were under the jurisdiction of Quasi. As he went on, the participants in the procession began to swell. Hearing about Chaitanya's defiance, his sympathisers, and opponents gathered to witness the scene on both sides of the streets. The procession reached the gate of Quasi's residence and dispersed peacefully. Quasi never expected such a big mob defiantly marching and approaching his residence. He thought it wise to keep his cool and ultimately withdrew the ban order.

It is said that Quasi went in person to meet Chaitnaya and offer his respects. Thus the crisis-ridden situation blew over.

A Cut-off Date at Kattwa

We have seen that Nimai returned from Gaya a thoroughly changed man. Though not yet formally initiated into *sanyas dharma* he gave up all the worldly ties and lived like a sanyasi. This transformation of her only son pained his old mother, Sachidevi. She tried by all means to dissuade him and tried to bring him back to the house and the world. Nimai's young wife Vishnupriya was at first worried about her husband's new path, but she soon came to terms with the situation and began to be a bhakta herself. Later when Nimai began to be a staunch Vaishnavite she also accepted the faith and spent a long life as a Vaishnavite Bhakta.

Though Nimai adopted the life of a sanyasi for all practical purposes, he was yet to be formally initiated to sanyasa asrama by a guru. Such initiation took place in Kattwa. In January 1510, Kattwa was a village not far from Nabadwip on the other side of Ganga. There lived in Kattwa a famous yogi called Kesawa Bharati. In many ways, Nimai's faith was different from that of Bharathi. However, Bharathi knew the rituals connected with the sanyasa asrama and was very experienced in conferring this privilege on those who approached him. Therefore, Nimai also approached him to enter sanyasaasrama. Kesawa Bharathi gave him proper instructions and conducted the usual rituals and conferred on him the sanyasasrama. When initiating a person who deserves the sanyasa asrama, it was usual, as it is, to give the acolyte a new name. The new name Nimai adopted was Sri Krishna Chaitanya.

Thus, he became a full-fledged sanyasi. After that, he never returned to his native Nabadwip. The first reaction of the people in Nabadwip to Chaitanya's formal rejection of worldly life and happiness was one of universal dismay. On hearing the news, the shops were closed and the people wept for Chaitanya. Some of them even gave up their daily jobs. His mother, Sachidevi is said to have observed fast for more than a week.

After accepting the sanyas, Chaitanya's plan was to go on a

pilgrimage in north India where Vrindavan was situated. He longed to visit and worship Vrindavan around Mathura and the neighbourhood of Mathura where Sri Krishna had his boyhood *leelas* with Radha, the Gopis, the cows and the cowherds. But hearing Chaitanya's plans, his mother Sachidevi dissuaded him. She requested him to go to Puri in Orrisa, which was nearer to Bengal. Bengalis regularly go to Puri on pilgrimage and return. Some Bengali devotees of Vishnu that is, of Jagannatha, go on pilgrimage to Puri almost as an annual ritual. In order to oblige his loving mother Chaitanya agreed to her proposal and went to Puri with some of his close disciples like Nityananda.

Nityananda

Among the many disciples of Chaitanya, two are the most important—Advaitaacharya and Nityananda. Whether they should be called disciples or colleagues may be a subject of debate. Both of them were older than Chaitanya. Advaitaacharya was too old to be active in the movement. Nityananda was older than Chaitanya by only about 8 years. After Chaitanya left Nabadwip, he went to Puri and stayed there worshipping Jagannatha. It was Nityananda who carried the torch of Vaishnavism into Bengal. Chaitanya's Vaishnavism was more an emotional outburst than a philosophical system.

Chaitanya's Pilgrimages

It was Nityananda who gave a philosophical foundation for Chaitanya's Vaishnavism. Nityananda also brought Vaishnavite practices into the social field. He opposed the social and caste inequalities. Chaitanya, too, though was against social inequalities he does not seem to have emphasized it, though there were Muslims and untouchables in his entourage. Nityananda enriched this attitude and made it a part of Vaishnavite propaganda. It was in 1510 CE that Chaitanya left for Puri. Before leaving for the sacred city, he met Advaitacharya and entrusted the care of his mother, Sachidevi and wife, Vaishnupriya to him. He was accompanied by Nityananda, Damodar Pandit, Jagadananda and Mukunda Datha. The journey was not safe and peaceful. Sultan Hussain Shah was engaged in a war with the king of Orissa. This war and the movement of the army created many impediments on the way. His first visit to Puri was very short. It took about 18 days and he returned to Bengal with his associates. He found himself irresistibly drawn to Puri. From 1513 CE onwards, Chaitanya made the pilgrimage an annual event. The followers who accompanied him were constantly increasing in number. The regular annual visits of Chaitanya (except in 1515 when Hussain Shah was again engaged in war against Orissa) had salutary effects on Orissa. Not only he drew inspiration from Puri's Jagannatha but also helped the spread of Vaishnavism in Orissa. Among those who were converted to Vaishnavism, there were not only ordinary devotees but also outstanding scholars.

Among those who were drawn towards Chaitanaya by his magnetic personality and intense bhakti was Vasudeva Sarvabhouma who was very much a Vedic scholar. Though he was permanently settled in Orissa, he originally belonged to Nabadwip. Sarvabhouma was almost 40 years older than Chaitanya. His full name was Vasudeva Sarvabhouma Bhattacharya. He was well known in Bengali intellectual circles. He was interested in the new philosophical school, *'Navya Nyaya'*, founded by Vignana Bikshu and others. From Nabadwip he went to Mithila to learn Navya Nyaya more deeply. He joined the school run by Pakshadhar Misra in Mithila. The Navya Nyaya philosophy was not only intricate and abstruse, but it was almost kept as an esoteric faith by its adherents. The students who joined Misra's school were not allowed to copy its texts. They were allowed only to read the texts. Among the books he memorized were *Tathva Chintha Mani,* which is a basic text of Navya Nyaya, and *Kusumanjali* which deals with aesthetics. After completing his studies, he returned from Mithila to Bengal and accepted a few students and taught them Navya Nyaya and thus his enormous memory power helped to retrieve Navya Nyaya from those who tried to monopolise it and made available to all those who wished to learn it. Among his favourite students was Raghunatha Siromani. Due to many reasons, Vasudeva was not able to continue living in Nabadwip. Being a Vishnu bhakta, Vasudeva went to Puri and permanently took up residence there.

Chaitanya met Vasudeva in 1510 itself, during his first visit to Puri. At the time, Vasudeva was living under the patronage of the King of Orissa as his court philosopher. When Chaitanya saw for the first time the black idol made of wood, he was overwhelmed by it. As he drew closer to the idol to embrace it, Chaitanya fell down chanting the name of *Krishna*. The priest of the temple thought Chaitanya to be a mad man and behaved in a cruel manner. Vasudeva was a witness to the scene. He nursed Chaitanya and took him home. The discussions with Chaitanya influenced Vasudeva and he accepted Chaitanya as his guide.

Vasudeva was touched by Chaitanya's sanyasa and its rigours and suffering. He tried to dissuade Chaitanya from his sanyasa and advised him to go to his mother and wife and lead a normal worldly life. The discussion and the debate between young Chaitanya and older Vasudeva continued for days. Chaitanya of course based his arguments on Vaishnavism and bhakti. Basing himself on Vedic and other traditional religious texts, Vasudeva argued vehemently to defend his opposition to sanyasa and rejection of worldly duties and life. The final result, to make it short, was that Vasudeva had to accept his defeat and proclaim his conversion to Vaishnavism. The younger man won and the elder one almost dramatically accepted defeat. After some years, Vasudeva Bhattacharya wrote a life history of his guide called *Chaitanya Charitam*.

This conversion of such an outstanding and famous scholar added to the prestige of Chaitanya.

Towards South and West

At Puri, Chaitanya decided to fulfill a long-time wish to undertake an all-India pilgrimage. He went first to the south and next to western India in a tour which took two years to complete. He did not take with him either his close associates or other disciples—as he used to do during his earlier travels and pilgrimage. Only a personal servant accompanied him. His name was Govind Karmakar. Though he was only a personal attendant, his association with Chaitanya converted him to Vaishnavism and sacred texts and he learned to write and sing songs. He wrote a detailed account of Chaitanya's two-year-long odyssey. Chaitanya did not take any heavy luggage except minimum personal needs and some of his favorite song books. Neither did he take any money for his expenses which were very limited. He accepted food and gifts from devotees. When such gifts increased beyond his requirements Chaitanya donated them to temples and needy people whom he met on the way.

During his travels, he visited pilgrim centers and met important saintly people and scholars and had discussions with them. He was especially gratified over the opportunity to meet Vaishnavites in south India and west India. Among the well known Vaishnava gurus and bhaktas, he met one, was Ramanandarayar in Andhra. Chaitanya knew about this scholar and devotee from Vasudeva Sarvobhouma at Puri. Chaitanya and Ramananda first met at a bathing ghat of river Godavari. The place was Rajamundry, which is even now an important city in Andhra. Ramananda was invited into the spiritual path by Raghavendra, who was a disciple of renowned Yogi Madhavendrapuri. When Chaitanya and Ramananda met, the latter was holding a high office under the King Prathaparudra of Orissa. Chaitanya spent many days as a guest in Ramananda's house. Ramananda's conversion to the special brand of Chaitanya's Vaishnavism was considered in Bengal as a big achievement and it contributed to the spread of his cult in Orissa and Andhra.

Though Chaitanya firmly stuck to his own brand of Vaishnavist cult, he was tolerant of faiths different from his. That is why he went to Karnataka and visited Udupi, where lived Madhwacharya, the exponent of *Dvaita Vedanta.* Chaitnya worshipped at the temple established by Madhwa. Sri Krishna was the deity there, to whom he offered puja.

After visiting various temples and passing through towns and villages accompanied by his solitary assistant, Chaitanya moved on to West India in Maharashtra and Gujarat. The same procedure of pilgrimage continued. His visit to the famous Pandharpur of Varkari Pilgrimage and the black deity Vithoba there, deserve special mention. After visiting Gujarat, Chaitanya concluded his two years pilgrimage and returned to Puri by the end of 1511 CE. In Puri, Chaitanaya's numerous disciples and followers came from distant places in continuous streams to pay respects to Chaitanya.

Puri is famous not only in India but also abroad for its *Rathotsava* (Car Festival). In this festival, a massive chariot with the idols of Jagannatha or Krishna, the deity of the Puri temple, and Krishna's wife, Subhadra and brother Balarama is carried along the streets and pulled by huge crowds of devotees. Stampedes, deaths and injury are not uncommon in this procession. Such a massive and irresistible crowd is called in English a 'Juggernaut', derived from the word Jaganatha. Chaitnaya's followers in Bengal used to come in hundreds or thousands to participate in the festival, worship in the temple and visit Chaitanya for his *darshan* and blessings. This has become an annual ritual of Bengali Vaishnavites, even after the death of Chaitanya.

Chaitanya did not want every one of his followers to give up *Grihasthasrama* (householder's duties) and become a sanyasi like himself, though those who felt intensely interested in such a pursuit were quite welcome to do so. He advised some of his disciples to marry and lead a householder's life which could facilitate the fulfillment of some duties of the movement which were essential to the development of the broad spectrum of Vaishnavism. Nityananda, as we noted earlier, was a social worker engaged in the efforts for abolition of inequalities. He rendered other services also as was approved by Chaitanya. Chaitanya thought that for these kinds of services Grihasthastama was ideal.

Now to the Dreamland

We have seen that when Chaitanya began his all-India pilgrimage, he wanted to go to north India and Vrindavan in particular. Vrindavan is considered to be the region where Krishna was born. It was the scene of his plays and pranks and his divine amours with Radha and other Gopis. No other place was holier than Vrindavan to a devotee of Radha and Krishna.

Chaitanya had to alter his plans to visit Vrindavan and go to Puri instead as insisted upon by his affectionate mother, Sachidevi. However, now a time had arrived when he could not resist visiting Vrindavan, the land of his dreams.

Though Chaitanya had not yet visited Vrindavan, he knew from occasional pilgrims who returned from there that Vrindavan was almost a deserted jungle, badly requiring repair and improvements, to both the shrines there as well as the places around. Chaitanya instructed his followers to do this job and recover its lost beauty and prestige. One of Chaitanya's favorite disciples called Lokanath was the leader of the team which undertook the renovation activities. There were two brothers, Sanathana and Rupa, who helped Lokanath. They were great scholars and were not Chaitanya's disciples when they began to cooperate with Lokanatha's endeavour. Later, they were converted to the New Vaishnavism of Chaitanya. It was Chaitanya who gave them the evocative names—Sanathana for the elder brother and Rupa for the younger. They accepted Chaitanya's advice to reside permanently in Vrindavan and look after its shrines and sacred spots associated with the life of Krishna and Radha. The two brothers jointly and severally wrote many books on Gaidi Vaishnavism, that is, Chaitanya's New Vaishnavism of the Bengal school. They wrote these books in Sanskrit, unlike most of the bhakti poets who wrote in local languages.

During his pilgrimage to Vrindavan, he reached a place called Ramakeli. It was in those days a renowned centre of administration with a garrison. We have in our narrative dealt with Gaida, a city on the the northern side of the Ganga. We have also seen that in those days that Bengal was known as Gaida. Ramakeli was in the neighbourhood of Gaida. Sanathana and Rupa were living there. Chaitanya's visit became a ceremony for the local people. Many came to pay respects to him and listen to his songs and advice. Sultan Hussain Shah's capital was not far away. Ramakeli was a stronghold of Brahmin priesthood. They were also humble supporters of Hussain Shah. Chaitanya's visit undermined the authority of the Brahmins and spread widely his simple teachings of Krishna bhakti. People were wonderstruck by the costly, elaborate and above all incomprehensible rituals of the brahmin priests. Attracted by Chaitanya's personality, devotion and the simplicity of his bhakti cult, a large number of people turned to him for solace and contentment. When Chaitanya left Ramakeli for his final destination in Vrindavan, a huge crowd gathered to see him off. He did not stay in north India for a long time. He was eager to return to Puri where he wanted to spend the rest of his life.

Before leaving for Puri, Chaitanya found time to visit the holy city of Prayag where the Ganga and Yamuna join and flow west. It is said that long ago the river Saraswathi also joined the Ganga at Prayag and that is why it is called *Triveni Sangama*. When Chaitanya visited this holy city, the historic Kumbhamela festival was in full swing. Many saints, devotees and scholars as usual had come to the Kumbhamela, which takes place once in 12 years. One such great devotee was Vallabhacharya from Gujarat. Though Vallabhacharya originally belonged to Andhra, his main centre of missionary activities was Gujarat. Vallabhacharya was an outstanding devotee of Krishna; but his Vaishnavism was quite different from Chaitanya's. Vallabhacharya had his own brand of Vaishnavism which concentrated on *Krishna Leela* and *Rasakrida* and other such aspects which were in the poems of Vidyapati and Jayadeva. Another scholar with whom Chaitanya met and exchanged ideas was Raghupati Upadhyaya.

On the way back to Puri, he visited Varanasi, the historic city of Indian scholarship and religious thought. Almost all the Indian schools of thought were represented by the scholars there. Vaishnavism, Saivism, Advaita Vedanta, Vishishtadvaita and Dvaitavedanta were all present in Varanasi through their respective Pandits. Brahminism was of course predominant because of this peculiar conglomeration of faiths and cults deeply embedded in Varanasi. Chaitanya could hardly make an inroad into these complex cults and practices. However, it is said that he had just won an important convert there to his credit. This was Prakashananda Saraswathi. Before conversion, he was an outstanding authority and believer in Vedantha. By 1515,

Chaitanya reached Puri and his North-Indian pilgrimage was over. He was then 30 years of age.

It is after his return from Vrindavan that Chaitanya made his personal acquaintance with King Prathaparudra of Orissa. Though Prathaparudra had heard of Chaitanya and his spiritual accomplishments, it was through his senior officer, Ramanandarayar, that he knew more about Chaitanya and his greatness. We have already discussed Chaitanya's meeting with Ramanandrayar at Rajamundry, near the river Godavari during his southern sojourn. Prathaparudra showed great respect to Chaitanya and heard his views with rapt attention. Even Chaitanya, no respecter of worldly power and position, was overwhelmed by Prathaparudra's behaviour. Prathaparudra asked him many questions about Vaishnavism and Chaitanya gave him convincing explanations. The news spread fast and wide and reached Bengal. It was a great boost to Vaishnavism both in Bengal and Orissa. After becoming a sanyasi at Kattwa, he spent about six years in different parts of India. He spent the rest of his life in Puri from 1515, that is, 18 years and he never left it. He passed away at the age of 48 in the year 1533 CE.

Vaishnavism and Bhakti in Orissa

While narrating the story of Chaitanya's Neo-Vaishnavism in Bengal we have covered a lot of ground on bhakti developments in Orissa. It was inevitable since Puri in Orissa was a spring board of Bhakti. The Jagannatha temple in Puri was a great centre of Krishna worship. Jagannatha was worshipped as Krishna during early medieval times. There is evidence that Jagannatha was a tribal god originally. It was also a centre of worship for Buddhists. The idol is sculptured in black wood instead of stone or metal as is the practice in Hindu temples. It is further proof of its tribal origins. During Chaitanya's time, the Buddhists claimed Jagannatha as an incarnation of Gautama Buddha. Thus, the Puri temple underwent many transformations and adapted itself to the dominant religious faith of the Oriyas. In this connection, we may also remember that some *Purana*s assert that Buddha was an incarnation of Vishnu as the tenth or eleventh in the line. *Amarakosa* the ancient Sanskrit dictionary tries to give credence to this belief. In Orissa, Jagannathadasa and Achutha, in their *Darubrahma* and *Sooryaveda* respectively advances this argument. Jagannanthadas was not a Buddist. He was a devotee of Krishna. This is clear from his version of the *Bhagavata Purana*. This popular sacred text attracted Chaitanya very much. Thus, all that Jagannathadasa tried to do was to weave the Buddhist tradition to the texture of his Vaishnavism.

This line of thought was widely propagated by five important devotees. These were collectively known as the 'group of five friends'. They were Jagannathadasa,Valethadasa, Achuthananda, Ananda and Yasotantadasa. We have already mentioned one or two of them. All of them had met Chaitanya and received his blessings. It is also very important that they wrote many of their works in Oriya, instead of Sanskrit. This helped not only ordinary people to understand their doctrines, but also abetted the growth of the Oriya language in the early years of its evolution.

The Legacy

The psalms and hymns of Chaitanya were collected in the sixteenth century itself. The first collection was the work of Radhamohan Thakur. He called it *Padamrita Samgram*. It was followed by another collection called *Padakalpatharu*. These psalms were generally known as *Padavali*. It became the basic stream which gave Bengali music its form and delicate nuances. The tradition of singing and dancing in groups and processions seems to have continued till the middle of the eighteenth century. The immense popularity of Chaitanya psalms and their indelible impact on Bengal society are also evidenced by his honourable title 'Maha Prabhu', conferred on him not by kings or feudal chieftains but by the common people at large.

As we have seen, Chaitanya's influence and popularity were not confined to Bengal. Orissa in the south and Vrindavan in the west were also his areas of activity. The revival and renovation of Vrindavan as a centre of pilgrimage was mainly due to his efforts. Though Puri and its Jagannatha temple were already famous pilgrim centers long before Chaitanya, it was he who gave it a new life and relevance.

By the latter half of the eighteenth and the first quarter of the nineteenth centuries, the fervour of people for Gaidiya Vaishnavism of Chaitanya began to decline according to Dilip Kumar Mukherjee. Thus, the Gaidiya Vaishnavism of Chaitanya that flourished in Bengal for about two and half centuries declined and turned to history.

27

Many Streams of Bhakti in Andhra

The Bhakti movement had no pioneering leaders in Andhra like Basava in Karnataka, Jnaneswar in Maharashtra or Chaitanya in Bengal. However, as the etymology of Telugu, the language of Andhra, shows it had Saivite Bhakti tradition from the sixth century CE. Neelakanta Sastri has the following to say on the origin of the Telugu language and its relation to other cultural areas as follows:

> In ancient times the Telugu country was often called Trilinga, the country which contained or was bounded by the three lingas of Kalahasti, Srisailam and Daksharama, and Telinga-Telugu as the name of the country and language may well be traced to this word. It is also suggested that Tel(n)ugu comes from **tene**, 'honey' or **tennu**, 'way'. The beginnings of the language can be traced from stone inscriptions of the fifth and sixth centuries A.D., and its basic elements have unmistakable affinities with Tamil and Kannada. But, from the beginning, the literary idiom depended very largely upon Sanskrit and the **Janasrayachandas**, an early work of prosody, fragments of which have recently come to light, though it includes some meters peculiar to Telugu and unknown to Sanskrit, is itself written in Sanskrit throughout; the author was most probably the Vishnukundin monarch Madhavavarman II (580-620), who had the title Janasraya. The inscriptions of the dynasty are in Sanskrit with an admixture of Prakrit and Telugu words.[96]

Owing to *linga* worship, the influence of Basava's Veerasaiva movement could encompass large sections of Telugu people from the very beginning. This wide-spread adulation of Saivism did not prevent Vaishnava Bhakti form penetrating from Karnataka in the west, and Tamizhakom in the South. Periyalvar was one of the most notable among the 12 Vaishnavite Alvars and his teachings were very popular in the southern parts of Andhra, especially when the Chola Kingdom extended its borders beyond the northern frontiers of Tamizhakom.

The Bhakti movement symbolized both a continuity as well as a break with the past. Even a radical movement like Basava's Veerasaivism at least nominally extolled Siva of traditional Hinduism. However, Andhra's rebellious Shudra poet Vemana rejected all Vedic and Hindu traditions altogether. He also added grist to the Bhakti movement though by a sort of 'back-seat driving'. The element of 'break with the past' in the Bhakti movement emerges from its rejection of Brahminical rituals and sacrifice in favour of simple devotion and submission to the chosen deity. All these streams constitute the composite character of the Telugu Bhakti movement. Next, we shall examine some of the Bhakti poets who represented in their poems, translations and transcriptions, the different streams which flew into the ocean of Andhra's Bhakti tradition.

Age of Nannayya

The Telugu language and literature came off age with the contribution of Nannayya, a poet, grammarian, thinker and courtier of 11th century CE. This period in the history of Telugu literature is known as the *Age of Nannayya*. Nannayya flourished during the latter part of the Eastern Chaluakya rule. It was an era of decline of Buddhism and rise of Brahmanical dominance in the secular and religious life of the Andhras. It would be more correct to say that Buddhism was absorbed into Hinduism and it lost its vitality and individuality. The famous philosopher, scientist and physician Nagarjuna was the spearhead of Buddhism in Andhra. Nagarjuna's Mahayana Buddhism went to the extent of *Madhyamika Vadha* and *Sunyavada w*hich were all directly opposed to the original materialist content of Buddhism. The consequent revival of Brahmanism and the Vedic culture were patronized by the rulers as an attempt to reverse the trend of political turmoil. Dr Salva Krishnamurthy says:

> Within a short time after the Eastern Calukya rule started in Andhra in the 7th c. AD. Kumarilabhatta, an Andhra, born in the village of Jayamangala in Ganjam district, appeared on the scene and revived the Vedic religion, the religion of Yajnas and Yagas. He is said to have studied all the Jain scriptures and works disguising himself as a Jain student and later on used his knowledge to demolish their religious theory. He wrote a commentary on Sabara's bhasya of Jimini's Poorva Mimamsa aphorisms in his works Slokavartika, Tantravartika and Brhattika. He was completely opposed to the non-Vedic religions and advocated action- oriented Vedic religion. It was Kumarila's work that made Hiuen Tsang record the decline of Buddhism and Jainism and the emergence of brahmanical temples in the country. Kumarila was followed by Sankara from Kaladi of Kerala and his commentaries on the prasthana-traya (namely Upanisads, Brahmasutra and Bhagavadgita) and his advocacy of Advaita philosophy completely changed the religious scene in the country. Jains in Andhra felt shaken to their roots and migrated to Sravana Belagola and Vatapi in Kannada country where they could get protection and encouragement. Pampa, Ponna and Nagavarma I. were Telugus who migrated from Andhra and became celebrated writers in Kannda. But Nagavarma I (c.990 AD) the author of Chandombudhi in Kannada, was an Andhra Brahman and not a Jain.
>
> With the construction of Brahmanic temples in Andhra the cultural scene became enlivened. The temples became centres of arts and learning. People belonging to the 72 niyogas came to reside around the temples—Sthanapatis, Pujaris, dancers and dance masters, singers, instrumentalists and other retinues connected with the temple. Kings, chieftains and commanders lavished their patronage on them. What may be called a 'Calukya Style' emerged in the construction of temples and their sculpture. One can see orchestra groups in the paintings of Jammidoddi, in Vijayawada and in the sculptured panels of Bikkavolu and Bhimavaram. Appropriate musical and folk poetic compositions can be inferred. Nagi-gitas (song sung by Naga-women) mentioned by Nannayyabhattu and 'gaudu-gitas' (songs sung after drinking toddy) mentioned by Nannicoda could be such compositions. The Attili copper plate inscription of Calukya Bhima

(910 AD) speaks of a donation of a land with a thousand arecanut trees, a big cultivable piece of land of 50-putties and home-stead to one lady called Callavva, who was extremely talented in both music and dance. This very inscription suggests the prevalence of the game of chess and the required pieces being prepared in mud. (Arudra in his book quotes the lines 'Yasya khadga jalavardhinimagnam Krsnavallabha balam sasapatnam, (mrnmayamtu caturangabaleva ksiprameva vilayagatamajau) and saya Komarraju Laxmana Rao had procured the bracketed portion from another inscription). Some indigenous Telugu literature should have flourished between the 6th and 10th centuries. Desi meters like Dvipada, Taruvoja, Ragada could have been musically oriented with an option for either yati or prasa. The Prakrt work 'Lilavati' dealing with the story of an Andhra Princess refers to the Desi School in story telling. This work is assigned to 6th/7th c. AD. So it is only correct to positively infer the presence of a desi tradition of literature in Andhra in lucid Janu-Tenugu.[97]

The Pioneer

We have explained in detail the turmoil and conflicts in Andhra in the era of Nannayya when Nannayya Bhakti flourished. Nannayya was so important a personality in the history of the Telugu language and literature that historians have honoured him by ascribing an entire era to him. As one who gave modern shape to Telugu and in the process wrote its first grammar text, the honour is befitting. Adept in both Sanskrit and Telugu, he wrote in both languages, earning the title of *Ubhaya Kavi*. He was a great scholar in traditional knowledge and also an original thinker. His translation—*Andhra Mahabharatamu*— of the Sanskrit epic *Mahabharata* was a significant contribution to the development of the Telugu language and religious thought.

An erudite Vedic scholar, he believed in the sanctity of the *Vedas* and conducted Vedic rituals. He claimed that he conducted the rituals of *yaga* or *yagna* to purify himself in order to undertake this sacred task of translating the *Mahabharata*. It is hard to include him in the bhakti tradition which rejected the elaborate and expensive Brahmanic rituals and sacrifices in favour of simple devotion to the chosen deity. However, some may argue that the very translation of the *Mahabharata* into Telugu, which made it accessible to the common people, itself was an indirect contribution to the spread of the bhakti cult.

The dates and other details of Nannayya's life are still a matter of dispute and conjecture. A consensus of modern scholars places him in the twelfth century CE. The eastern Chalukya Emperors were ruling the Telugu country, parts of Karnataka and Maharashtra and the northern border lands of Tamizhakam. Nannayya was the royal priest and court poet of the Chalukyas under Raja Narendra, a great patron of scholars, poets and artists of every variety.

The conflicts and turmoil described earlier had affected the stability of Raja Raja Narendra's kingdom and those who thought a Hindu revival would help bring about a unity and tranquility to his state. Hindus were divided into Saivites, Vaishnavites, Veerasaivites, et cetera, besides the challenge they continued to face from Buddhism and Jainism. It was part of his endeavour to revive Hinduism that he undertook the translations of Hindu religious texts, including the epics and *Purana*s into Telugu. The king allocated the job of translating the *Mahabharata* to the senior court-poet Nannayya.

Though Nannayya accepted the royal assignment with pleasure, he found many hurdles on his way. Telugu was yet to be completely free from the bonds of the Dravidian family and was also heavily dependent on Sanskrit vocabulary. It was unsystematic for narrative purposes and confused in semantics. As a beginning to his efforts to bring some order into the language and retrieve it from such a chaotic situation, Nannayya wrote *Andhra Sabda Chinthamoni*. It is the first grammar text of Telugu but written in Sanskrit. In his prodigious efforts to develop the language and enrich it, Nannayya had a close collaborator—Narayana Bhatta. Nannayya acknowledges his help generously in his works. Summarising Nannayya's role and place in Telugu literature S. Raghavachari writes:

> The credit of shaping the language and making it worthy for construction of a great epic belongs to Nannayya. The sanctity and soaring imagination of Valmiki, the intellectual quality of Vyasa the high seriousness of Milton, the emphatic narrative of Homer, all these came in one poet-Nannayya –who without doubt can be called the father of Telugu poetry.[98]

Though Raghavachari, in his enthusiastic admiration for Nannayya, crosses the bounds of scholarly restraint, there is no doubt that his incomplete translation—or perhaps transcription—establishes Nannayya's poetic genius though his comparisons seem a little odious.

Tikkana

Tikkana of the thirteenth century flourished almost two centuries after Nannayya. There were great differences between the two in talents and characteristics as we shall presently see. In spite of this, both Nannayya and Tikkana have often been bracketed by historians for their seminal contributions to Telugu literature.

Tikkana was not only a poet of eminence, but also a philosopher, statesman, diplomat and warrior. His diplomatic talents were employed not only in politics but also religious disputes. To prove the unity of the 'godheads' and to unite the two sects of Veerasaivas and Vashnavites Tikkana advanced the concept of *Hariharanatha*. Hari is Vishnu and Hara is Siva and Natha meant Lord. So Tikkana's concept meant the unity of Vishnu and Siva as a single godhead. Though Tikkana had believed in the *Vedas* and conducted its rituals like *Somayaga*, he claimed a respectable place in the galaxy of bhakti poets on account of his contribution with salutary results in religious faith and practices.

Tikkana's administrative acumen and diplomatic skill were in full bloom when he functioned as the minister and army commander of King Muhammaduddin who ruled Nellore. In a conflict with a rival claimant, Muhammaduddin lost his throne. Tikkana, making full use of his diplomatic skills and logical arguments, convinced the neighbouring ruler Ganapathideva of the Kakatiya dynasty that justice and fair play demanded support to Muhammaduddin's case. Tikkana won over Ganapathideva, and with his support, restored Muhammaduddin to his throne.

Tikkana's favourite works of Sanskrit were the *Ramayana* and the *Mahabharata*. He translated the *Ramayana* into Telugu poetry and called it *Nirvachanethara Ramayana*. He also translated

15 chapters *of Mahabharata*. Another book attributed to him is called *Vijayasena,* a book of Telugu poems. He also wrote books of literary theory. One of them is about prosody in Sanskrit called *Kavagbandhanam*.

Nannayya, in his incomplete translation of the *Mahabharata,* closely followed the original without giving his imagination free play. Sanskrit words abound in it, too. However, he can surely claim credit for some conscious innovations. He left out in his translations some details from the original but embellished it with his own ideas and values. Tikkana made the women characters like Gandhari, Kunti and Draupadi more vibrant and assertive than they were in the original Sanskrit text. As far as Tikkana's language is concerned, though there is an unavoidable presence of Sanskrit words, pure Telugu words appear more than in Nannayya's works. Tikkana uses not even the elitist or chaste Telugu but uses '*jana Telugu*', the common man's speech. Though Tikkana was attached to kings and courts as minister, army commander and diplomat, he did not consider them worthy of dedication of great works of art, literature and philosophy, though such acts to them would have helped to advance his career or fill his coffers, Tikkana dedicated his *Mahabharata* not to them but to his deity, Hariharanatha.

Raghavachari gives us a brief evaluation of Tikkana's character and ideals:

> Tikkana's character is a blend of several interesting characteristics. He was an ascetic, yet he lived n luxury; he was a great philosopher who had his eyes always on the Kingdom of heaven; yet he vigorously tackled all the problems he faced in his Kingdom; He was one of the greatest of scholars, yet his literary style is the most unpretentious, he was a warrior himself, yet he always preached the ideal of unity viewed through his life and letters, he is a towering personality of an almost super-human calibre.[99]

Bopadeva

Chronologically, Bopadeva comes between Nannayya and Tikkana. Belonging to the thirteenth century, Bopadeva is known for his commentaries and analyses of the *Bhagavata* which is more associated to the Bhakti movement than either the *Mahabharata* or the *Ramayana*. Therefore Bopadeva, along with Pothana, are considered the most important Telugu poets of the Bhakti movement. Though the *Bhaghavata* is seen as closer to Vaishnava tradition as against the Saivite, some poets like Pothana interpret the *Bhagavata* as sacred to both the bhakti trends.

Bopadeva was born in a Brahmin village called Vedapura in Vidharba on the banks of river Varada. This village was famous those days for its many scholars, Ayurvedic physicians and poets of eminence. The royal physicians Kesava and Dhanesa belonged to this village. They were all attached to the court of the Yadavas of Devagiri, which was later known as Daulatbad. Kesava, his father Mahadeva and teacher Bhaskara were patronised by King Singhana who ruled from 1210–47 CE. Bopadeva's literary activities expanded to the reigns of Singhana's successors also. The two *Bhagavata* works, *Harilila* and *Muktaphala* were written under the patronage of Ramaraja. Bopadeva did not translate the *Bhagavata* but wrote commentaries and analyses of *Bhagavata* and a few books on it, including those mentioned above. Bopadeva's extant works included *Harilila, Bhagavata, Muktaphala* and commentaries and interpretation of Pushpadanta's *Sivamahimastava*. The fact that he also wrote commentaries on *Sivamahimastava* shows that his bhakti was not confined to Vishnu alone. This proves that Bopadeva anticipated the theory advanced by Tikkana that Vishnu and Siva were not two deities but one. Tikkana called the syncretic deity *Hariharanatha*, that is, the Lord who unites in himself both Hari and Hara or Vishnu the Preserver and Siva the Destroyer respectively. This concept also includes monotheism—a favourtie ideal of many bhakti saints like Kabir.

Bopadeva was a great scholar. It is evident not only from his detailed analysis and interpretation of the *Bhagavata* but also by his proficiency in grammar and prosody. After Nannayya, the Telugu language developed fast and new usages and style came into vogue. Therefore, Nannayya's grammar was fast becoming out of date. Bopadeva updated the grammar of Telugu. The well-known modern Sanskrit scholar V. Raghavan concludes his study of Bopadava in the following words:

This aesthetics of **Bhakti** Rasa given in the **Muktaphala** and its commentary is the most important contribution of Bopadeva and I have taken note of it in my books 'The Number of Rasa, and 'Bhoja's **Sringara Prakasa'**. Bopadeva's **Bhakri**-aesthetic, like his **Mughdhabodha** grammar, exerted great influence in Bengal and the Bhakti cult of the Chaitanya school. The most prominent Chaitanya-rhetorician Rupa Gosvamin, in his work on this subject, **Ujjvalanilamani**, expresses his indebtedness to Bopadeva **and his Muktaphala**. In his commentary on the **Bhagavata**, the **Vaishnavatoshini**, Santana Gosvamin refers to Bopadeva's **Muktaphala**. Other Bengali Vaishnava writers also like, Jiva Gosvamin and Gopala Bhatta mention Bopadeva. The Bengali **Bhaktamala** includes an account of Bopadeva.

Although Bopadeva's erudition is versatile, with specialty in grammar and medicine, his real greatness lies in something deeper than mere scholarship. The **Bhagavata** is his Bible and **Krishna Bhakti** the anchor of his heart.[100]

Errana

The poetic trio who one after the other completed the *Andhra Mahabharata* included Nannayya, Tikkana and Errana. Though he belonged to the fourteenth century, he is placed among the trinity owing to his great stature. Also known as *Yellapragada* or *Errapragada,* Errana was born in a Brahmin family of Saivite tradition. He was a worshipper of Vishnu, though his parents were Saivites. He was a court poet of Prolaya Vemareddy who ruled during 1325–53 and founded Reddy dynasty (1325–1424), whose kingdom spread to Guntur, Prakasam, Nelloor and Kurnool districts of the state of Andhra Pradesh.

Besides completing the translation of the *Mahabharata* he wrote *Vaganu-Shasana, Kavibrahma* and *Prabhanda Parameswara* and was conferred the title Prabhanda Parameswara. He translated *Hari-Vams*a from Sanskrit to Telugu which is the concluding part of *Mahabharata*. His *Narasimha Purana* is the story of the incarnation of Lord Vishnu as the half-man half-beat who slays the evil King Hiranya Kasipu who tortured the boy Prahlada for worshipping Vishnu.

Bammera Pothana

The birth and growth of the modern Telugu, like most of the other modern languages in India, is related to the Bhakti movement and the translation of Sanskrit epics and *Puranas*. In Telugu, this process started with the translation of the *Mahabharata* by Nannayya who left it incomplete as we have seen. It was continued by Tikkana and completed by Errana, the poetic *trio* of early Telugu. Tikkana also translated the *Ramayana*. The translation of *Srimad Bhagavataa*, the basic text of Vaishnava Bhakti was done by Bammera Pothena. Later, another translation of the *Bhagavata* was made by Bopadeva, as discussed earlier.

Pothana belonged to a Neog Brahmin family and therefore was also known as Pothayya. His father was Kesana and mother Lakhamamba. Regarding his birth place, scholars are unanimous. The consensus is that he was born in Warangal in Telengana region (1450–1510). According to the first historian of Telugu literature, Kandukuri Viresalingam, Pothana flourished in the middle half of the fifteenth century.

Though a Brahmin by birth, Pothana and his family were poor and resorted to physical labour for their livelihood. Pothana also worked on his small plot of land to earn his living. Although he was poor and could not aspire to be rich, he rejected opportunities to get rich when be became famous. Pothana had only contempt for the high and mighty, as is clear from his following words:

> There is only one poet (Pothana) who did not dedicate his work to wicked Kings and received from them villages, valuables and the like, but willingly dedicated his Bhagavatha to Sri Hari and escaped from the punishment of Yama.

Pothana also said that 'it is good for the poet to be a tiller of the soil and support his family from its income'. That he was not making necessity a pretence for his claims to moral superiority is quite clear from his life. King Sarvajina Singa Bupala desired that Pothana's *Bhagavatha* is dedicated to him. No doubt such dedication would have earned him a lot of money and other gifts to alleviate his poverty. The king sent his messengers to

Pothana with the suggestion. Pothana did not accede to the king's request. The king naturally was angry at the impertinent behaviour of the poet. It is said that he ordered the copies of *Pothana Bhagavatha* to be burnt. It is not known whether the king's men could lay their hands upon the great book. Anyway, that it survived the king's wrath is evident.

There is no doubt that Pothana was an outstanding poet in the bhakti tradition. Who exactly was his chosen deity for worship or which school of bhakti did he adhere to? It is difficult to answer. His religion was a fascinating cocktail of different cults and faiths. He was a Saiva to begin with, as he derived his faith from his parents and other predecessors who were all staunch Saivites. By the time of his youth, he became a Vaishnavite to write his version of the *Bhagavatha,* considered a Vaishnavite text. Towards his old age, Pothana became an ardent Advaiti. However, these changes did not cause him to discard the earlier faith. All co-existed with one another. His Saivism did not conflict with his Vaishnavism. He worshipped both Siva and Vishnu with a liberal attitude. This is evident from his *Bhagavatha* itself.

What urged him to undertake the translation of the *Bhagavatha*? Paying due respects to his predecessors Pothana explains:

> Nannayya, Tikkana and other poets have translated the Puranas into Telugu. But do not know what amount of Punya I have done in that the Bhagavatha shall therefore translate this work and make my birth fruitful and avoid re-birth.

Pothana's bhakti was not aimed at his personal salvation. It is permeated with an intense passion for the well-being of humanity. As we have seen, his views on different deities were not sectarian but liberal. It would seem that his frequent invocation of the names of deities is but a garb to embellish his love of human beings and the ethical life. Read this short passage to understand the essence of his Bhakti ideal:

Why should one be born, if
Siva is not worshipped,
Hari is not praised,
Compassion and truth not felt inwardly.

To complete the picture of Pothana's life and letters, we have to mention some controversies on his *Bhagavatha*, during his time and later. Some scholars and grammarians find fault with him for grammatical errors and semantic defects. Some people surmise that such errors and defects were due to his lack of formal education. Some others attribute these defects to his followers and disciples who added some of their own lines to the master's original. However, nobody disputes his poetic talents or genius or the quality of his mellifluous poetry. Such defects, even if true, are only like the dark spots on the moon, which spreads its soft and luxuriant rays that envelope the earth.

This is also proved by the pervasive influence exercised by Pothana among many of his contemporaries and later readers. Among them, the great Thyagaraja was one. The admiration and affection for Pothana crossed the boundaries of the Telugu country. In Tamizhakam also, his name and fame persisted till modern times. The great revolutionary Tamil poet of the twentieth century, Subramanya Bharati extolled Pothana as equal to Kamban, author of the Tamil *Ramayana* and Thiruvalluvar, author of the Tamil classic, *Thirukural*.

Pothana is a household name in Andhra and his *Bhagavatha* is still read and enjoyed by scholars and common bhaktas alike.

Vemana, The Rebel Poet

Among the many saints, scholars and social reformers of the Bhakti movement, Vemana stands out as a rebel sharply different from all others except in the matter of poetic genius. According to C.P. Brown, an authority on Vemana's life and letters, Kumaragiri Vema Reddy, popularly known as Vemana was born in c. 1352 in Rayalaseema and died in Katarupalli. His father was Kumaragiri Vema, then the King of Kondaveedu in present-day Andhra Pradesh. Since he practised Yoga, he was also called Yogi Vemana. As he was a Yogi he was buried upon death and not cremated.

Vemana flourished in Andhra during the fourteenth century. Though he was immensely popular in his time and later, it is intriguing that he did not find a place in the history of

Telugu literature till very recently. V.R. Narla, a modern scholar in his study of Vemana writes as follows:

> "VEMANA, by any test, is a great poet; judged by popularity, he is by far the greatest of the Telugu poets—early, medieval or modern. None else, not even the honey-throated Potana, is half as popular. Vemana is a prince among commoners, and he speaks to myriads of commoners in their own accents, and they open out their hearts to him. They may wince occasionally under the lash of his tongue, but they know that he means well, and they love him all the more. While loving him as a poet, they revere him as a philosopher and a saint, and quote him frequently to score a point, to emphasize a truth, or to underline a moral. No wonder, a Western scholar like G.A. Grierson, who had devoted a lifetime to the study of Indian languages and literatures, found that Vemana "is today the most popular of all Telugu authors, and there is hardly a proverb or a pithy saying which is not attributed to him."
>
> Vemana's popularity is by no means confined to the common men and women of Andhra; it extends to those of the neighbouring areas as well. Long ago, some of his verses were translated into Tamil and Kannada. He may or may not have been the first Telugu poet who has translated into other languages but certainly no other Telugu poet is translated into so many languages.[101]

Does it not seem rather odd that Vemana was ignored by historians of literature by a sort of conspiracy of silence during the colonial rule? The foreign administrators of education tried to rescue Vemana from oblivion, prescribe his works for the academic curriculum and include Vemana's works in the syllabus for the study of Telugu literature. But the conservative teachers especially from the Brahmins deliberately kept them in dark and refused to teach them till the first decade of the twentieth century. It would be interesting to examine the reasons for this exclusion.

One important reason which incensed the Brahmins and the conservatives was Vemana's contempt for the *Veda*s, Vedic sacrifices, *Purana*s and the mythical heroes as is proved by the following verses:

> *Though he should daily read or hear*
> *The Veds, the sinner still is vile.*

Will not its blackness still appear
Though coal in milk be washed a while?

Religions counted by the score
There are. But yet not one is god
Faith makes our worship please our God.

They read the Shasters, write them out,
And learn the truths that in them lie.
And yet of death they are in doubt:
They know not even how to die!

You smear your face and arms with ash,
Hang silver idols round your neck!
All this may help to swell your cash,
But in the coming world will wreck.

"Thou art unclean! O, touch me not!"—
They cry. But who can draw the line?
What man was born without a spot?
In each man's flesh sin has a shrine.[102]

Vemana also ridiculed the idol worship. He asks:

What animals ye are who worship stones
And care not for the God that dwells within !
How can a stone excel the living thing
That praise intones ?

What strange delusion draws your mind to dream
That God doth dwell in senseless images ?
Is broken stone, which neither hears nor sees,
Fit house for Him ?

Yet men take earth, make idols, set the clod
In honor, count as gods and worship them !
How can they dare so blindly to contemn
Their inward God ?

What fools! They take a stone from off the hill,
And after knocking it about with hands and feet,
With chisels cut it and with hammers beat:
Then chants they trill.

The living useful bull you starve and beat;

But when 'tis carved in stone you it adore !
How gross such sinful folly is ! Abhor
So clear a cheat.

While He, the worshipful, dwells in the heart,
Why pile your gifts in temple made of stone ?
Can gods who, in and out, are rock alone
E'er taste a part ?[103]

Another reason for the marginalisation of Vemana was that he was a Sudra-poet and that he was strongly against the caste system. There is a conservative tradition that poems written by Sudras have to be ignored and if possible destroyed. In the words of Narla, we find the following explanation:

> ...Thirdly, Vemana is a Sudra; and no less an authority on Telugu poetics than Appakavi has laid down the rule that the work of a Sudra poet should be rejected out of hand without examination. Such indeed was the contempt of the high castes for Sudra poets in general that of the 500 first edition copies of **The Verses of Vemana**: **Moral**, **Religious** and **Satirical**, which Charles Philip Brown of the Madras Civil Service printed in 1829 for the College Board, 450 disappeared mysteriously. (The remaining fifty were presented to him as editor's copies.) It took Brown ten years to discover that, with the active connivance of the high-caste pandits of the College Board; the missing copies were rolled up as waste paper and tucked away in the lumber room of the College Library.[104]

Among Vemana's many poems and renouncements of the caste system, the following may be quoted.

If we look through all the earth
Men, we see, have equal birth.
Made in one great brotherhood,
Equal in the sight of God.

Food or caste or place of birth
Cannot alter human worth.
Why let caste be so supreme ?
'Tis but folly's passing stream.

Viler than the meanest race
Is the man before whose face

Others only Sudras are.
Hell for him shall ne'er unbar.

Empty is a caste-dispute:
All the castes have but one root.
Who on earth can e'er decide
Who to praise and whom deride?

Why should we the Pariah scorn,
When his flesh and blood were born
Like to ours ? What caste is He
Who doth dwell in all we see?[105]

In spite of the rebellious nature of his personality and poems, Vemana is often compared with Tiruvalluvar, Kabir and Sarvajna who were all peaceful in their temperament, though radical social reformers. On his life in the galaxy of bhakti poets, Narla gives us the following assessment.

> In his temperament, thought and mode of expression, Vemana is nearer to Sarvajna than either to Tiruvalluvar or to Kabir. What brings them so near is perhaps their common background. As young men, both were philanderers. Both were first much enamoured of, and then disgusted with, **devadasis**. Again, both of them veered round suddenly from a life of pleasure to a life of religion, but the **devadasis** continue to occupy their thoughts so much that they miss no opportunity to curse the poor wretches, who are, after all, the victims of a cruel social order. It may also be added that the blind spot of both was woman. Whether Vemana or Sarvajna was prior in point of time is a moot question, but Rallapalli, who has made a critical study of both, thinks that there are more reasons for the presumption that it was Vemana who influenced Sarvajna, rather than for its reverse. Anyway, in spite of their many similarities, Vemana and Sarvajna were not mere copies nor echoes of each other; the latter was more of a realist and more worldly-wise than the former, and they differed in their emphasis on certain basic ideas and ideals.[106]

Bhadrachala Ramadas

Bhadrachala Ramadas (c 1620–80) CE was a great mystic bhakta poet of Andhra. He was also a tragic figure who had to spend about 10 years in a dark prison cell where he was given food through a hole in the wall. He was towards the close of his life when was not only pardoned by the king but also honoured by being sent home on a palanquin with a retinue.

Ramadas was born in Nadakondanappalli in the present Telengana region, then within the kingdom of Golkonda ruled by Muslim kings. The Muslim kings of Golkonda were generally very tolerant and stood for Hindu-Muslim unity. They were great patrons of poets, artists, musicians and dancers. Ramadas flourished during the reign of King Abul Hasan, who was popularly known as Tani-Shah (1674–99). Tani Shah means a jovial king.

King Abul Hasan Tani Shah, like his dynasty, was not only tolerant to Hindus, but respected their customs and rituals and used to participate in their festivals. He was very fond of Ramadas and used to converse with him on his faith and bhakti. He had many Hindu officers under him including a Brahmin Minister. Madanna was Ramadas's uncle, who tried to help his nephew when he was in trouble. Though the name his parents gave him was Gopanna, owing to his intense devotion to Rama he later adopted the name Ramadas. The Bhadrachalam temple which gave Ramadas spiritual sustenance later led him to penury.

Even before Ramadas reached adulthood, he began to express his spiritual inclinations. He moved around with devotees and often gave them feasts and gifts. He made little attempt to look after the family property and gradually became too poor to continue his hospitality towards the devotees. He was in need of a job to make both ends meet and also continue services to the devotees. His uncle, Minister Madanna, was at hand to help. Madanna persuaded the king to appoint his nephew as the Tehsildar of the *firka* (a few taluks) of Bhadrachala. Ramadas also got under his jurisdiction his beloved Rama temple at Badrachalam. Ramadas began his duties as Tehsildar efficiently and collected taxes et cetera due to the king regularly and diligently without fail.

As time passed, Ramadas began to lose interest in his official duties and was irresistibly drawn to the pursuit of bhakti and worship. Ramadas noticed that the temple of Rama was in a dilapidated condition due to lack of care and repair. He undertook to renovate the temple with the money he collected as taxes. Thus it became difficult for Ramadas to remit the share of the taxes so collected to the king's exchequer. No wonder Ramadas's action invited punishment from the king. He was arrested, tried and sent to prison. He wrote a hymn in *Saveri* lamenting to Rama. Following is the prose translation of his lament.

What wrong did I do?
Did I make the earrings
the rings for all the ten fingers,
the diadem for myself?
It is for your acceptance,
Oh, Sita Rama, that I did all this!

King Abul Hasan Tani Shah could not forgive the unexpected and deliberate lapse of his erstwhile friend Ramadas. Ramadas' uncle, Madanna, could not help his nephew who was indisputably at fault. It was in prison that some of the best songs and psalms in the entire Telugu literature were composed by Ramadas which made him immortal. The story of the condonation of Ramadas's lapse and his release from prison are shrouded in myths and legends. One of them is that Lord Ram and brother Lakshmana appeared before Tani Shah in the dead of night, posing to be servants and messengers of Ramadas. They paid the entire amount due to the king's treasury on the spot. The flabbergasted king knew that they were not servants of Ramadas and went straight to the prison to order his release. Ramadas was provided with a royal palanquin and sent ceremoniously to Bhadrachala. Needless to say he did not accept the defaulted payments Ramadas had to pay the exchequer. Of course, all these are only legends passed from generation to generation right upto this day.

Ramadas's songs and bhakti influenced such a great man as Thyagaraja, one of the patriarch's of Carnatic music. Though Thyagaraja was born in Chola Desa, that is, Tamizhakam, he was a Telugu, writing and singing in the Telugu language. Thyagaraja is said to have exclaimed the glory and greatness of Ramadas. Following words bear testimony to this:

Had I been Ramadas, Sita would have come forward to speak to you on my behalf.

*** ***

O ye common folk of the world! Why not buy the medicine of Rama-jogi? (the mendicant from whom medicines and antidotes could be had; the prescription meant here, as given by God Rama is himself, His Name and Worship). When, with love, you take this remedy of the Rama-mendicant, it completely destroys pride, jealousy, avarice, and the accumulation of Karmas. The remedy of Rama-jogi, which is unequalled in the world and destroys the formidable fetters of life, the remedy which cannot be obtained even by spending crores of rupees and is ever remembered by the unequalled devotees of the Lord; the remedy at Bhadradri (the shrine in Andhra for renovating which out of state funds, the Saint was imprisoned), and which helps attainment of salvation and which is ever worshipped with devotion by Ramadasa.

28

Dadupanthis and Panchavani

Dadu (1544–1603) and his followers occupy an important place of their own in the history of north India's Bhakti movement. He was a contemporary of Akbar the Great who was attracted to Dadu, his personality and teachings. The sect he founded had a chequered history. It is very interesting that the transformations of bhakti-panth took on many forms including the political and the military. Dadu was a non-conformist *Nirguna Bhakta* and very much dedicated to Hindu-Muslim brotherhood. However, ultimately it became a militant Hindu movement, especially after his death. So it provides a subject for a special case-study of the Bhakti movement.

Dadu was an adopted child of a Brahmin family in Ahmedabad and was brought up as a Brahmin. But there are some intractable problems about his name. 'Dadu' is a Turkish word; it means brother, or servant. A contemporary book named *Dabistan-i-Mazahib* calls him a *naddaf*. His family was engaged in cotton carding. The book gives us a brief account of Dadu's life as follows:

> Dadu was by birth a naddaf and lived at Naraina (a town in Marwar). He adopted the ascetic life in the time of the Emperor Akbar and made many disciples. He forbade the practice of idolatry among his followers. He also prohibited the eating of flesh and sought to avoid causing pain to any living creature. He did not require the abandonment of secular pursuits, nor forbid marriage. People were free to remain celibate or to marry, to withdraw from the world's business or engage in it as they saw fit and his disciples embraced both classes.[107]

Dadu was a family man with children. He looked after his family with the resources he earned from his occupation. Later, when he became a well-known teacher himself, he did not advise celibacy to his followers and gave freedom of choice. He emphasised the dignity of labour and advised them to work and earn their livelihood. Though some accounts give the impression that he was a disciple of Buddha or Vridhanand, Dadu does not seem to have acknowledged them. He recognised only the *satguru*, that is, God himself. Dadu had great contempt for the 'human Gurus' who misled their disciples and lived at their expense. According to him, the disciple was a cow and the human guru, the milkman. The milkman draws the milk and drinks it. He claimed that Allah or Ram were not different entities and were in fact his guru.

From this, it is quite evident that Dadu was deeply influenced by Kabir. Dadu did not have much respect for the traditional scriptures either. He found them all distorted and garbled by the so-called believers. Therefore, he composed or compiled his own collection of sacred sayings from different religions and bhakti sources. This collection is named as *Panchavani*, the sayings of five saints. *Panchavani* contains the aphorisms and advice of Kabir, Namdev, Ramadas, Mandas and Dadu himself. As the compiler, Dadu wrote a small introduction to *Panchavani*. He says in it:

> Very dear to me is the true word of Kabir. To hear it is pure bliss: greatly do I delight in it. To Him who was Lord of Kabir is my soul wedded. In thought, word and deep, I acknowledge no other.' He stated, 'who vanquishes the hostile army of the passions, such was Kabir in this age of darkness.' He also stated, 'Poor Kabir spoke his message and passed on, having given much wise counsels'.[108]

On Life and Bhakti

Dadu claimed himself to be neither a Hindu nor a Muslim. He did not deny god. A thorough surrender to one's god and rendering good to fellow human beings was to him the path of true bhakti. He did not believe or attach much importance to the concept of heaven or hell as his emphasis was to live life ethically and usefully. He says:

> *You will not have this body again*
> *and again, O, foolish one. Why*
> *do you surrender it idly? ... How*
> *priceless is life? O, Man, such a*
> *life will not come again, why*
> *then cast away the precious jewel?*[109]

Dadu's emphasis on the reality and glory of this life gives substance to his spiritual ideas and the need for an ethical life devoted not only to God, but to the humanity in general. This also presages a reflection of caste and religious distinctions and all forms of inequality. The process of this spiritual and ethical advance is explained in the following verse by Dadu:

> *Day by day be intoxicated with Ram,*
> *Day by day let your love increase;*
> *Day by day drink the essence of Ram,*
> *Day by day behold the mirror within the body;*
> *Day by day forget the limitations of the body,*
> *Day by day let the senses be repressed;*
> *Day by day let the devices of the mind perish,*
> *Day by day will the glory be revealed.*
> *When the soul leaves the company of the body and takes its seat in the regions of Hari, Then is it devoid of fear: no limitation can possess it.*[110]

Since Dadu extolled the dignity and necessity of labour, he did not subscribe to the traditional caste system which allotted to each caste a special task as its duty. Krishna, in the *Bhagavad Gita,* called it *Swadharma* and said that one should stick to one's Swadharma (caste duty) even if it was inferior to Paradharma (the duty of other castes). Dadu rejected this without mentioning Krishna, Gita or Manu.

Dadu's love and concern were not confined to human beings. It encompassed the entire universe. He did not eat meat or fish for he could not suffer the pain of the creature killed. It is also said that Akbar issued orders restricting the killing of animals at Dadu's instance. Dadu Panthis did not bury or cremate the dead bodies. They took them to jungles for animals to feed upon.

State and Politics

Unlike Kabir, Dadu was not averse to politics or state authority. He considered it necessary to keep law and order by an authority to ensure peaceful life for people devoted to god. As already mentioned, Akbar was very much impressed by Dadu's teachings and Dadu reciprocated the compliment by giving respect to him. His involvement in politics caused Dadu some difficulties especially in Rajasthan where a number of autonomous kingdoms were fighting with each other.

In Rajasthan, he had lived in the Sambhar region for a long time before leaving for Amber, the capital of Jaipur. The king of Jaipur and its people gave him a rousing welcome on the banks of the Mota Lake. Raja Bhagawan Das, king of Jaipur, was a commander of Akbar's Army. Through Bhagawan Das, Akbar came to know about Dadu. In 1584, Dadu received an invitation from Akbar from his new capital at Fatehpur Sikri near Agra. Dadu accepted the invitation and had a detailed conversation with the emperor. Akbar's chief courtiers and historians, Abu Fazal and Birbal, along with Bhagawan Das, joined the conversation. Though Akbar's recognition of Dadu was a high water mark in the saint's religious and secular career, he also attracted severe opposition from the conservatives of both Hindu and Muslim communities. Though Bhagawan Das was an admirer and well-wisher of Dadu, his successor Mansingh was not so. There were many differences between the two and on the death of Bhagawan Das, Dadu shifted base to Mewar where he had many disciples among whom were also members of the royalty. He was received with love and affection. Dadu passed away in 1602 at Naraina at the age of 59.

As it happened to many sects, many internal squabbles broke out among Dadu Panthis after the founder's demise. One was between his disciples from the Rajput and non-Rajput communities. The conflict was mainly on the adoption of Rajput traditions and attire. Naraina was a sort of headquarters of Dadu Panthis where, during the annual festivals, debates used to take place on Dadu's teachings and life.

29

Kerala: A Latecomer

Utpanna Dravide Bhakti.
Vriddhim Karnatake Gata

As seen in the above stanza, the Bhakti movement had begun in the deep south of India and from there it spread to Karnataka with increased vigour. Later, it traversed to the western, northern and eastern parts of India before heading south again to reach Andhra. In all this India sojourn, we left out Kerala which should have been the second cultural area to cover by our survey. However, the movement's entry into the region which forms present-day Kerala occurred much later. One probable reason could be that Malayalam—language of Kerala—is the youngest in the Dravidian language family. The second reason was that the Bhakti movement in Kerala was much weaker than in other areas.

The earliest inscriptions in Malayalam first using the *Vattezhuthu* alphabet were not older than the tenth century CE. The first poem in Malayalam called *Rama Charitham,* which belonged to the thirteenth century, is a mixture of the old Malayalam and Tamil languages. Subsequently, the Sanskrit language, which had penetrated into Malayam in a big way, had given rise to a mixture of those two languages called *Manipravalam.* Poems in *Manipravalam* were mainly escapist literary works created to suit the taste of the idle upper classes. Many of them were only about carnal pleasures, prostitutes and their patrons like *Chandrotsavam, Unniyachi Charitham,*

Unnichiruthevi Charitham et cetera. However, these works are very important in discussions on the Bhakti movement, for bhakti poetry was seeking to save society from the depths of moral decadence to which it had sunk. *Leela Tilakam* by an anonymous author, written probably in the early fifteenth century, is a prosody of *Manipravala* literature.

During this period, there were compositions in Sanskrit for the traditional performing arts like *Chakyar Kooth,* and later there were songs to be sung for theatrical art forms like *Kathakali* and another genre, the *Chambu,* in which poetry and prose appear alternatively. All these were based on episodes in the *Purana*s though it is difficult to categorise them as Bhakti poetry.

Genuine Bhakti poetry in Malayalam began with Cherusseri Namboodiri during the early fifteenth century. His major work is *Krishnapattu* or *Krishna Gatha* based on the *Bhagavatha Purana*. *Krishna Gatha* was written in simple Malayalam, accessible to children and elders alike. Cherusseri's melodious diction and the intense bhakti for Krishna make it an extremely popular bhakti text in Malayalam. During this period lived the Niranam poets called Kannasa Panickers who belonged to Niranam in the present Pathanamthitta district which also became popular as a Christian pilgrimage destination. There were three Panickers: Niranam Rama Panicker, Malayinkeezhu Madhava Panicker and Vellangalloor Sankara Panicker to whom are ascribed the Kannassa works of the *Ramayana, Bhagavat Gita* and also the *Bharatamala* respectively. Some scholars are of the view that though all the three originally had belonged to Niranam, two of them—Madhava and Sankara—later took residence respectively in Malayinkeezhu in Trivandrum District and Vellangallur which was either in the present-day district of Thrissur or in Ernakulam District. Irrespective of whether they belonged to the same family or flourished in their different places, one factor brings all of them together: their bhakti ideology, the style of language and the meter in which they wrote their poems. Kannasa poets were the first to begin the work of freeing Malayalam from Tamil and also *Manipravalam*. Not only did they part company with the *Manipravalam* language style, but also its carnal themes to set in motion the Bhakti movement which was brought to its final form by Thunchathu Ezhuthachchan considered to be the father of modern Malayalam language. Ezhuthachchan freed Malayalam from the trammels of Tamil though he used Sanskrit words judiciously.

The most important Bhakti poets in Malayalam after Kannasa and Cherusseri were Ezhuthachchan, Melpathoor Narayana Bhattathiri and Poonthanam Namboodiri. According to tradition, Melpathoor, Ezhuthachchan and Poonthanam were contemporaries during the sixteenth century though some modern scholars dispute this contention (for example Koladi Govindan Kutty in his study *Bhakti Prasthanam Malayalam Kavikaliloode* (published by Kerala Sahitya Academy, 2004). Melpathoor Narayana Bhattathiri, who was a great devotee of Krishna, the presiding deity of the Guruvayur Temple in Thrissur district of central Kerala used to write in Sanskrit. He was a great scholar and wrote a book on Sanskrit dramas called *Prakriya Sarvaswom.* His grammar is said to have improved upon the great Sanskrit grammarian Panini and his interpreter Pathanjali. His devotional works, *Narayaneeyam* tells the story of Krishna as given in the *Bhagavatha Purana.* But since it is in Sanskrit, *Narayaneeyam* is hardly accessible to the common folk of Kerala. Writing devotional poems in Sanskrit was a deviation from the usual bhakti poets who wrote mostly in the spoken languages of common people. Therefore it is debatable whether *Narayaneeyam* could be included in the category of bhakti literature.

Ezhuthachchan

Thunchathu Ezhuthachchan who had lived in the middle of the sixteenth century is arguably the greatest and earliest poet of modern Malayalam literature. Modern Malayalam language took its form and vocabulary from Ezhuthachchan's works which include the *Adhyathma Ramayana, Mahabharata* and the *Bhagavatha Purana.* However, many modern scholars suspect if it was the scholarly Ezhuthachchan who wrote the Malayalam *Bhagavatha,* given the many grammatical and idiomatic mistakes it contains. Ezhuthachchan is also credited as the author of works like *Harinama Keerthanam* and *Padya Ratnam.*

Ezhuthachchan's real name is still unknown. He came to be called later as Ramanuja, literally meaning the younger brother of Rama, his guru. Most poets of his time were Namboodiri Brahmins like Cherusseri, Punam, Mazhamangalam, Poonthanam, Melpathoor Bhattathiri et al. who were supposed to be 'twice born' (dwija) Brahmins. Members of lesser communities like the Nairs were not considered so and hence were not entitled to wear the Brahmin's sacred thread—*poonool*. **Within** the Nair community, too, Ezhuthachchan was said to have belonged to a lower sub-caste called *Chakkala*. This community's members used to earn their living from crushing oil seeds. Nairs and especially members from the Chakkala sub-caste were not entitled to learn the *Vedas* or Sanskrit. Being a *Sudra*, the lowest echelon in the pan-Indian *chathurvarnya* caste hierarchy, Ezhuthachchan was not entitled to write 'sacred hymns'. Ezhuthachchan, in his work, humbly apologises for his 'impertinence' in writing about the sacred scriptures and *Purana*s.

Ezhuthachchan was born in Tirur in present-day Malappuram District. There are a few acres of land here still called *Thunchan Parambu* believed to be the compound in which Ezuthachchan lived. Towards the close of his life, he migrated to Chittoor in Palakkad district where he established a monastery (*math*) and lived there probably till his death. These places and Thunchan Parambu continue to be considered sacred spots where children are traditionally initiated to learning the *adyakshara* (starting alphabets).

The sixteenth century was a time of conflicts, decadence and turmoil in Kerala. Except a large area in Kurumbanad in the northern and Guruvayur in the southern parts of present-day Kerala, which were ruled by the relatively more powerful native kingdom of the Zamorins of Kozhikode, the entire region was divided into small principalities embroiled in continuous internecine wars. The Zamorins too had waged many wars to expand their mini-empire. In 1498, the Portuguese navigator, Vasco-da-Gama, with his soldiers landed at Kappad a few kilometers north of Kozhikode. It was a significant event in the history of Kerala as well as India. For it marked the beginnings of Western powers' interference in the internal politics of this region and even inside the indigenous Christian faith and traditions. The Arabs were the traditional foreign traders in Kerala before the advent of Gama and they were friendly with the Zamorins.

The iniquitous caste system of the Hindu society had prevailed in Kerala region from time immemorial. It gradually took a worse and virulent form which continued till the twentieth century. Swami Vivekananda, who was acquainted with the caste system prevalent all over India, had condemned Kerala's caste hierarchy as the worst. He called Kerala a lunatic asylum when he visited the southern parts towards the close of the nineteenth century. It was in this asylum that Ezhuthachchan was born.

Ezhuthachchan's works hardly reflect these political situations. Nor does he directly attack the caste system, though there are many oblique references to the forms of discrimination. Kunchan Nambiar, exponent of *Ottam Thullal*—a performing art, refers to the foreign penetration into Kerala and also lampoons the caste system. What was the specific contribution of Ezhuthachchan in this regard? It was already mentioned that Ezhuthachchan had retrieved Malayalam from the trammels of Tamil and Sanskrit, although he was not averse to making use of Sanskrit words. However, his semantics were quite different from that of Sanskrit. His most important contribution was the rejection of *Manipravala* and the erotic extravaganza which marked many of those works. Rejecting the *Manipravala* in his style and the content, Ezhuthachchan extolled dharma along with bhakti. His *Ramayana* itself was neither heavily dependent on Valmiki's *Ramayana*. He based himself on a much later work, the *Adhyathma Ramayana*, in which unlike in Valmiki's work, Rama is depicted as a reincarnation of Vishnu. In Valmiki's Ramayana, Rama was an ideal son and an ideal ruler. The *Adhyatma Ramayana* is considered a work of a Brahmin poet who belonged to either Maharashtra or Andhra. Ezhuthachchan, in the beginning of his *Ramayana* and in some of the chapters, goes into ecstasy over his object of worship and repeats the name 'Rama' uninterruptedly. He wrote in the indigenous *Kilipattu* meter borrowed from the folk songs created and sung by ordinary people. *Kilipattu* literally means the song of the bird. There are many theories on why he chose a bird to narrate his poetry. Some people hold that Ezhuthachchan chose this medium because he was from a Sudra caste not entitled to write a scriptural work which was the prerogative of Brahmins. Most poets before and after Ezhuthachan were from the Brahmin caste of Namboodiris.

The essence of Ezhuthachchan's poetic message is given by P.K. Parameswaran Nair as follows:

> It was spiritual solace that Ezhuthachan offered to his compatriots. His whole being was so thoroughly saturated with the most ardent devotion for the 'Supreme Being' in 'His' different manifestations that whenever he sang His tales, he would also sing of the infinite peace that is in 'His' name. So sincere was he in his outpourings and so sweet the melody of his numbers, that he was irresistible to the masses, and his exhortations carried with them immediate conviction. Above all, the tone he set for his poetry was not the *rasa* of the *Manipravala* kind, achieved as it was with a lot of superficial trappings and a sensuous imagination, but edifying emotions adorning the eternal verities which a mystic alone can realise and delineate.
>
> If at a time when the erotic was the dominant *rasa* and entertainment was the sole purpose of literary activity, a poet could meditate on the destinies of man and the mysteries of life and come forward with such questioning as
>
> If the phenomenal world were true—
> The earth, its kingdoms, the mortal garb
> Of man, his riches and the rest—
> It only means how embroiled thou art ;
> And if it meet not thy reasoning's,
> What then indeed does it profit thee?—
>
> it means for certain that such a one, Ezhuthachan, elevated the thought-processes of the people to a higher level and imparted to their literature a more solemn diction than was ever attained before.[111]

As we have already noted, the Bhakti movement in Kerala was a latecomer compared to the rest of the country. Nevertheless it was certainly a continuation of the pan-India movement which started probably in the sixth century CE with Thirumoolar in Tamil and continued for about a thousand years the close of which witnessed Ezhuthachchan's emergence. About this background Nair again observes as follows:

> But this return to matters of the spirit was not a feature exclusive to Kerala, there were parallel forces working throughout the country in the sixteenth and seventeenth centuries. This was the period when the Vaishnava poets were enriching most literatures of India with their mystic outpourings; in Bengla there were the disciples of Ramanuja, a continuous line, and of many a caste; there were in the north Kabir, Surdas and Tulsidas writing in the various earlier forms of Hindi. The tide of devotional literature was steadily rising in the South as well. The sojourn of Sri Krishna Chaitanya –he came to Kerala also—heralded a renaissance in the cult of Krishna worship. But even before his arrival there were, in most of the languages of this zone, poets who made substantial contributions to the devotional literature in their respective languages. Thus Tukaram and Sridhara retold Vaishnava tales for the Marathi audience; Jagannatha for the Oriya; and Kanakadasa and Venkitadasa for the Kannada. And of course, Tamilnad had no dearth of Vaishnava poets even before the days of kamban.
>
> Devotional literature had its votaries in Kerala from the days of **Ramacharitam**, but it was with Ezhuthachan that it became an active principle in the cultural life of the community.[112]

Although Ezhuthachchan had deviated very much from Valmiki's *Ramayana* to infuse into his poem his spiritual enthusiasm, he stuck close to Vyasa when writing the *Mahabharata*. Certainly it was a marvelous summary of the Vyasa *Mahabharata* which is the largest epic in Sanskrit. Despite being true to the original, Ezhuthachchan did not fail to allow a free play for his imagination and poetic competence. For example, the episode in which Sakunthala leaves her foster father, Kanwa's, ashram for the palace of the King Dushyantha he writes:

> *Woe-begone and disconsolate*
> *at parting from her sire, the sage,*
> *and wiping off the tears which came*
> *trickling down her high rich breasts*

and offering him her obeisance
with folded hands, and with her son
circumambulating him,
and bidding farewell with smothered words,
Sakuntala rose to leave.
And then the sage took on his lap
her son and hugged him rapturously
and kissing his head many times, he blessed :
"Long be thy life and goodness infinite !"
And wishing him well in many more ways
he chanted benisons with ritual pots;
and when slowly his hands caressed
his daughter and he said, "Be thou happy!"
tears streamed from his eyes, his heart
shed its ascetic severity;
sighs rose freely and distressing thoughts
rocked his bosom : in short, the sage
was swamped with human sympathies
and felt within his inmost being
an agony born of affection.

Poonthanam: Bhakti and Society

As already mentioned, *Kilipattu* was a popular meter in folk songs from which Ezhuthachchan borrowed. The tremendous success of Ezhuthachchan's classic works led many poets of lesser caliber to imitate him. Obviously most of them have been long forgotten. The last in these series was written after a century by Kerala Varma. His major work was Ramayana. He also wrote *Pathala Ramayana, Bana Yuddha, Moksha Siddhi Prakarana,* et cetera. It was Poonthanam Namboodiri (1547–1640 CE) who became famous for his devotional poems following the bhakti tradition of Ezhuthachchan.

Poonthanam was a Namboodiri Brahmin. His real name is not known; 'Poonthanam' is his household's name. His *illam* or house is preserved in Keezhalloor village in Malappuram District as is his memorial by the state government.

Poonthanam was a great devotee of Krishna and a frequent visitor to the famous Krishna temple at Guruvayur. It is said that his own son had died at a very young age and this tragedy affected him deeply. To console himself, he once wrote: *when the young Krishna is playing in your heart, why should one have another kid?*

Poonthanam's intense bhakti for Krishna made him a follower of Ezhuthachchan. As mentioned earlier, the legends have it that he was a contemporary of Ezhuthachchan. Yet, Poonthanam's language, diction and meter were fundamentally different from Ezhuthachchan's. Poonthanam wrote in extremely simple Malayalam which may even be described as colloquial. There are few Malayalees, literate or non-literate, who cannot recite at least a few lines by Poonthanam. Tradition attributes almost a dozen works to him of which *Jnanappana, Santhana Gopalam, Bhasha Karnamritham,* et cetera, are the most well-known. Among others, many are irretrievably lost.

All these works were exceptionally short. Each may comprise 80–100 pages in print. The most famous of them, *Jnanappana,* means 'songs of wisdom'. In the guise of criticising non-believers, Poonthanam huffs at those addicted to creating wealth and enjoying worldly pleasures. Though a Brahmin himself, he sharply ridicules those Brahmins who are so proud of their caste identity and pretend themselves to be the God Brahma. He expresses contempt for those overwhelmed by self-importance. Poonthanam also makes fun of those who are servile to those in power.

The following lines from *Jnanappana* bring home the above arguments:

> *What had happened till yesterday*
> *and what will happen tomorrow*
> *I know not, not when this body*
> *seen today, will cease to be.*
> *He Thou art Who turns to naught*
> *those who were the moment before,*
> *sets a man on palanquins*
> *in a couple of days or four*
> *and makes the king who dwelt in palaces*
> *bundles on the shoulders bear.*

These lines reflect the sentiments of the poor and oppressed sections of society. Poonthanam was not only a bhakti poet but a critique of the social inequalities and hypocrisy as well. He can be considered a social reformer. Though himself a Brahmin, he was no admirer of Brahmin rituals and practices. Poonthanam belonged to the poor strata among the Brahmins and was considered to belong to the lower rungs of the caste.

Poonthanam does not seem to have followers or imitators, unlike Ezhuthachchan. There were critics who thought Poonthanam's poetry lacked quality or finesse. One of them is the poet and historian of Kerala literature, Ulloor S. Parameswara Iyer. However, with changing times when simplicity and directness in literature gained popularity and heavy terminology and bombastic style became passé, Poonthanam's literary stature rose again. The charges leveled against his poetry have been more than compensated by Poonthanam's sincerity and honesty.

30

Conclusion

Following is an attempt to address the question posed in the title of this book: *Bhakti Movement: Renaissance or Revivalism?* Renaissance literally means re-birth and the term has been most often used in history with reference to the re-birth of ancient Greek and Roman culture and its impact on European society, culture, language, literature, art and religion. The *Oxford English Dictionary* gives the following meaning to the word renaissance:

i. The great revival of art and letters under the influence of classical models which began in Italy in the fourteenth century and continued during the fifteenth and the sixteenth centuries; also the period during which the movement was in progress.
ii. Any revival or period of marked improvement and new life in art, literature, et cetera.

Modern scholars maintain that the mere revival of classical (Greek and Roman) traditions can hardly be termed Renaissance. The definition gives the impression that Renaissance and Revivalism are almost similar. Actually, it is to the contrary as they are diametrically opposite to each other. The concept of revivalism ingrained in the concept of Renaissance has been rejected by modern writers. They consider renaissance as a new and massive upsurge in the societal value-system with its direct impact in almost all fields like arts, culture, politics or religion. In Europe this upsurge is considered to have begun in the fourteenth century and came to close by the late sixteenth century, paving way for great movements like religious reformation and scientific revolution. It started in Italy and spread to the North and then the North-West of Europe.

Friedrich Engels, in his incomplete book *Dialectics of Nature,* explains the nature and significance of Renaissance in the following words.

> It was the greatest progressive revolution that mankind had so far experienced, a time which called for giants and produced giants—giants in power of thought, passion and character, in universality and learning. The men who founded the modern rule of the bourgeoisie had anything but bourgeois limitations. On the contrary, the adventurous character of the time inspired them to a greater or lesser degree. There was hardly any man of importance then living who had not traveled extensively, who did not speak four or give languages, who did not shine in a number of fields. Leonardo da Vinci was not only a great painter but also a great mathematician, mechanician, and engineer, to whom the most diverse branches of physics are indebted for important discoveries. Albrecht Durer was painter, engraver, sculptor, and architect, and in addition invented a system of fortification embodying many of the ideas that much later were again taken up by Montalembert and the modern German science of fortification. Machiavelli was a statesman, historian, poet, and at the same time the first notable military author of modern times. Luther not only cleaned the Augean stable of the Church but also that of the German language; he created modern German prose and composed the text and melody of that triumphal hymn imbued with confidence in victory which became the Marseillaise of the sixteenth century. The heroes of that time were not yet in thrall to the division of labour, the restricting effects of which, with its production of one-sidedness, we so often notice in their successors. But what is especially characteristic of them is that they almost all live and pursue their activities in the midst of the contemporary movements, in the practical struggle; they take sides and join in the fight, one by speaking and writing, another with the sword, many with both. Hence the fullness and force of character that makes them complete men. Men of the study are the exception—either persons of second or third rank or cautious philistines who do not want to burn their fingers.[113]

From Engels' description, it is quite clear that the Renaissance in Europe was not a Revival of classical learning but a new upsurge witnessed in Europe's cultural firmament. The word Renaissance meaning 'new birth' is a result of the misconception that arose from a wrong evaluation of the early historians of the so called Renaissance.

Some Indian scholars influenced by the European concept too have allowed themselves to be misled. But there are also scholars and languages in India where this concept is used correctly. The following list which gives the terms in different Indian languages which denote Renaissance prove this.

Assamiya	-	Punarjagarana, Navajagarana
Bengali	-	Navajagaran
Gujarati	-	Punarutharan
Hindi	-	Punarjagaran
Kannada	-	Navodaya
Malayalam	-	Navothanam
Oriya	-	Navajagarana, Abhyuthana, Punarjeevana
Punjabi	-	Punarjagrithi
Sanskrit	-	Punajeevanam
Sindhi	-	Sugathi, Badhari
Tamil	-	Marumalarchi
Telugu	-	Punarjeevanam
Urdu	-	Misa Adhaniya

For convenience sake, we use here the word 'Renaissance' though it is not appropriate in the strict sense of the term from a historical point of view.

In contrast to Renaissance, Revivalism hardly marks a positive upsurge in the societal value system. Instead, it denotes an attempt to bring back the outdated values of a bygone era with or without some marginal changes. Therefore, while Renaissance is revolutionary in its thrust and nature, Revivalism denotes an attempt to halt social progress and hence a reactionary phenomenon. With these complexities and nuances of terminology, it is not easy to apply these concepts to a movement which enveloped a subcontinent known for its myriad diversities. Besides its spread in many languages and cultural areas, the movement's span belonged to a period a thousand years ago in the past. This era had witnessed major changes in the politics and administration of the country. While some religions like Buddhism and Jainism had declined, others like Christianity and Islam rose to heights during the period. The traditional and all pervasive Hinduism, dominated as it was by the Brahminic core, came into conflict with the Bhakti movement in many ways.

Another difficulty in analysing and evaluating the Bhakti movement is common to the analysis of any religion. The outward forms of religious practices often conceal their social and political essence. What the British historian A.L. Morton writes about the English Revolution of the seventeenth century is also applicable to the Bhakti movement in India. He says:

> Few things have made it more difficult for us to understand fully the English Revolution of the seventeenth century than the religious forms in which political issues were often, though of course not inevitably, framed. This can lead us into all sorts of errors. Because the great religious controversies of the age may seem to us unreal and frequently grotesque, we may brush them aside altogether, may say, these people were hypocrites or self-deceivers who simply did not know what they were about. Or we may fall into the opposite error, like those nineteenth-century historians who coined the phrase 'the Puritan Revolution': that is to say we may take the religious issues merely at their face value and fail to see the political and class implications which lay beneath them. Often we manage to combine both sorts of errors into an inextricable confusion, and either way, we degrade the Revolution and fail to see the grandeur and seriousness of the men who made it.[115]

II

We began the story of the Bhakti movement from Tamizhakom, the earliest centre of the Bhakti movement led by the Nayanars and Alvars between the sixth and tenth centuries CE. As seen before, Narayanan and Veluthat have assessed the movement in Tamizhakom as revivalist which then paved way for the return of Brahmanic Hinduism, rendering death-blows to Buddhism and Jainism. This led to the establishment of big temples under the control of Brahmins with big landed estates donated to them by kings and emperors.

However, can it be said that each and every form of the movement in its different manifestations in various parts of India were equally Revivalist? It would be a folly to consider Basava who challenged the base of traditional Brahminism in Karnataka as revivalist. We have also seen the two main radically different trends in Karnataka's Bhakti movement—Saguna and Nirguna—which were conformist and non-conformist respectively. Basava in Karnataka, Kabir in Varanasi and Ravi Dasa in north-west India were Nirguna bhaktas. They opposed the Brahmanic rituals, the caste system and did not accept the difference between Hindus and Muslims. Ramananda and the Ramanandis opposed all types of caste discriminations. It would be very wrong to designate them as revivalist or reactionary. Narayanan's and Veluthat's condemnation of the Bhakti movement in Tamizhakom cannot be applied to the Nirguna bhakti. Therefore, even if the Tamil Bhakti movement is taken as an exception (an exception that can be applied to the views of certain other bhakti protagonists and isolated areas) the movement generally took the form of protest and resentment against decadent Buddhism. It has also many points of affinity with the Muslim Sufi Movement. Shahabuddin Iraqi says:

> The Bhakti movement in medieval northern India started as a protest against orthodoxy. The nature and scope of the movement was almost the same as that of Sufism. But, whereas the Sufis did not go against Islam, Quran or Prophet, the bhakti as particularly those of Nirugna school, emerged as a reaction against Hinduism or Brahmanism. It was, in fact, due to the long term socio-religious bias and humiliation faced by the people of lower strata that spiritual leaders of this class not only challenged the religious system of traditional Hinduism but also took over the leadership in their own hands and broke the religious monopoly of the Brahmans. So to believe that all the leaders of the Bhakti movement were peaceful socio-religious reformers seems inappropriate. In fact, the idea of reform formed their ethical and ideological base, while their mission was to deal with practical aspect of life, having

> certain aims and objectives in mind. Some turned to political and even militant action for the attainment of their objectives.[116]

The bright picture of the Bhakti movement in its prime had gradually begun to dim to the point of extinction by its final phase. In the history of India as well as other countries, this fall from the glorious pinnacle is not an isolated episode. Most religions are born as revolutionary in character or as a Renaissance movement revolting against the prevailing decay of culture, morals and faith of the establishment. However, as time passed they ignored the teachings of the founding fathers, Buddha, Jesus, Mohammed and almost restored the old mores. The Bhakti movement also had its glorious pinnacle and then fell into decay. Iraqi, who paid wholehearted tributes to the Bhakti movement, concludes with its decline if not demise as follows:

> A subtle change took place in the inner character of the Bhakti movement after the demise of the teachers. These men, along with their contemporary followers, rejected formal doctrines, distinctive marks, initiatory rites, and prescribed modes of worship. Their doors were open to all without distinction of caste or community. But, after them particular rituals were adopted by particular groups. The divine position that was later given to them created a suitable background for their own worship in all the cults formed in their names. The **Bijak** for the Kabirpanthis, the **Guru Granth** for the Sikhs and the **Panchavani** for the Dadupanthis occupied not only the position of scriptural authority but also became objects of formal worship. **Arti** was adopted by Hindu devotees who were familiar with the temple service. This led to the growing approximation of the cult to traditional Hinduism, in a different form.[117]

Though rise and decline are inevitable for all popular movements, it also has to be remembered that no movement/revolution disappears altogether without leaving its long lasting traces on society. Many revolutions have failed not very long after they blossomed forth. The English Revolution in the seventeenth century looked as if it was a failure after restoration of monarchy. The French Revolution of 1789 was sabotaged by Napoleon when he came to power four years afterwards. In the case of the October Socialist Revolution of Russia, it was upturned in 1991 after 73 years. Can we say that all these were futile exercises? The English Revolution though had failed and monarchy was restored, no English monarch has ever dared to challenge the authority of the Parliament since then. In the case of the French Revolution, it is universally accepted that the entire history of the nineteenth century is marked by the series of struggles for freedom and democracy which were inspired most by the French revolution's famous slogan: ***'Liberty, Equality and Fraternity'***. Regarding the collapse of the Soviet Socialist System, the October Revolution still remains an inspiration and guide throughout the world.

The Bhakti movement is no exception to this tradition. The Bhakti movement in all cultural areas in India, whether of the Saguna or the Nirguna variety, gave rise to the modern Indian languages. Languages are not only instruments of formal communication but instrument of power as well. Upper classes/ castes or foreign powers had succeeded in subjugating people through the use of elite languages like Sanskrit and foreign languages like Persian and English. It is through the promotion of people's languages and literature that common people can be empowered. This task in India was accomplished by the Bhakti movement. All these prove that the movement, with all its limitations, left its indelible mark on Indian life and culture. Certainly the movement had elements of Revivalism. But the elements of Renaissance it contains weigh much more and they deserve the credit for providing a form, character and unity to India.

Bibliography

1. Satish Chandra, *Historiography, Religion and State in Medieval India*, Har Anand Publications, 1996.
2. John B. Thomson, Preface to *Language and Symbolic Power* by Pierre Bourdieu, Harvard University Press, 1991.
3. A.K. Majumdar, *Bhakti Renaissance*, Bharatiya Vidya Bhavan, Mumbai, 1965.
4. K.C. Varadachari, *Aspects of Bhakti*, University of Mysore, 1956.
5. Ibid.
6. S.M.S. Chari, *Philosophy and Theistic Mysticism of Alvars*, Motilal Banarasidass, Delhi, 1997.
7. David N. Lorenzen, (Ed) *Bhakti Religion in North India: Community Identity and Political Action*, State University of New York Press, 1995.
8. Ibid.
9. Christian Lee Novetzke, *History, Bhakti and Public Memory: Namdev in Religion and Secular Traditions*, Eastern Book Corporation, 2009.
10. R.S. Sharma, *India's Ancient Past*, Oxford University Press, 2008.
11. Ibid.
12. D.D. Kosambi, *An Introduction to the Study of Indian History*, Popular Book Depot, Mumbai, 1956.
13. M.G.S. Narayanan and Kesavan Veluthat, *Bhakti Movement in South India*, Indian Institute of Advanced Studies, Shimla, 1978.
14. Heinrich von Stietencron, *Hindu Myth, Hindu History: Religion, Art & Politics*, Permanent Black, Delhi, 2005.
15. H.H. Wilson (Trans.), *Parasara's Vishnu Puranam*, Parimal Publications, Delhi, 2005.
16. Kesavan Veluthat, *The Political Structure of Early Medieval South India*, Orient Longman, Delhi.

17. Ibid.
18. Greg M. Bailey, *The Mythology of Brahma*, Oxford University Press, New Delhi, 1985.
19. Mahadev Chakravarti, *Siva in the Pre-Vedic Harappa Civilization*, Motilal Banarasidass, Delhi, 1986.
20. Ibid.
21. Ashley Montagu, *Man's Most Dangerous Myth: The Fallacy of Race*, Oxford University Press, 1974.
22. K.N. Neelakanta Sastri, *A History of South India*, Oxford University Press, New Delhi, 1955.
23. Friedhelm Hardy, *Viraha Bhakti: The Early History of Krishna Devotion in South India*, Oxford University Press, New Delhi, 1986.
24. S. Vaiyapuri Pillai (Ed), *History of Tamil Language & Literature*, Madras University, 1956.
25. Ramendranath Nandi, *Social Roots of Religion in Ancient India*, K.P. Bagchi & Co., Calcutta, 1986.
26. Ibid.
27. S. Vaiyapuri Pillai, op. cit.
28. M.G.S. Narayanan and Veluthat, op. cit.
29. Neelakanta Sastri, op. cit.
30. Hephziba Jesudasan and Jesudasan, *History of Tamil Literature*, YMCA Publishing House, Calcutta, 1961.
31. G.Vanmikanathan, *Appar: Makers of Modern Indian Literature*, Sahitya Akademi, New Delhi, 1983.
32. Ramendranath Nandi, op. cit.
33. Hephziba Jesudasan & Jesudasan, op. cit.
34. Sundaram Manickam, *Nandanar*, CLS, Madras, 1995.
35. V.I. Lenin, *The State and Revolution*, 1916.
36. S.M.S. Chari, op. cit.
37. Arthur P. Bali, *Studies in Indian and Asian Civilizations*, Indian Institute of Advanced Studies, Shimla, 1978.
38. M. Chidambara Murthy, *Basavanna*, National Book Trust, New Delhi, 1972.
39. A.S. Adke, *Vachans of Akka Mahadevi*, Dharwar, 1973.
40. Chidambara Murthy, op. cit.
41. Parita Mukta, *Upholding Common Life*, Oxford University Press, 1997.

42-44. Ibid.

45. Bhav Prakash, *Chaurasi Vaishnav ki Varta*, 1689.
46. J.R. Verma, *Devotional Poets and Mystics-II*, Publications Division, Ministry of Information and Broadcasting, Government of India, 1978.
47. Darshan Singh, *A Study of Bhakta Ravidasa*, Punjabi University,

Patiala, 1996.
48. William R. Pinch, *Peasants and Monks in British India*, Oxford University Press, 1996.
49. R.P. Tiwari.
50. Darshan Singh, op. cit.
51. Darshan Singh, op. cit.
52. Prabhakar Machwe, *Marathi: The Language and its Linguistic Traditions*, Indian and Foreign Review, 1985.
53. Kusumavati Deshpande and M.V. Rajadhyaksha, *A History of Marathi Lirerature*, Sahitya Akademi, 1998.
54. Ibid.
55. Elenor Zelliot, *Palkhi*, Disha Books, Hyderabad, 1990.
56. Durga Bhagvat.
57. Bhalchandra Nemade, *Sant Tukaram*, Sahitya Akademi.
58. *Songs of Chokhmala*, The Book Review Literary Trust, New Delhi, 2002.
59-64. Ibid.
65. R.L. Handa, *History of Hindi Language and Literature*, Bombay, 1978.
66. Savitri Chandra Sobha, *Social Life and Concepts in Medieval Hindi Bhakti Poetry*, Chandrayan Publications, New Delhi, 1983.
67. Ibid.
68. M.A. Karandikar and others, *Guru Nanak*, Publications Division, Government of India, 1969.
69. G.S. Talib, *Guru Granth Sahib*, Punjabi University, Patiala, 1969.
70. Ibid.
71. Shahabuddeen Iraqi, *Bhakti Movement in Medieval India: Social and Political Perspectives*, Centre for Advanced Study, Aligarh Muslim University and Manohar Publications, 2008.
72. Ibid.
73. Mahmoud M. Ayoub, *Crisis of Muslim History, Religion and Politics in Early Islam*, Oxford University Press, UK, 2003.
74. Shahabuddeen Iraqi, op. cit.
75. Hamid Hussain, *Sufism and Bhakti Movement: Eternal Relevance*, Manak Publications, 2007.
76. Hamid Hussain, op. cit.
77-79. op. cit.
80. Ajit Bhattacharjee, *Kashmir: The Wounded Valley*, UBS Publishers, New Delhi, 1991.
81. Prananabananda Jash, *History of Saivism*, Roy & Choudhury, Calcutta, 1974.
82. Ajit Bhattacharjee, op. cit.

83. Ajit Bhattacharjee, op. cit.
84. J.L. Kaul, *Devotional Poets and Mystics*, Part I, Publications Division, Ministry of Information and Broadcasting, Government of India.
85. Maheswar Neog, *Sankradeva*, National Book Trust, New Delhi, 1967.
86. Ibid.
87. Ibid.
88. Ibid.
89. Sukumar Sen, *History of Bengali Literature*, Sahitya Akademi, 1971.
90. Sukumar Sen, *Chandidas*, Sahitya Akademi, 1971.
91. Suniti Kumar Chatterjee, *Jayadeva*, Sahitya Akademi, 1973.
92. Ibid.
93. Ibid.
94. Sukumar Sen, op. cit.
95. Ibid.
96. K.A. Neelakanta Sastri, *A History of South India*, Oxford University Press, New Delhi, 1975.
97. Salva Krishnamurthy, *History of Telugu Literature*, Institute of Asian Studies, Chennai, 1994.
98. S. Raghavachari, *Nannayya-Tikkana, Ramayana, Mahabharata* and *Bhagavata Writers*, Publications Division, Ministry of Information and Broadcasting, Government of India, 1998.
99. V.R. Narla, *Vemana*, Sahitya Akedemi, 1969.
100. Ibid.
101. Ibid.
102. Ibid.
103. Ibid.
104. Ibid.
105. Ibid.
106. Ibid.
107. Shahabuddeen Iraqi, op. cit.
108. Ibid.
109. Ibid.
110. Ibid.
111. P.K. Parameswaran Nair, *History of Malayalam Literature*, Sahitya Akedemi, 1967.
112. Ibid.
113. Frederich Engels, *Dialectics of Nature*, 1883.
114. A.L. Morton, *The World of Ranters, Religious Radicalism in the English Revolution*, Lawrence & Wishart, London, 1970.

Index